UNIVERSITY OF NORTH CAROLINA AT CHAPEL HILL
DEPARTMENT OF ROMANCE LANGUAGES

NORTH CAROLINA STUDIES
IN THE ROMANCE LANGUAGES AND LITERATURES

Founder: URBAN TIGNER HOLMES

Distributed by:

UNIVERSITY OF NORTH CAROLINA PRESS
CHAPEL HILL
North Carolina 27514
U.S.A.

NORTH CAROLINA STUDIES IN THE
ROMANCE LANGUAGES AND LITERATURES

Number 204

METAPHORIC NARRATION:
THE STRUCTURE AND FUNCTION OF
METAPHORS IN
A LA RECHERCHE DU TEMPS PERDU

METAPHORIC NARRATION: THE STRUCTURE AND FUNCTION OF METAPHORS IN *A LA RECHERCHE DU TEMPS PERDU*

BY

INGE KARALUS CROSMAN

CHAPEL HILL

NORTH CAROLINA STUDIES IN THE ROMANCE
LANGUAGES AND LITERATURES
U.N.C. DEPARTMENT OF ROMANCE LANGUAGES

1978

Library of Congress Cataloging in Publication Data

Crosman, Inge Karalus.
  Metaphoric narration.

  (North Carolina studies in the Romance languages and literatures; no. 204)
  Bibliography: p.
  1. Proust, Marcel, 1871-1922. A la recherche du temps perdu. 2. Proust, Marcel, 1871-1922—Technique. 3. Narration (Rhetoric). 4. Metaphor. I. Title. II. Series.

PQ2631.R63A784   843'.9'12   78-12573
ISBN 0-8078-9204-1

I. S. B. N. 0-8078-9204-1

DEPÓSITO LEGAL: V. 2.659 - 1978   I.S.B.N. 84-499-2027-2
ARTES GRÁFICAS SOLER, S. A. - JÁVEA, 28 - VALENCIA (8) - 1978

For my parents, Ewald and Hildegard Karalus

ACKNOWLEDGEMENTS

This book owes its genesis to two of my professors in the Graduate Faculties of Columbia University. To the late Justin O'Brien, whose seminar on A la recherche du temps perdu *inspired a lasting interest, I am grateful for encouragement to undertake the study of Proust's imagery. I am particularly indebted to Michael Riffaterre for a firm grounding in style analysis, and the thorough critical reading he gave my manuscript. I wish to thank Philip Kolb of the University of Illinois, and Albert Salvan of Brown University for their helpful suggestions and welcome interest in my work.*

Time in which to write this book was provided by a fellowship from the American Association of University Women, for which I am grateful. Thanks are also due to Williams College and Brown University for timely grants. My final debt is for the patient criticism and encouragement of my husband, Robert.

CONTENTS

	Page
INTRODUCTION	13

Chapter
			Page
I.	THE SINGLE METAPHOR		23
II.	THE BRIEF CONCEIT		35
	A.	Same Parts of Speech Establishing the Semantic Domain.	35
	B.	Verb-Subject-Object Reinforcements	37
	C.	Specific Functions of the Conceit as Conceptual Model	41
		1. Conceit Clarifying References to Time	41
		2. Conceit Clarifying a Descriptive Tableau	45
III.	THE CONTINUED METAPHOR		56
	A.	Aphoristic Conceit Extended for Illustration	57
	B.	Extensions Clarifying the Semantic Domain	59
	C.	Metaphorical Tableau	60
	D.	Continued Metaphors within a Symbolic Context	61
	E.	Continued Metaphors within a Context Associating Similar Temporal Experiences	63
IV.	METAPHORICAL EXPANSION AND MULTIPLE SETS OF METAPHORS.		67
	A.	Metaphorical Expansion	67
	B.	Cumulative Series of Metaphors	71
		1. Clarifying Function of Additional Transposition	72
		2. Syntactical Integration of Additional Metaphors	74
		3. Juxtaposition of Antithetical Images	76
		4. Juxtaposition of Different Images	81
V.	ACCUMULATED METAPHORS		85
	A.	Simple Structures	87
		1. Accumulated Metaphors from the Same Semantic Domain	87
		2. Accumulated Metaphors from Different Semantic Domains	88

Chapter			Page
	B. Complex Structures		92
	1. Extension to an Additional Accumulation		92
	2. Juxtaposition of Two Syntactically Dependent Groups.		94
	3. Combined Accumulations		98
	C. Multiple Structures		105
VI.	METAPHORICAL EXTENSIONS TO SYMBOLIC TABLEAU		108
	A. Synaesthetic Metaphors Symbolic of Mental Contiguity		109
	B. Metaphors Animating Abstractions		118
	1. Duration		118
	2. The "Self."		127
	C. Metaphorical Extensions within the Symbolic Portrayal of the Novel's Characters		133
	1. Dehumanization		133
	2. Characters Functioning as Symbolic Figures		143
	D. Symbolic Implications of an "Actual" Scene or Event		160
	E. Symbolic Descriptions of Art		169
VII.	METAPHORS AND SIMILES IN THE SAME TEMPORAL CONTEXT		173
	A. Single Simile within Metaphorical Passages		176
	1. Simile Enhancing a Single Aspect of the Metaphorical Image		176
	2. Simile Playing an Essential Role		179
	a. Brief Simile Specifying the Code of the Metaphorical Transposition		179
	b. Simile Extending to a Descriptive Tableau		183
	c. Simile Introducing a Separate Image		186
	3. Borderline Cases between Simile and Metaphor		188
	a. *Etre comme*		188
	b. *Comme*		191
	c. *Comme si*		194
	B. Multiple Similes within Metaphorical Passages		196
	1. Multiple Similes from the Same Domain		196
	2. Multiple Similes from Different Domains		202
CONCLUSION			215
BIBLIOGRAPHY			219

INTRODUCTION

Of the many aspects of Proust's style that have been, or might be studied, the Proustian metaphor has a special claim to our attention. For Proust, style was the true medium of an artist's vision, and metaphor was the essence of style. He considered it the animating principle of all literary art, and declared that metaphor was no less than the technique whereby art might transcend time.[1] A careful reading of *A la recherche du temps perdu* reveals that metaphors, in particular those that have been called to the reader's attention through stylistic emphasis, extension, or repetition, are at the heart of the creative process of the novel.

Before we rejoice at Proust's critical insight about what he was doing when he proclaimed metaphor the animating principle of his novel, we should keep in mind that he had a rather broad view of metaphor, since he does not make a distinction between metaphor, simile, and metonymy.[2] One explanation for this lack of precision

---

[1] See Marcel Proust, *A la recherche du temps perdu*, "Bibliothèque de la Pléiade" (Paris: Gallimard, 1954), III, 889. While this observation on metaphor is put forth within a context of sensory analogies, an earlier reference to metaphor is more inclusive (I, 835) and deals with the "metamorphosis" of things represented in art. The famous statement "Je crois que la métaphore seule peut donner une sorte d'éternité au style" appeared first in an article ("A propos du style de Flaubert") submitted to the *Nouvelle Revue Française*, 14, No. 76 (1920), 72-90, and later reprinted in *Chroniques* (Paris: Gallimard, 1927), p. 193. For further information on Proust's comments on imagery, consult Stephen Ullmann's article "L'Esthétique de l'image dans 'Contre Sainte-Beuve' de Marcel Proust," in *Festschrift Walther von Wartburg zum 80. Geburtstag*, ed. Kurt Baldinger (Tübingen: Max Niemeyer Verlag, 1968), II, 269, and Jean Milly, "Proust et l'image," *Bulletin Société Marcel Proust*, No. 20 (1970), pp. 1031-1043.

[2] See Gérard Genette's "Métonymie chez Proust, ou la naissance du Récit," *Poétique*, No. 2 (1970), p. 156, footnote 1 where we are reminded that the

is that he may merely be following the trend of traditional rhetoric.[3] A more revealing explanation would be that Proust seems more interested in the principle of association that underlies all of these tropes, and that he is less concerned with their particular linguistic formulation. The fact that he frequently uses both simile and metaphor within the same passage to jointly set up an association between two realms of discourse supports this idea.[4] One should also bear in mind that some of Proust's figures are at once metaphoric and metonymic, for instance, when it is clear from the context at hand that the metaphoric transfer is based on the conceptual contiguity between things, impressions, or ideas.[5] What is important to study in such cases is how the context of the novel develops double semantic implications. Thus the distinction, as well as the close relationship, between simile, metaphor, and metonymy are important for a full understanding of the meaning and function of these figures in *A la recherche*.

Though it would be ideal to consider all of these tropes as they appear in the novel, the wealth of figures to be dealt with would make this an impossible task for a single scholar. My primary aim in this study is to focus on the Proustian metaphor, not ignoring, however, the presence of metonymics or similes within the passages under consideration.

Since it is essential that each metaphor be studied within its relevant context, I further had to limit the scope of my investigation, and decided to concentrate on the metaphors connected with the theme of time.[6] One might ask whether it is worthwhile to

---

expression *faire cattleya*, which Proust calls metaphor, is a metonymy in the context of *A la recherche*.

[3] See Gérard Genette, "La rhétorique restreinte," *Communications* 16 (1970), pp. 165-171, and Gerald Kamber and Richard Macksey, " 'Negative Metaphor' and Proust's Rhetoric of Absence," *Modern Language Notes*, 85 (1970), 858-883.

[4] The joint functions of metaphor and simile are discussed in Chapter VII.

[5] For a discussion of this, see Gérard Genette, "Métonymie chez Proust ou la naissance du Récit," pp. 156-173.

[6] My decision was not an arbitrary one. This theme is central to the novel, and is closely related to others, since the passage of time is responsible for the constant change — and the observer's changing perspective — of emotions, ideas, social relationships, and physical appearances. That Proust's — and the hero-narrator's — conception of the novel is largely dependent upon his awareness of the nature of time is apparent from an observation he once made during an interview with Elie-Joseph Bois: "Vous savez qu'il y a une géo-

limit the scope of the study in order to analyze metaphors within their context.[7] This procedure is essential when we admit that the context is indispensable, first of all, in identifying metaphor, in distinguishing it from other semantic relationships, such as metonymy or synecdoche.[8] Moreover, all the metaphors introduced into a given passage must be considered if we are to understand how and to what extent the domains of figurative and literal language are related, and what meaning we are to derive from this juxtaposition. Some recurrent metaphors need to be considered within the larger context of the novel, since their repeated association with a particular concept points to a conceptual equation between image and idea.[9]

Before proceeding further, a definition of terms is in order. The view held by many that metaphor is a reduced, elliptical simile is an unjustified oversimplification.[10] The statement is true neither when we examine metaphors and similes within their syntactical

---

métrie plane et une géométrie dans l'espace. Eh bien, pour moi, le roman, ce n'est pas seulement de la psychologie plane, mais de la psychologie dans le temps..." (Philip Kolb and Larkin B. Price, Ed., *Marcel Proust: Textes retrouvés* [Urbana: University of Illinois Press, 1968], p. 217). Cf. *A la recherche*, III, 557 for a similar remark.

[7] The importance of studying a figure of speech within its context has repeatedly been stressed. For example, André Abbou, "Problèmes et méthode d'une stylistique des images," *Le Français Moderne* (July, 1969), pp. 213-223; Harald Weinrich, "Semantik der kühnen Metapher," *Deutsche Vierteljahrsschrift*, 37 (1963), 340-341; Heinrich Henel, "Metaphor and Meaning," in *The Disciplines of Criticism*, ed. Peter Demetz, Thomas Greene, and Lowry Nelson, Jr. (New Haven: Yale University Press, 1968), p. 94; Michael Riffaterre, "Stylistic Context," *Word*, 16 (1960), 207-208; Paul Ricœur, *La Métaphore vive* (Paris: Seuil, 1975).

[8] Metaphor is based on similarity, while metonymy is based on the contiguity of two things or concepts within the same mental framework. See Roman Jakobson and Morris Halle, *Fundamentals of Language* (The Hague: Mouton & Co., 1956), p. 76; and Stephen Ullmann, *Semantics* (Oxford: Basil Blackwell, 1962), pp. 212-20.

[9] The term "image" is used within this study to designate a figure of speech — primarily in reference to metaphors and similes. Cf. R. A. Sayce, *Style in French Prose* (Oxford: Clarendon Press, 1965), p. 57, and Stephen Ullmann, *Language and Style* (New York: Barnes & Noble, 1964), pp. 176-178.

[10] Simile may at this point summarily be defined as the verbal expression of a conceptual analogy between two things or concepts that are both represented in the context, and that are explicitly joined by a grammatical link indicating the conceptual relationship. The two compared elements must be from different domains. For a distinction between simile and the more general category of comparison, see Marsh H. McCall, *Ancient Rhetorical Theories of Simile and Comparison* (Cambridge: Harvard University Press, 1969), pp. vii-viii of the Preface.

framework, nor when we consider their semantic implications. A metaphor is not necessarily a briefer, or more elliptical statement than the standard simile introduced by *as* or *like* (French *comme*), since a metaphor may be introduced through such explicit syntactical devices as the copula *to be (être)* or a preposition.[11] The semantic implications of a metaphor must be determined from the given context within which it appears, and cannot merely be generalized as "analogy," "similarity," or "identification."

To define metaphor, a flexible and general enough definition is necessary. In her analysis of metaphor, Christine Brooke-Rose gives the general and simplified definition that "any identification of one thing with another, any replacement of the more usual word or phrase by another, is a metaphor."[12] Though this definition is broad enough to describe the metaphorical process, it does not tell us what happens semantically. This specification is important, since metaphor is basically a semantic phenomenon.[13] It should be made clear that the substitution or identification of terms does not take place within the same realm of discourse. The transfer must take place between objects or concepts belonging to two distinct domains. We are thus suddenly confronted with the intrusion of a word or words belonging to a semantic domain clearly distinguishable from the subject matter at hand.[14] This aspect of metaphor was defined in more analytical terms by W. B. Stanford:

---

[11] Among recent studies, Stephen Ullmann still upholds this view by quoting and accepting G. Esnault's definition from *Imagination populaire, métaphores occidentales*: "La métaphore est une comparaison condensée par laquelle l'esprit affirme une identité intuitive et concrète" (*Language and Style*, p. 180).

[12] *A Grammar of Metaphor* (London: Secker & Warburg, 1965), p. 17.

[13] Max Black points this out in *Models and Metaphors* (Ithaca: Cornell University Press, 1966): "to call a sentence an instance of metaphor is to say something about its *meaning*, not about its orthography, its phonetic pattern, or its grammatical form" (p. 28).

[14] "Semantic domain" is used interchangeably in this study with the term "code" as defined by Roman Jakobson in "Linguistics and Poetics," in *Style in Language*, ed. Thomas A. Sebeok (Cambridge, Mass.: M.I.T. Press, 1964), p. 353. Referring in particular to speech, Jakobson defined "code" as words used to convey a message between addresser (the speaker) and addressee (the listener) in terms familiar to both, so that the listener is able to "decode" (interpret) the speaker's communication. Applied to literary analysis, "code" designates the written verbal sequence referring the reader to a given subject in terms familiar to him through conventional language or literary tradition. It is, in short, a vehicle of communication between writer and reader.

Metaphor is the process and result of using a term (X) normally signifying an object or concept (A) in such a context that it must refer to another object or concept (B) which is distinct enough in characterstics from A to ensure that in the composite idea formed by the synthesis of the concepts A and B and now symbolized in the word X, the factors A and B retain their conceptual independence even while they merge in the unity symbolized by X. [15]

Since reference to X, A and B would be tedious, and in the end confusing, I prefer to use the by now well-known terminology introduced into the study of metaphor by I. A. Richards in his *Philosophy of Rhetoric*: "tenor" (the literal term) and "vehicle" (the term unexpectedly introduced into the given context and obviously belonging to another semantic domain). [16] Richards specifies that "the whole double unit" (tenor and vehicle) constitutes metaphor. [17] He fails to mention, however, that the tenor is often missing in a metaphorical statement. A more comprehensive definition should state that we require both the vehicle and the verbal sequence of the tenor's semantic domain — with or without the tenor itself — to have metaphor.

That the conceptual implications of metaphor cannot be generalized as analogy or likeness, and that metaphors do not necessarily "represent analogies, correspondences, and similarities which are given in the order of existence or in our thinking" has been pointed out more than once. [18] Since metaphor is a semantic phenomenon,

---

[15] *Greek Metaphor* (London: Oxford University Press, 1936), p. 101. The semantic distinction between A and B as a pre-requisite for the metaphorical process is also stressed by Danielle Bouverot, "Comparaison et métaphore," *Le Français Moderne* (July, 1969), pp. 231-232.

[16] *The Philosophy of Rhetoric* (London: Oxford University Press, 1936), p. 96.

[17] *Ibid.*, p. 97. Many critics, however, do not follow the same terminology. Miss Brooke-Rose, for instance, calls the tenor "the proper term," and the vehicle "the metaphoric term" (*A Grammar of Metaphor*).

[18] Harald Weinrich, "Semantik der kühnen Metapher," p. 337; Heinrich Henel, "Metaphor and Meaning," pp. 94-95. For similar observations, see I. A. Richards, pp. 107-09, p. 118, p. 127, and Max Black, pp. 35, 37, 39 and 43.

Proust was aware of the fact that some metaphors are solely based on subjective impressions, not on logical or ontological analogies. While praising the Comtesse de Noailles for her use of metaphor in the collection of verse

it should be studied on the level of words, with regard to the individual context at hand, and not according to pre-established philosophical and ontological concepts. The meaning to be derived from a given metaphorical statement must be determined by the context, where such interpretive aids as the presence of the tenor, subsidiary metaphors and other tropes, metalinguistic commentaries or other literal reinforcements may give significant clues.

The introduction of the vehicle into the given context orients the reader's conception of the subject matter at hand, as the new domain invoked by the vehicle introduces a set of characteristics common to it — called by one scholar "the system of associated commonplaces." [19] In the confrontation of the verbal sequence of tenor and vehicle a process of selection, modification, and emphasis is at work, so that the metaphor organizes our conception of the meaning to be conveyed. [20]

A metaphorical statement presents us with a semantic equation that may be stated implicitly or explicitly, depending on the grammatical structure of the individual metaphor. In the case where

---

entitled *Les Eblouissements,* he speaks of metaphors that convey a first, often false, impression entirely based on subjective experience (*Correspondance Générale* [Paris: Plon, 1931], II, 237-38).

[19] Max Black calls this semantic process "interaction," a term previously used by I. A. Richards (*Philosophy of Rhetoric,* pp. 100-101). Black makes the important observation that a metaphorical statement "has two distinct subjects — a 'principal' subject and a 'subsidiary' one," and that "these subjects are often best regarded as 'systems of things,' rather than 'things.'" He explains that "metaphor works by applying to the principal subject a system of 'associated implications' characteristic of the subsidiary subject" (p. 44).

Hedwig Konrad makes a similar observation when she points out that "Le mot est naturellement loin d'être seulement le symbole adéquat d'un trait dominant, il est avant tout le symbole d'une *structure*. Ainsi la transposition d'un mot fondée sur la seule parenté d'un trait dominant ne peut être regardée, ni au point de vue logique, ni au point de vue psychologique, comme normale" (*Etude sur la métaphore* [Paris: Librairie Philosophique J. Vrin, 1958], pp. 82-83).

[20] Max Black, p. 44. Black singles out and defines the various elements that enter into the metaphorical process (*Models and Metaphors,* p. 47).

In studying the metaphorical process I reject R. A. Sayce's theory of the "angle of an image," determined, according to him, by the semantic distance between tenor and vehicle (*Style in French Prose,* p. 62). Since it is impossible to determine the conceptual distance between tenor and vehicle with any exactness, such a criterion cannot be used to determine the relative value of an image, which Sayce unfortunately bases on this subjective "distance" — i.e., the wider the angle, the more original and better the image.

the vehicle directly replaces the tenor, the equation is implicit. In the case of a metaphorical statement through the copula (i.e. A *is* B), the equation is obviously explicit.[21] Prepositions that set up a relationship of dependency between tenor and vehicle, or between the vehicle and an element of the tenor's verbal sequence, may also identify and equate tenor and vehicle to a certain degree. Equation is again implicit in the direct syntactical juxtaposition of tenor and vehicle in apposition.[22] The metaphor's context, therefore, is important in determining the grammatical and conceptual relationship between the verbal sequence of tenor and vehicle.

Proust's use of imagery has not hitherto been studied within the relevant context, as defined above, and no major study has been devoted to metaphor alone.[23] However, studies that give us a comprehensive view of Proust's imagery in general do exist. An excellent one is Stephen Ullmann's analysis of imagery in *Du côté de chez Swann,* which gives us valuable information about the themes that give rise to images, the sources from which they were drawn, the use of imagery as a means of portrayal, and the predominant patterns and tendencies of Proust's figurative language.[24]

---

[21] See Brooke-Rose, *A Grammar of Metaphor,* for a discussion of what the author calls "simple replacement," pp. 26-27.

For a summary of the various syntactical devices used to convey semantic equivalence in metaphor, see Michael Riffaterre, "La Métaphore filée dans la poésie surréaliste," *Langue Française* (September, 1969), p. 50; Danielle Bouverot, "Comparaison et métaphore," pp. 224-227; and Heinrich Henel, "Metaphor and Meaning," pp. 109-111.

[22] For a detailed analysis of the various prepositional structures, see Brooke-Rose, pp. 146-190, especially pp. 154-160 where she examines the genitive link construction with *of* in a relationship of identity. Apposition is discussed on pp. 93-99.

[23] Only two short articles study the Proustian metaphor within its context. Gottfried Wäber's "Die Bedeutung der Proustschen Metapher, aufgezeigt an der Darstellung des gealterten Herzogs" (*Die Neueren Sprachen,* 14 [1965], 431-437) focuses on one passage of sustained metaphor portraying the aged Duc de Guermantes. Françoise Bloch-Sakai's article "Remarques sur la métaphore proustienne" (*Etudes de Langue et de Littérature Française* [March, 1967], pp. 104-116) analyzes the evolution, within Proust's work, of several recurring metaphors. Monique J. Layton briefly discusses certain structural peculiarities of Proust's metaphors in her article "Structure de certaines métaphores dans Proust" (*Révue d'Esthétique* [October, 1972], pp. 425-441).

[24] *The Image in the Modern French Novel* (New York: Barnes and Noble Inc., 1963), Chapter Three, pp. 225-238. Ullmann examines a particular aspect of Proust's imagery in his *Style in the French Novel* (Cambridge: Cambridge University Press, 1957), Chapter V: "Transposition of Sensations in Proust's Imagery."

A more extensive study is Victor Graham's *The Imagery of Proust,* which includes all of *A la recherche.* He examines primarily the themes connected with images (Chapter Two), and their sources (Chapter Three). An analysis of the type and function of the Proustian image, my main concern, is relegated to a brief fourth chapter ("Techniques"). The Conclusion includes various tabulations and charts disclosing the number and percentages of the distribution of images according to context, type, concreteness or abstractness, to quality — including sensory categories and mental images — and according to source.[25] A frequency count of figurative language within a literary work is difficult to assess, since it does not reveal the relationship and interaction of tropes that appear within the same passage.[26]

A third book on Proust's imagery, Irma Tiedtke's *Symbole und Bilder im Werke Marcel Prousts,* distinguishes between simile, metaphor, and symbol.[27] In Part One ("Bildhafte und symbolische Wirklichkeit") she studies the symbolic implications present in the material realm depicted in *A la recherche,* while in Part Two ("Spiegelung der geistigen Bedeutung der Wirklichkeit in den Bildern") she concentrates on the domains from which the images and symbols are derived.[28]

On Ullmann's approach to the study of imagery, see his *Language and Style,* Chapter IX, "The Nature of Imagery," pp. 174-201.

[25] *The Imagery of Proust* (Oxford: Basil Blackwell, 1966), pp. 257-264. For a review of this book, see André Abbou, "Problèmes et méthode d'une stylistique des images," pp. 212-223.

[26] For a discussion of the statistical approach, see Lillian Herlands Hornstein, "Analysis of Imagery: A critique of literary method," *PMLA,* 57 (1942), 638-653.

[27] See pp. 14-20 of *Symbole und Bilder* (Hamburg: Paul Evert Verlag, 1936) for a definition of these terms.

[28] Studies of Proust's style that include a section on imagery, are: Jean Milly, *Proust et le style*; Jean Mouton, *Le Style de Marcel Proust* (Chapter Three: "Les Images"); Käthe Zaeske, *Der Stil Marcel Prousts* (Chapter One, Section F: "Der ästhetische Ausdruck" studies metaphor, simile, personification, antithesis); Madeleine Remacle, *L'Elément poétique dans "A la recherche du temps perdu"* (Chapter Five, Part C studies comparisons and metaphors in a brief section). In *La Théorie du symbole littéraire,* Emeric Fiser discusses those of Proust's images that are based on sensory analogies connected with the experience of involuntary memory.

I should also mention three articles on the Proustian metaphor that concentrate on identifying the various vehicles connected with a given subject: Stephen Ullmann, "Images of Time and Memory in *Jean Santeuil,*" in *Currents*

In short, some excellent work has been done on the themes and sources of Proust's imagery, but little has been done on the structure and function of a particular class of imagery, such as metaphor. Since such a study should provide intensive analysis of each metaphor in its surrounding context, its breadth should be correspondingly limited. I have therefore limited myself to an important group of Proust's metaphors, those connected with the theme of time. By restricting scope, however, we can get a much closer look at how Proust's metaphors are constructed, at how they function as effective conveyors of insight and feeling, and how they orient the reader's interpretation of *A la recherche*.

The division of this study into seven chapters is based on the different structures and combinations of metaphors. Within these broad categories, further subdivisions were introduced to distinguish secondary structural peculiarities, and to single out the various functions of metaphor within the novel.

In studying the "single metaphor" (Chapter I), I deal exclusively with those passages in which only one part of speech is metaphoric. Within the extended structures of metaphor, the "brief conceit" (Chapter II) constitutes the simplest structure. My definition limits "brief conceit" to two or more metaphors from the same semantic domain, working together in the same syntactic unit. While the brief conceit consists of metaphors all of which function as essential components in establishing the basic code, the "continued metaphor" (Chapter III) presents us with several metaphors from the same semantic domain, one or more of which, however, have an explanatory, qualifying or tautological function in relation to the original metaphor or metaphors establishing the code. In discussing multiple sets of metaphors (Chapter IV), I distinguish between their various functions. "Accumulated metaphors" (Chapter V) are defined as metaphors that are closely related within the same syntactical framework, since they all have the same grammatical function in relation to a particular element

---

of Thought in French Literature: Essays in Memory of G. T. Clapton, ed. J. C. Ireson (Oxford: Basil Blackwell, 1965), pp. 210-226; Reino Virtanen, "Proust's Metaphors from the Natural and Exact Sciences," *PMLA*, 69 (December, 1954), 1038-1059; Elisabeth Gülich, "Die Metaphorik der Erinnerung in Prousts *A la Recherche*," *Zeitschrift für französische Sprache und Literatur*, 75 (1965), 51-74.

of the sentence. Metaphorical images that acquire added significance through repetition or through various types of context determination are studied in a separate chapter (VI). I have devoted one chapter (Chapter VII) to the study of various structures and functions of simile in relation to the metaphor or metaphors appearing within the same context.

Chapter I

THE SINGLE METAPHOR

I shall first examine the case of the single metaphor, the simplest metaphorical structure. In this study the term single metaphor refers to those passages in which only one part of speech is metaphoric. Although any part of speech may be metaphoric, all but one of the single metaphors dealing with an abstract notion of time are nouns or verbs. Only a few of Proust's time metaphors, however, fall into this category, since he is fond of elaborating on a notion of time by extending his metaphors or by reinforcing them with similes.

Unless they are clichés, single metaphors have a strong contextual determination or reinforcement that points to their intended meaning.[1] All of the single noun metaphors appear in the genitive link with the preposition *de*.[2] This structure immediately identifies or specifies the time aspect, as vehicle and tenor are directly juxtaposed and grammatically linked: *cours des âges, forme du Temps, courbe du temps, cloisons de cette heure, plénitude d'une après-midi, distance ... des années,* and *sceau du Temps.*

How these metaphors function is in each case to be learned from the surrounding text. *Cours des âges,* which out of context

---

[1] Proust uses such stereotype metaphors as *passé lointain, temps éloigné, moment éloigné, lointaines années, temps écoulé, temps immémoriaux, espace de ... années,* and variants of these expressions. See I, 719, 829; II, 14, 85, 205, 350, 383, 532, 1162, 1168.

[2] I am here following the general definition given by Christine Brooke-Rose in *A Grammar of Metaphor* where genitive link is described as a "part-relationship between two nouns, which is essentially one of provenance from or attribution to," and which may be a relationship of identity (pp. 146-147).

appears to be a stereotype metaphor,³ is given its original vigor in the Proustian passage, which must be quoted at length if we are to participate in the renewal of the metaphor:

> Un de mes rêves était la synthèse de ce que mon imagination avait souvent cherché à se représenter, pendant la veille, d'un certain paysage marin et de son passé médiéval. Dans mon sommeil je voyais une cité gothique au milieu d'une mer aux flots immobilisés comme sur un vitrail. Un bras de mer divisait en deux la ville; l'eau verte s'étendait à mes pieds; elle baignait sur la rive opposée une église orientale, puis des maisons qui existaient encore dans le XIVᵉ siècle, si bien qu'aller vers elles, c'eût été remonter le cours des âges.⁴

The schematic, allegorical tableau of the gothic city in the sea prepares and determines the interpretation of *cours*. The verbs *aller* and *remonter* immediately preceding *cours des âges* orient our visual response, especially the verb *remonter* since it is directly linked to the metaphor, its direct object. Within the water context, *cours,* reinforced by *remonter,* definitely takes on one of the concrete, literal meanings listed in the nineteenth-century *Larousse,* such as "mouvement, direction d'un liquide," "parcours d'un fleuve," and "course, marche rapide."⁵ Hence *cours des âges* constitutes part of the tableau's visual detail. Thus a used metaphor is restored to its original vigor as its full imaginal content is called upon by the preceding pictorial setting.

Sometimes the larger context of the novel is needed to determine the full meaning of a metaphor. In the following example the entire section of the "Matinée Guermantes" and a passage from "Combray" constitute the significant framework within which the metaphor must be considered. The metaphor's immediate context

---

³ The nineteenth-century *Larousse* lists this stereotype expression as a common usage for "succession du temps et des choses qui se composent d'une série d'instants." See Pierre Larousse, *Grand Dictionnaire universel du XIXᵉ siècle* (Paris: Librairie Classique Larousse et Boyer, 1869), V, 369.

⁴ Marcel Proust, *A la recherche du temps perdu,* "Bibliothèque de la Pléiade" (Paris: Gallimard, 1954), II, 146. All subsequent quotations from *A la recherche* are from the same edition. Volume and page numbers will be given in parentheses after each quotation.

⁵ Pierre Larousse, *op. cit.,* V, 369.

explicitly points to the broader context which is to be taken into consideration:

> Alors, je pensai tout d'un coup que si j'avais encore la force d'accomplir mon œuvre, cette matinée ... qui m'avait, aujourd'hui même, donné à la fois l'idée de mon œuvre et la crainte de ne pouvoir la réaliser, marquerait certainement avant tout, dans celle-ci, la forme que j'avais pressentie autrefois dans l'église de Combray, et qui nous reste habituellement invisible, celle du Temps. (III, 1044-45)

Forme du Temps takes on a concrete, physical meaning within the narrative framework of the "Matinée Guermantes" explicitly referred to by the narrator, while the relative phrase modifying *forme* further particularizes its implications through a specific reference to the Church of Combray. These two references call forth images of time visible in the reader's memory. The "Matinée Guermantes" has shown him the horrible metamorphosis of young men and women into old caricatures of themselves, as the Church of Combray previously revealed the wear and tear of the ages: the worn stones, the threadbare rugs, and the dusty stained-glass windows (I, 59-61).

Another example of single metaphor draws on the broader context of the "Matinée Guermantes." The narrator takes up the same idea of rendering time visible, a notion he again expresses by means of a single genitive link metaphor: "Du moins, si elle [la force] m'était laissée assez longtemps pour accomplir mon œuvre, je ne manquerais pas de la marquer au sceau de ce Temps dont l'idée s'imposait aujourd'hui" (III, 1151).[6] The metaphor *marquer au sceau du Temps* is a composite of the cliché *marquer au sceau* and the genitive link expressing the attribution to time, supplying us with a key to its meaning. This combination is quite effective, for the stereotype endows the notion of time with the concrete, visual content which it receives from the larger context of the "Matinée Guermantes," where people and things are described bearing the "seal of time."

The metaphorical expression *marquer au sceau du Temps* appears to be Proust's own combination. At any rate, even if it

---

[6] This passage was omitted from the main text of the Pléiade edition of *A la recherche,* and appears under "Notes et Variantes" as an alternate, incomplete and deleted version.

were a previously used expression, Proust's specific usage is original in its symbolic implications, which are specifically derived from the vision of Time projected by the work as a whole. The expression is striking because its cliché aspect stands out in a sentence where the tone is serious.[7] Since the exact insertion of this passage into *A la recherche* has not been determined, the surrounding context cannot be discussed. Yet the passage was written for the final paragraphs of the novel, where the symbolic content of *sceau du Temps* is significantly reinforced by the continued metaphors of men perched on top of the total of years lived.[8]

Context again plays a crucial role in interpreting the following metaphor. *La distance des années,* in itself a conventional expression, is given vigor by its presence within a syllepsis:[9]

> je reconnus, peint lui au contraire en bleu sombre, simplement parce qu'il était plus loin, le clocher de l'église de Combray. Non pas une figuration de ce clocher, ce clocher lui-même, qui, mettant ainsi sous mes yeux la distance des lieues et des années, était venu, au milieu de la lumineuse verdure et d'un tout autre ton, si sombre qu'il paraissait presque seulement dessiné, s'inscrire dans le carreau de ma fenêtre. (III, 698)

The syllepsis consists in this instance of the double genitive link attributed to *distance,* in relation to which *des lieues* is literal, and *des années* metaphorical. The dual semantic role of *distance* within the condensed syntactical structure is striking, since the reader has just been conditioned by the initial genitive link to take *distance* literally.

The special attention given to *distance* by the syllepsis and the narrative content of the broader context both alert the reader that

---

[7] The effectiveness of the stereotype *marquer au sceau* within this particular context has been discussed by Michael Riffaterre in "Fonctions du cliché dans la prose littéraire," *Cahiers de l'Association Internationale des Etudes Françaises,* No. 16 (1964), p. 89.

[8] See *A la recherche,* III, 1047-48. See *infra,* pp. 155-160 for a discussion of the continued metaphors within this passage.

[9] In this instance we are dealing with a most common, conventional syllepsis in which the part of speech to which the two elements of the syllepsis are linked performs a double semantic function, as its literal and figurative meanings are called upon. For other uses of syllepsis, see *infra,* p. 46, n. 13 and p. 106.

THE SINGLE METAPHOR 27

distance, besides being literal and metaphoric, is also symbolic. The different vantage point from which the narrator views the steeple, observing it from Tansonville rather than from his own room in Combray, is symbolic of significant changes, social and other, that Time has brought with it.

In addition to a genitive link that states the relationship between tenor and vehicle, a single metaphor may be clarified by accompanying explanatory remarks. In one of several passages where an aspect of time is described in terms of visual perception, the metaphor *courbe du temps* is reinforced by descriptive elaboration explaining the image:

> ils ne se rendaient pas compte de la courbe du temps qui faisait que ceux d'aujourd'hui voyaient ces gens à leur point d'arrivée tandis qu'eux se les rappelaient à leur point de départ. Et quand eux, les anciens, étaient entrés dans le monde, il y avait là des gens arrivés dont d'autres se rappelaient le départ.[10]

In the light of the preceding figure *courbe du temps,* the explanatory relative clause is read on two levels: *point de départ* and *point d'arrivée* refer to the mental distance existing in the perceiver's mind between successive generations of Parisian high society, and it reinforces the spatial analogy of physical distance, which explains the metaphor twice, once from the double present point of view of the newcomers and the oldtimers where a difference in years is translated into a difference of optical range. The second sentence merely reinforces the image and extends the curve.[11]

A few genitive link metaphors are borderline cases between the single metaphor and extended structures. In two examples, single metaphors are reinforced by an accompanying verb form, and there-

---

[10] According to the editors of the Pléiade edition, this passage appears on a separate sheet and its insertion in the novel cannot be determined (III, 1143).

[11] Proust once before expressed the same notion in similar terms based on the laws of perception in distance:

> c'est ainsi que ce que nous apercevons à l'horizon prend une grandeur mystérieuse et nous semble se renfermer sur un monde qu'on ne reverra plus; cependant nous avançons, et c'est bientôt nous-même qui sommes à l'horizon pour les générations qui sont derrière nous; cependant l'horizon recule, et le monde, qui semblait fini, recommence. (III, 929)

fore do not stand entirely alone. Yet the metaphorical development is not sufficient to allow one to speak of a small conceit, a category that shall be treated separately.

Here, as in the previous examples, the genitive link is formed by the preposition *de* followed by a time expression that clarifies the metaphor. Semantically these genitive links function like appositions, since the two parts of the metaphorical expression stand in a relationship of identity.[12] In the case of the metaphors *cloisons de cette heure* and *plénitude d'une après-midi,* hour becomes a unit of confinement, and the very essence of *après-midi* is *plénitude,* as is evident from the context in each case. In the first instance:

> nous allons être rien qu'à lui, lui faire des serments d'amitié qui, nés dans les cloisons de cette heure, restant enfermés en elle, ne seraient peut-être pas tenus le lendemain.... (II, 397)

Enfermés reinforces the concrete aspect of *cloisons,* and underlines its salient characteristic. The sudden "materialization" of the abstract temporal notion and the intrusion of the prosaic term *cloison* create a stylistic contrast that commands the reader's attention. Further contrast exists on the cognitive level, as the reader is asked to conceptualize a given period (of time) as a separate entity detached from the continuous flow of time. As a hyperbole and concrete translation of the notion of confinement, *cloison* strikingly conveys the central idea of the entire passage.

How *plénitude* becomes identified with *après-midi* and *fin de journée* is learned from the surrounding context:

> Et même celles qui n'avaient pas commencé dans le mystère, comme mes relations avec Mme de Souvré, si sèches et si purement mondaines aujourd'hui, gardaient à leurs débuts leur premier sourire, plus calme, plus doux, et si onctueusement tracé dans la plénitude d'une après-midi au bord de la mer, d'une fin de journée de printemps à Paris, bruyante d'équipages, de poussière soulevée, et de soleil remué comme de l'eau. (III, 974)

---

[12] Heinrich Henel calls this type of genitive link metaphor "appositional metaphors" and points out, as does Miss Brooke-Rose (pp. 154-160), that the two terms of the metaphor are "virtually identified" ("Metaphor and Meaning," p. 109).

THE SINGLE METAPHOR

Our conception of *plénitude* is primarily determined by the three images that qualify une *fin de journée*. The juxtaposition of three evocative images — each conveying an essential part of the spring day atmosphere — translates the "fullness" of an experience into verbal terms, focusing our attention on its essential qualities. It also reveals which impressions are closely related within the narrator's mind.[13]

This example of genitive link metaphor is unique in that it has a double complement (*une après-midi au bord de la mer* and *fin de journée à Paris*), each of which relates the notion of *plénitude* to a specific experience. The close syntactical structure translates the conceptual relationship between different moments within time. Such a juxtaposition of two separate experiences within time translates the narrator's interest in common essences. In his quest for time lost, chronological time is unimportant, for what matters is the essence of an experience.

The fact that all of the single noun metaphors appear in the genitive link structure seems to reveal the author's tendency to be explicit, since each metaphorical expression is at once modified by a term pointing to the tenor. The immediate juxtaposition of tenor and vehicle confronts us with an evident semantic shift that aids us in identifying the metaphor, while the direct mention of the temporal aspect under consideration through the genitive link guides our interpretation of the metaphorical statement.

The genitive link, which may express a relationship of provenance from, attribution to, or equivalency, is primarily used as a statement of identity in the examples just studied.[14] In *forme du Temps, courbe du temps, plénitude d'une après-midi, distance des ... années* time is fully identified with each of the metaphorical elements. The other instances of genitive link metaphor are also partly statements of identity, though there is enough ambiguity that they may also be read as salient characteristics attributed to time.

The other main category of single time metaphor is the verb metaphor. The five examples I have found are all active verbs of

---

[13] The multiple impact of an experience was previously stated as a general truth: "Une heure n'est pas une heure, c'est un vase rempli de parfums, de sons, de projets et de climats" (III, 889). See also I, 84-87; 345-346; 426.

[14] *Supra*, p. 23, footnote 2.

movement used figuratively within an abstract context: *chevaucher, interférer, empiéter, fondre,* and *renverser.* These verbs appear in a context of expository prose where they stand in sharp contrast to an abstract cadre.

The first example appears within the impersonal cadre of a generalization derived from personal experience. The narrator's objective viewpoint is obvious from the various impersonal pronouns he employs (*on, vous*):

> Les différentes périodes de notre vie se chevauchent ainsi l'une l'autre. On refuse dédaigneusement, à cause de ce qu'on aime et qui vous sera un jour si égal, de voir ce qui vous est égal aujourd'hui, qu'on aimera demain, qu'on aurait peut-être pu, si on avait consenti à le voir, aimer plus tôt, et qui eût ainsi abrégé vos souffrances actuelles, pour les remplacer, il est vrai, par d'autres. (I, 626-627)

The aphoristic initial sentence whose *ainsi* seems to be pointing to a previous illustration is actually vague, unprepared. There appears to be a hiatus between this sentence and the preceding statement to the effect that the narrator's parents were annoyed with him for refusing a dinner engagement where he would have met Mme Bontemps and her niece Albertine. Only the reader who has already read the novel will see a narrative anticipation in the first sentence, since he knows that Albertine will replace Gilberte in the hero's affections. At first reading we require the long explanation of the second sentence, which illustrates in literal terms what has just been stated metaphorically as a general rule. The general concept emerges from this sentence, but our comprehension of it is strongly colored by the unique verb metaphor of the preceding statement. The concrete quality of *chevaucher* ("to straddle") as a dynamic verb of action organizes our point of view about the notion of time. The verb carries an image of a distinctive posture or position, which is transferred to its subject, *périodes*. The verb works alone as the only element that personifies an abstraction. Its specific content is therefore solely responsible for acting on the noun to which it is linked, and by standing alone it forces us to focus on its metaphorical action. This results in a bold confrontation of widely different semantic domains not readily joined, an effect further enhanced by a contrast of styles. The term *chevaucher,* belonging to the realm of activity or technical description (position of shingles, teeth), stands in contrast with the abstract, theoretical vocabulary of the entire passage, and stands especially opposed to *périodes,* its abstract subject.

The interruption of the narrative by general, aphoristic observations is a frequent device in *A la recherche.* A general truth or conclusion is advanced before the reader has been given a complete account of an episode. The above passage, for instance, prefigures the narrator's future relationship with Albertine, and derives a general law from it.

Proust's use of another verb form, *interférer,* is quite original within an abstract context, since nineteenth-century dictionaries define it only as a technical term belonging to the realm of optical physics. *Interférer* was then defined as the action of "produire une interférence." The phenomenon of "interference" is characteristic of a certain behavior of light waves which, according to Littré, results in "une suite de bandes alternativement brillantes et obscures." [15]

Yet the Proustian context in which *interférant* appears does not bring out its scientific implications:

> Souvent (notre vie étant si peu chronologique, interférant tant d'anachronismes dans la suite des jours), je vivais dans ceux, plus anciens que la veille ou l'avant-veille, où j'aimais Gilberte. (I, 642)

The participial verb form is limited in scope by its subject *vie* and its direct object *anachronismes,* whose abstract nature robs the verb of its original sensory quality and prevents a visual interpretation.[16] The context points to a meaning which comes close to "interpolating" or "inserting," yet a substitution of these terms within this passage would change its impact.[17] *Interférant* is a highly original

---

[15] Emile Littré, *Dictionnaire de la langue française* (Paris: Gallimard-Hachette, 1967), IV, 1088.

[16] Proust, who seems fond of the term, uses it again in another context, which definitely brings out its visual implications. Cf. III, 68-69.

[17] The Robert dictionary added a new, figurative meaning to the definition of *interférence* with a quotation from Proust: Paul Robert, *Dictionnaire de la langue française,* IV, 164. The figurative use of *interférence* is thus less striking today than it was in Proust's time when the only standard definition of the term was a technical one. Proust uses the term "interpolate" in another context dealing with the same notion of anachronism. Cf. I, 386-387.

term in its new context, a term not yet neutralized by common usage.

The metaphor's primary purpose here seems to be conceptual. It is part of a structure (the parenthetical phrase) interpolated into the narration to express a general truth about time and to supply a concise explanatory note to the narrative content.

The third example of single verb metaphor works very much like the previous two: an active verb of movement stands out in an explanatory passage. In addition, the figurative connotations of the verb reinforce the statement:

> Or cette cause [félicité], je la devinais en comparant ces diverses impressions bienheureuses et qui avaient entre elles ceci de commun que je les éprouvais à la fois dans le moment actuel et dans un moment éloigné, jusqu'à faire empiéter le passé sur le présent, à me faire hésiter à savoir dans lequel des deux je me trouvais.... (III, 871)

The phrase *jusqu'à faire empiéter le passé sur le présent* commands the reader's attention, since it introduces a personifying element into an otherwise abstract passage. The verb *empiéter* transfers its potential of action to its subject and indirect object, which are thus both animated. The uniqueness of the temporal experience is further underlined by the pejorative notion of "violation" contained in the figurative implications of *empiéter,* implications that orient the reader's conception of the extraordinary experience. Finally, further emphasis is given to the verb by its difference in lexical *niveau* from its direct and indirect object: the prosaic implications of *empiéter* stand in contrast to *passé* and *présent,* aspects of time usually found in an abstract, more elevated context.

Empiéter is less striking within its context than *interférer,* since it has been weakened by common usage. Yet as the central stylistic device in an otherwise neutral passage, it draws our attention, and shapes our point of view toward the particular aspect of time under discussion.

These single verb metaphors all share certain characteristics.[18] All of them are verbs of action that transfer part of their active

---

[18] Two other single verb metaphors work much the same way as those already discussed: 1) "Et pour mieux fondre tous mes passés, Mme Verdurin

impact onto the abstract nouns to which they are linked. These nouns are thereby personified, and their interrelationship with the verb adds a concrete element to an otherwise abstract explanatory or discursive passage. The verb in each case is the text's striking element, since it stands in sharp contrast to the rest of the passage. A certain amount of tension results from the joining of an abstract expression of time to a verb of action. The tension is further enhanced by a difference in lexical *niveau*: the verbs belong to a prosaic context, and the notion of time is expressed in an abstract, intellectual context. As the central stylistic element in each passage, the verb metaphor commands the reader's attention. It also dominates the intellectual content, since the trope's concrete nature helps us conceptualize the abstract notion.

I have found only one example of the single metaphor as adjective. This example is a borderline case, belonging as much to the verb category as to the adjective: "c'était cette notion du temps évaporé, des années passées non séparées de nous, que j'avais maintenant l'intention de mettre si fort en relief..." (III, 1046).

The verbal adjective *évaporé* is ambiguous here, since its implications are not clarified by the context. The term's primary meaning refers us to the phenomenon of effervescence or volatilization. This reference to a specific activity animates the abstract temporal notion and emphasizes it, but the figure seems less original when we recall that one of the established figurative meanings of *évaporé* is *dissipé*. As a synonym of time "lost" or "vanished," *temps évaporé* might seem stereotype, yet it is still striking since common usage has adopted *temps écoulé,* the combination *temps évaporé* being relatively unfamiliar. Our conception of *évaporé* is restricted, however, by the phrase immediately juxtaposed to *notion du temps évaporé,* whose genitive structure it expands and whose implications it modifies: "cette notion du temps évaporé, des années passées non séparées de nous." While *des années passées* is a tautological repetition in literal terms of *temps évaporé,* the additional qualification *non séparées de nous* seems contradictory within the context of

---

tout comme Gilberte avait épousé un Guermantes" (III, 1031). 2) "...c'est bien plutôt quelque chose qui semble en soi n'avoir aucune importance et qui renverse pour eux l'ordre du temps..." (III, 728).

Renverser, like *empiéter,* has lost some of its original dynamic impact, since its figurative meaning is part of common usage.

evaporation, which logically implies disappearance.[19] Only the broader context of the final section of *A la recherche* resolves this apparent contradiction. Though the years pass quickly and seem to disappear — a notion the narrator translates into *temps évaporé* — they have left on each of us a permanent imprint that does not allow us to ignore these years, to detach ourselves from them. The paragraph in which this figure of "evaporated time" appears speaks of the memories left by these years, whereas the preceding and following paragraphs translate their destructive residue, their ever-growing burden into the precarious image of men on stilts (III, 1046-48).

---

[19] Although the more definitive Pléiade edition uses *temps évaporé*, the expression *temps incorporé* used by earlier editions makes more sense within the present context.

CHAPTER II

THE BRIEF CONCEIT

A. SAME PARTS OF SPEECH ESTABLISHING THE SEMANTIC DOMAIN

Within the extended structures of metaphor, the brief conceit constitutes the simplest one. I shall define this category by limiting it to two or more metaphors sharing the same semantic domain and working together within the same syntactical framework. Most metaphors forming a simple conceit play an auxiliary role within their context, since literal statements are mainly responsible for preparing the temporal notion. Their main function is to emphasize and clarify the temporal concept through a concrete image. When metaphors are the prime carriers of meaning, the transpositions are more extensive than the brief conceit.

The first two conceits consist of nouns mutually reinforcing each other. For example, a short conceit of two noun metaphors in apposition expresses the narrator's notion of a particular emotional state: "La perte de toute boussole, de toute direction, qui caractérise l'attente, persiste encore après l'arrivée de l'être attendu..." (II, 738). *Direction* clarifies the code introduced by *boussole*, since the two nouns exist within the same mental context. Their relationship is metonymic, one being the instrument, the other standing for the realm of activity where the instrument is employed. The conceptual link between these two nouns belonging to the same semantic domain is enhanced through the syntactical link of the grammatical structure they share: each forms a genitive link with *perte*. The anaphora *toute* further underlines this syntactic parallelism. The renewal of the stereotype *perdre la boussole* from a verbal statement in the past tense (e.g. *Il a perdu la boussole*) to the substantival form lends the figure added effect, as does, of course, the addition of *direction*.

In the second example, the two noun metaphors express a very personal conception of anachronism. The narrator elucidates this notion by contrasting two genitive link metaphors:

> ce n'était qu'à l'instant — plus d'une année après son enterrement, à cause de cette anachronisme qui empêche si souvent /le calendrier des faits de coïncider avec celui des sentiments / — que je venais d'apprendre qu'elle était morte. (II, 756) [1]

The insistence on the same code through *celui,* which refers us back to *calendrier,* draws our attention to the two genitive links. The key elements are thus thrown into relief. Whereas *anachronisme* explicitly states the temporal aspect in literal terms, *calendrier,* as the archetypal time-telling device, provides the reader with a striking conceptual model. [2] The proliferation of the conventional calendar — which by definition serves as a universal point of reference — into two separate entities concretizes and dramatizes the notion of anachronism.

The immediate literal context prepares the imagery by clearly indicating the time gap: "plus d'une année après son enterrement." This literal indication and the metaphorical phrase in question are syntactically joined and set off by the dashes that isolate this parenthetical interpolation from the rest of the sentence. The narrator thus interrupts his narration to focus the reader's attention on the temporal phenomenon. Besides that, the syntactical disjunction also orients the reader's conception of anachronism, since explanation precedes narration.

---

[1] The slanted line is used to set off the metaphorical statement from its surrounding context.

[2] The term "conceptual model" is used within this study to refer to the narrator's use of a well-known object whose salient characteristics — usually its distinct shape, form or function — are used to concretize an abstract notion. The reference to a specific object — or in some instances a geometric figure or a schema — guides the reader's conceptualization of the abstract notion.

B. Verb-Subject-Object Reinforcement

In a brief conceit where a noun or nouns (subject, direct object, indirect object) work in conjunction with a verb, the effect may be bolder, the image more easily comprehended, because the verb particularizes, personifies or actualizes the noun to which it is linked.

In some instances it is the conceit's textual integration that emphasizes the metaphors. A disjunctive syntactical structure heightens our awareness of the metaphors appearing in it, and emphasizes the temporal notion:

> Quand je vivais, d'une façon un peu moins désintéressée, pour un amour, un rêve venait rapprocher singulièrement de moi, / lui faisant parcourir de grandes distances de temps perdu, / ma grand'mère, Albertine que j'avais recommencé à aimer.... (III, 914)

This disjunctive phrase is especially striking because of the unexpected descriptive reinforcement of its stereotype expressions: *temps perdu* is a cliché, and the noun *distances,* used in connection with time, is likewise a conventionalized metaphor. Yet the combination *distances* and *temps perdu* is not stereotype, especially since *distances* is reinforced by its adjective *grandes* and its verb *parcourir,* stressing its spatial content. The verb actualizes and lends dynamic content to its direct object and the genitive link it forms with *temps perdu.* In this new combination, the stereotype *temps perdu* is renewed and concretized, thus gaining in expressive force.

In another instance, a brief conceit is interpolated into the middle of a sentence appearing within a narrative passage. The disjunctive element, by abruptly stopping the narration, forces the reader's attention on the insertion. As in the preceding example, a conventional conceit translates the abstract notion into concrete terms that help us understand it.[3] Though conventional, the conceit

---

[3] The conceptual image concretizing the abstract may be as prosaic and obvious as the following archetypal time-telling device which is directly inserted into the literal context by the conjunction *tandis que*: "tandis que, présage de celui-ci [le réveil], fait résonner son tic tac ce réveille-matin intérieur que notre préoccupation a réglé si bien" (II, 87). As in the conceit

is effective, because the sudden introduction of an animated image, which dramatizes each aspect of the temporal notion, commands our attention:

> Sa vie et celle d'Albertine, si tard connues de moi, toutes deux à Balbec, et si vite terminées, s'étaient croisées à peine; c'était lui, me redisais-je en voyant que / les navettes agiles des années tissent des fils entre ceux de nos souvenirs qui semblaient d'abord les plus indépendants, / c'était lui que j'avais envoyé chez Mme Bontemps quand Albertine m'avait quitté. Et puis il se trouvait que leurs deux vies avaient chacune un secret parallèle et que je n'avais pas soupçonné.... (III, 848)

This conceit from weaving introduces a dynamic, concrete nucleus into the temporal context that orients the reader's conception of the notion under discussion. The conceit is easily interpreted, because the reader is already familiar with a similar one, that of the Fates' spinning and cutting off the thread of life. The specific reference to the action of years on memory is syntactically and semantically made very clear, since the genitive link of the initial metaphoric expression (*les navettes agiles des années*) immediately clarifies the transposition. Once years turn into "shuttles," the verb "weave" and the direct object "thread," which lengthen and reinforce the code, are automatically accepted.[4]

The narrator frequently communicates his conception of an emotional state of being within a given duration by means of concrete images whose impact directs the reader's conception of the temporal notion. Most of these images are prosaic and lack poetic ambiguity, particularly since each image is exploited for a salient characteristic. Yet their use within a temporal context is original and striking, and the repeated use of some of these images

---

from weaving, the brief conceit relies on the metaphorical code set up jointly by subject, verb and direct object, whereas the relative clause attached to *réveille-matin* points to the pretext which gave rise to the image, a role played by the genitive link *des années* in the above conceit.

[4] Further on in *Le Temps retrouvé* the author re-introduces this conceit to express the same notion of man's retrospective awareness, as the years go by, of his complex interrelationships with people and events. This time the code from weaving is extended to express the intricate nature of such interrelationships. See III, 1030, and *infra*, p. 70, of this study where the passage in question is treated as a "complex conceit."

and their variants points to certain conceptual constants within *A la recherche*.

Within the structure of the basic conceit, such original transpositions largely rely on the mutual verb-noun reinforcement. To compensate for their brevity, these conceits are carefully reinforced by the immediate context.[5] The following one, for example, is preceded by a literal statement that initiates the imagery:

> presque autant que le doute anxieux, l'absence de doute rend intolérable l'attente du plaisir infaillible parce qu'elle fait de cette attente un accomplissement innombrable et, par la fréquence des représentations anticipées, / divise le temps en tranches aussi menues / que ferait l'angoisse. (II, 383)

The analogy to *angoisse* within this passage does not reinforce the metaphorical imagery. It closely relates two emotional states, however, since they share the same image, *tranches,* reinforced by *divise* and *menues.* This rather prosaic image stands in striking contrast to the abstract subject (*absence de doute; angoisse*) and direct object (*temps*). Introduced at the end of an abstract passage, these metaphors unexpectedly confront the reader with a concrete image whose graphic and dynamic nature acts upon the notion of time. Besides the tension created by bringing together the tangible, prosaic (*tranches*) and the abstract (*temps*), further tension is due to the reader's conventional conception of duration as a continuous whole, and the unexpected, new conceptual image of duration as minutely and sharply divided matter.

The message to be derived from this metaphorical transposition is reinforced by the prepositional phrase immediately preceding it: "par la fréquence des représentations anticipées" announces the specific durational aspect under consideration, and acts as a qualifying phrase to the verb *divise.* Such explicit contextual reinforcements within metaphorical passages dealing with time stress the author's insistence on the notion to be communicated.

---

[5] The narrator already introduced the temporal notion earlier in the same passage: "C'est qu'en général, plus le temps qui nous sépare de ce que nous nous proposons est court, plus il nous semble long, parce que nous lui appliquons des mesures plus brèves..." (II, 382).

A similar notion of temporal discontinuity translated into a concrete image is again reinforced by an explanatory apposition immediately following the conceit, restating the notion in literal terms.[6] The brief conceit relies, as in the previous example, on the object-verb reinforcement for its full imaginal appeal:

> Jamais il n'avait supposé que ce fût une chose aussi récente, cachée à ses yeux, qui n'avaient pas su la découvrir, non dans un passé qu'il n'avait pas connu, mais dans des soirs qu'il se rappelait si bien, qu'il avait vécus avec Odette, qu'il avait crus connus si bien par lui et qui maintenant prenaient rétrospectivement quelque chose de fourbe et d'atroce; au milieu d'eux, tout d'un coup, / se creusait cette ouverture béante, / ce moment dans l'île du Bois. (I, 366)[7]

The striking, concrete image communicates Swann's sudden emotional upheaval as he discovers a discrepancy within his mental representation of the pleasant evenings spent with Odette, a period whose temporal continuity up to now had been the guarantee of a continuous emotional tie between himself and Odette. While the anthropomorphizing adjectives *fourbe* and *atroce* transfer Swann's attitude onto *soirs* and reveal his emotional state indirectly and in abstract terms, the metaphorical image translates the subjective impression into concrete terms. The dynamic action verb *creuser*, particularized by the prepositional phrase *au milieu d'eux,* and reinforced by *ouverture béante,* turns evenings into a block of matter. *Ouverture*, magnified by the adjective *béante*, stands in sharp contrast to the concrete, continuous "time block." The "materialization" of a drastic conceptual transformation through an image representing a gap within homogeneous matter significantly empha-

---

[6] In this instance, the subjective insight into time is Swann's. The narrator-hero, whose experiences often echo Swann's, uses similar images to describe his emotional states.

[7] Cf. I, 385 where temporal discontinuity is likewise expressed through the concrete imagery of a short conceit: "l'heure du départ: elle me / semblait inciser à un point précis de l'après-midi une savoureuse entaille, / une marque mystérieuse...." The metaphorical structure is here similar to the one quoted above: the verb-diret object team sets up the basic code, whereas the prepositional phrase attached to the verb *inciser* further specifies its realm of action. The vague apposition juxtaposed to *entaille* does not lengthen the code, it merely adds an abstract emotional equivalent.

sizes the conceptual contrast and allows us insight into the abruptly changing attitude.

C. Specific Functions of the Conceit as Conceptual Model [8]

1. Conceit Clarifying References to Time

In several passages an ambiguous or vague expression referring to time is clarified by a conceit of two or more metaphors. For instance, a different mode of being within time, first expressed through the vague metaphor *zone différente,* is clarified by a brief conceit providing the reader with a conceptual model:

> Mais quand nous arrivions à Rivebelle, aussitôt, — à cause de l'excitation d'un plaisir nouveau, et me trouvant dans cette zone différente où l'exceptionnel nous fait entrer / après avoir coupé le fil, patiemment tissé depuis tant de jours, qui nous conduisait vers la sagesse / — comme s'il ne devait plus jamais y avoir de lendemain, ni de fins élevées à réaliser, disparaissait ce mécanisme précis de prudente hygiène qui fonctionnait pour les sauvegarder. (I, 809)

Couper le fil dramatically stresses the concept of discontinuity, since it provides us with a concrete representation of the sudden reversal: *fil,* reinforced in its aspect of continuity by its qualifying phrase *patiemment tissé depuis tant de jours,* is violently acted upon by the verb *couper,* whose abrupt action turns the model of continuity into its opposite.[9]

As in several previous examples studied above, the metaphorical imagery is part of an interpolated, explanatory remark introduced into the middle of a sentence. By interrupting the narrative in order to introduce a literal explanation reinforced by a concrete

---

[8] For a definition of the term "conceptual model," see *supra,* p. 36, footnote 2.

[9] See III, 848 and 1030 where Proust uses the same conceit from weaving, although in a different temporal context. This conceit appears to be a conceptual constant to which the author resorts when dealing with certain aspects of time.

image clarifying the abstract notion under discussion, the context focuses our attention on the discursive and cognitive. The disjunctive phrase containing the conceit is clearly set off from the rest of the sentence through the dash, which emphasizes the syntactical break. The reader's attention focuses on the disruptive element, and the conceit to which his attention is thus drawn determines his conception of the temporal notion. The juxtaposition of an additional disjunctive statement — the conditional sentence — in delaying the resumption of the narrative by elaborating on the notion of discontinuity, adds further emphasis to the temporal notion.

The explanatory function of the next conceit is obvious from the causal syntactical structure introducing it. As in the previous example, the conceit functions as a precise conceptual model specifying the temporal aspect previously introduced by several abstract time expressions:

> je jouissais en imagination de toutes les matinées pareilles, passées ou possibles, plus exactement d'un certain type de matinées dont toutes celles du même genre n'étaient que l'intermittente apparition et que j'avais vite reconnu; / car l'air vif tournait de lui-même les pages qu'il fallait, et je trouvais tout indiqué devant moi, pour que je pusse le suivre de mon lit, l'évangile du jour. / Cette matinée idéale comblait mon esprit de réalité permanente, identique à toutes les matinées semblables, et me communiquait une allégresse que mon état de débilité ne diminuait pas.... (III, 26)

The vague temporal phrases "toutes les matinées pareilles, passées ou possibles," "un certain type de matinées," "même genre," and "intermittente apparition" introduce and designate in literal terms the notion of time to be dealt with. The hero's very personal intuition of this temporal experience is then communicated by means of a conceptual conceit. The subject *l'air vif* stands here as a metonymy for the specific atmospheric conditions of the day, described at length in the preceding paragraph. As the subject of the conceit, *l'air vif* recalls and closely links the stimulus of the sensory analogy to its metaphorical translation. By narrowing down the conceit of the "book" to *évangile,* the temporal notion is further clarified. In fact, *évangile du jour* is given the dominant position within the conceit by appearing at the end of the sentence, after a syntactical delay. Thus *évangile,* besides reinforcing and continuing the code established by *tourner* and *pages,* also imposes further precision on the reader's interpretation of the conceit: the particular pages of the *évangile* ("les pages qu'il fallait") are only read on special days. This is the essence of the message dealing with very special days.[10]

The conceit is immediately followed by a literal statement resuming the general remarks on special days. As in the earlier sentence, we are confronted with abstract, general time expressions: *matinée idéale, réalité permanente,* and *matinées semblables.* The implications of the ambiguous expression *matinée idéale* are largely determined by the context, since the term is specifically used to refer to and encompass the temporal experience already clarified by the previous sentence. The immediate context further determines our conception of *matinée idéale,* as *réalité permanente* — in turn qualified by "identique à toutes les matinées semblables" — points to its salient characteristic.

Without being explicitly introduced as an explanatory image, a conceit may serve as an obvious conceptual model. The graphic nature of the image introduced into a passage dealing with *temps idéal* (to refer to imaginary time) as opposed to experienced time exemplifies this. The hero has just become aware of this distinction by realizing that time and space work together:[11]

---

[10] The temporal conceit based on the book appears to be a conceptual constant in *A la recherche.* In *Nom de pays* (I, 386-387, discussed *infra,* pp. 75-76) Proust uses the variant *calendrier* to express the notion of temporal anachronism based, as in the above example, on a change in weather. In II, 756 (*supra,* p. 36) *calendrier* is once more used in a context of subjective anachronism.

Proust uses another conceptual constant when speaking of "intermittence," namely several conceits based on music. See II, 396 for an extended conceit based on orchestration, and III, 25 for one based on the violin, which immediately precedes the *évangile* metaphor. Since these conceits reinforce each other in concretizing the same notion, they may be considered as belonging to the accumulative series of metaphors to be discussed in Section B of Chapter IV.

[11] Our subjectivity in regard to physical manifestations of time is conveyed by a brief conceit from the spatial domain:

> pour M. de Létourville j'étais donc, non un camarade, mais un vieux monsieur; et de M. de Létourville... étais-je donc / séparé par l'écartement d'un invisible compas auquel je n'avais pas songé et qui me situait si loin du jeune sous-lieutenant / qu'il semblait que, pour celui qui se disait mon "petit ami," j'étais un vieux monsieur? (III, 928)

je sentis que c'était vers la semaine qui commençait le lundi... que se dirigeaient pour s'y absorber, au sortir du temps idéal où elles n'existaient pas encore, les deux cités Reines / dont j'allais avoir, par la plus émouvante des géométries, à inscrire les dômes et les tours dans le plan de ma propre vie. / (I, 392)

The expression *temps idéal* refers to the hero's imaginary time conception, as stated by the preceding explanatory context: "Temps qui se refabrique si bien qu'on peut encore le passer dans une ville après qu'on l'a passé dans une autre." The expression is further clarified through the direct contrast to "experienced time" whose unique days are described as follows: "ils se consument par l'usage, ils ne reviennent pas, on ne peut plus les vivre ici quand on les a vécus là." This is the extent of the explicit textual preparation for the following conceit from geometry dealing with the notion of "actual time." By inserting the qualifying phrase "par la plus émouvante des géométries" before the metaphorical transposition, the author supplies us with the key for the figurative code. We then know to which realm *inscrire* and *plan* refer us. The clear and logical presentation of the imagery is further evident from the syntactical link to *cités Reines* clarifying the provenance of the metonymies *dômes* and *tours*. As symbols developing the semantic implications of *Reines,* they refer us to the regal aspect of the two religious and cultural centers.

The reader is also aware of the fact that these cities now represent space, real space, as opposed to imaginary space, for the narrator tells us in the passage preceding the conceit that these cities occupy "une certaine place déterminée de la terre." From this careful preparation it is clear that the graphical image from geometry serves as a conceptual model stressing and concretizing the important idea that time and space are to be considered together.[12] By insisting on the multidimensional aspect of reality just

---

The genitive link *d'un invisible compas* — a metonymy which refers us to the spatial domain — reinforces *écartement*. A similar image referring to a spatial measuring device appears in I, 482 (*aiguille*) and II, 738 (*boussole*).

[12] In *La Fugitive* and *Le Temps retrouvé,* Proust repeatedly uses the metaphor *plan* in a temporal context. Within the structure of the short conceit, I have found two more examples where time and space are brought together by the imagery: "je n'avais longtemps considéré que les positions différentes qu'elle occupait dans mon souvenir dans le plan des années" (III, 496). In

THE BRIEF CONCEIT 45

conceived by the hero, the geometrical graph impresses this notion upon the reader and throws it into relief within the narrative account of the hero's life, where the new temporal discovery plays a major role.

2. Conceit Clarifying a Descriptive Tableau

Several brief conceits are preceded or followed by descriptive details representative of a definite time and place. These descriptive images reinforce the conceit by illustrating the time aspect under discussion with recall images from the past. Repeated and selected to represent a certain period, they acquire symbolic overtones. To illustrate the relationship between the conceit and the surrounding imagery, a more extensive quotation is needed, as in the following passage describing Swann's remembrance of the past:

> il retrouva tout ce qui de ce bonheur perdu avait fixé à jamais la spécifique et volatile essence; il revit tout, les pétales neigeux et frisés du chrysanthème qu'elle lui avait jeté dans sa voiture, qu'il avait gardé contre ses lèvres — l'adresse en relief de la "Maison Dorée" sur la lettre où il avait lu: "Ma main tremble si fort en vous écrivant" — le rapprochement de ses sourcils quand elle lui avait dit d'un air suppliant: "Ce n'est pas dans trop longtemps que vous me ferez signe?"; il sentit l'odeur du fer du coiffeur par lequel il se faisait relever sa "brosse" pendant que Lorédan allait chercher la petite ouvrière, les pluies d'orage qui tombèrent si souvent ce printemps-là, le retour glacial dans sa victoria, au clair de lune, / toutes les mailles d'habitudes mentales, d'impressions saisonnières, de réactions cutanées, qui avaient étendu sur une suite de semaines un réseau uniforme dans lequel son corps se trouvait repris. / (I, 345-346)

The initial sentence, "il retrouva tout ce qui de ce bonheur avait fixé à jamais la spécifique et volatile essence," introduces the tem-

---

the following example, the experienced narrator multiplies these "planes" to hint at the complexity of man's existence within time, which, according to him, requires a "psychologie dans l'espace" rather than a "psychologie plane." He thus speaks of "ces plans différents suivant lesquels le Temps, depuis que je venais de le ressaisir dans cette fête, disposait ma vie" (III, 1031). See also II, 1005 and III, 557.

poral subject in general terms. The following series of recall images discloses the various sensory impressions that constitute the "volatile essence" of Swann's former happiness, and illustrates the significant extent to which the past has been recaptured. The metaphorical conceit of the "intricate network" is an emphatic translation of the conceptual contiguity between various impressions closely associated with an experience. Besides serving a cognitive function by translating a complex state of consciousness into concrete terms, the conceit based on *mailles* and *réseau* also "dramatizes" the overpowering impact of the momentary intrusion of the past. Swann suddenly finds himself enmeshed by the sensory and mental impressions associated with the past experience: "toutes les mailles d'habitudes mentales, d'impressions saisonnières, de réactions cutanées, qui avaient étendu sur une suite de semaines un réseau uniforme dans lequel son corps se trouvait repris."

The metaphors' intended message is apparent from the immediate context at hand, the triple genitive link with *mailles: mailles d'habitudes mentales, d'impressions saisonnières, de réactions cutanées.* The *de* links refer back to and categorize the content of the preceding descriptive imagery, and translate the close conceptual relationship between sensory and mental processes.[13] The close syntactical relationship between tenor and vehicle is a frequent structural element in Proust's time imagery, which fulfills primarily a cognitive function.[14]

The conceit's temporal content is further clarified by the prepositional phrase *sur une suite de semaines,* which particularizes the verb *avaient étendu* and in turn its direct object *réseau,* thereby closely joining the literal and metaphoric. Because of this close syntactical juxtaposition of literal and metaphoric discourse, the temporal implications of *uniforme* are brought out by the adjective's proximity to *suite de semaines.* The prepositional phrase "dans lequel son corps se trouvait repris" further particularizes the conceit

---

[13] This triple genitive link is an example of Proust's use of syllepsis as a losely knit syntactical structure translating a relationship of identity between the various terms. The metaphorical function of Proustian syllepses is discussed by Justin O'Brien, in "Proust's Use of Syllepsis," *PMLA,* 69, no. 4 (September, 1954), 751. See *supra,* p. 26, and *infra,* p. 106 for further examples of Proust's use of syllepsis.

[14] See pp. 215-218 of the Conclusion for the cognitive function of Proust's metaphors.

of the network, which now becomes a trap. The metaphorical extension again emphasizes the overpowering presence of the past, which entirely dominates Swann.[15]

When a conceit is introduced into a descriptive tableau to state a general law, it invests the account of a particular experience with symbolic significance. This is the more evident when the metaphors have an obvious conceptual function:

> Quand à dix heures du matin on venait ouvrir mes volets, je voyais flamboyer, au lieu du marbre noir que devenaient en resplendissant les ardoises de Saint-Hilaire, l'Ange d'or du campanile de Saint-Marc.... Je ne pouvais apercevoir que lui, tant que j'étais couché, mais / comme le monde n'est qu'un vaste cadran solaire où un seul segment ensoleillé nous permet de voir l'heure qu'il est, / dès le premier matin je pensai aux boutiques de Combray, sur la place de l'Eglise, qui le dimanche étaient sur le point de fermer quand j'arrivais à la messe, tandis que la paille du marché sentait fort sous le soleil déjà chaud. (III, 623)

The paragraph's initial sentence — which immediately precedes this quotation — is a comprehensive statement announcing the topic of the next three pages over which this passage extends: "j'y goûtais des impressions analogues à celles que j'avais si souvent ressenties autrefois à Combray, mais transposées selon un mode entièrement différent et plus riche." What follows is a juxtaposition of two images, one representing Combray, the other Venice. Their contrast, the "mode différent," is clear from the visual contrast of "marbre noir" and "l'Ange d'or," while the poetic metamorphosis of *ardoises* into *marbre,* which takes us from the factual to the imaginary realm, links the two images within the narrator's subjective evaluation. Yet the notion of "analogous impressions" between two such different settings is not evident from this juxtaposition, and so the narrator introduces a conceptual conceit, followed by a representative image of Combray.[16]

---

[15] The conceit based on *réseau* is used several times in *A la recherche* to communicate a temporal experience. Although the term *réseau* is used, its semantic reference varies. Cf. I, 407; I, 720, and III, 1030. See pp. 68 (I, 407) and 70 (III, 1030) for further discussion of this metaphor.

[16] Though the quotation under discussion focuses on the common essence attributed to Combray and Venice by the hero-narrator — an essence which

The conceit translates a complex temporal relationship between man and his surroundings into a familiar artifact, the sundial. However, no obvious conceptual link between the image of the sundial and the immediate context guides the reader's interpretation of the passage. It is not apparent why the fragmentary view of Venice ("Je ne pouvais apercevoir que lui," i.e. "l'Ange d'or") is syntactically linked to the conceit and to the following evocative image from Combray. This *non sequitur* on the cognitive level produces a certain tension, since the grammatical link through *mais comme* sets up a relationship of dependancy between the phrases, thereby categorically informing us that there is a conceptual relationship between the visual impression and the aphoristic metaphorical transposition that states the hero's personal experience as a general law. What is missing is an explicit statement pointing at the conceptual transition from sensory impression to mental interpretation. The key to the relationship between the conceit and the rest of the passage may be inferred, however, from the textual juxtaposition of the Combray and Venice imagery. The significance of this descriptive device becomes more evident when we recall a passage from *Du coté de chez Swann* (I, 64-65) where the specific visual aspect of the tower of Saint-Hilaire becomes a time-telling device. The striking image of the "black sun" within this context has inscribed this passage in the reader's memory and aids his interpretation of the later image, *marbre noir*: "quand, le dimanche, je les [ardoises] voyais, par une chaude matinée d'été, flamboyer comme un soleil noir, je me disais: 'Mon Dieu! neuf heures!' " [17] The narrator proceeds to tell us that the specific aspect of the tower as seen from his window

---

is at the base of the temporal notion under discussion — the pertinent context of this passage (which constitutes one long paragraph: pp. 623-625) insists on the differences between the two locations. One scholar maintains that these differences are more important than the common essence described in this passage (Gérard Genette, "Proust palimpseste," in *Figures* [Paris: Seuil, 1966], p. 46).

[17] While Proust's use of the image *soleil noir* is based on a sensory perception — the reflection of the sun from the black tiles of the steeple — and is basically a metonymy, Romantic and Symbolist poets have used the same image as a striking paradox, as a hyperbole of disaster and melancholy. For instance, Gérard de Nerval uses the image within a description of melancholy: "Ma seule étoile est morte — et mon luthe constellé / Porte le *soleil noir* de la mélancolie" (El Desdichado). See also Victor Hugo, *La Légende des siècles* (Inferi); Théophile Gautier, *Poésies diverses* (Melancolia); Charles Baudelaire, *Petits Poèmes en prose* (Le désir de peindre); and Heinrich Heine (Nordsee).

was the sensory impetus which would simultaneously evoke in him the particular aspect of the rest of the village on a sunny Sunday morning.

When the reader remembers this passage, the juxtaposition of certain descriptive details from the Combray setting to that of Venice emphasizes the underlying analogy. Thus the hero's similar situation — the fragmentary view from a window disclosing a radiant tower — and the insertion of the most representative image from the Combray of sunny, Sunday mornings ("je voyais flamboyer, au lieu du marbre noir que devenaient en resplendissant les ardoises de Saint-Hilaire") are symbolic pointers preparing our interpretation of the conceit's message. The conceit actually generalizes, in metaphoric terms, what the narrator has already told us in the literal, descriptive passage just quoted from *Du côté de chez Swann*.[18] We are bound to recall this passage because of the descriptive details accompanying the sundial conceit and the direct mention of Combray and of Sunday morning: "je pensai aux boutiques de Combray, sur la place de l'Eglise, qui le dimanche étaient sur le point de fermer...." Recalled within the Venice context, the imagery evoking Combray becomes symbolic of a sensory and conceptual analogy and serves as a specific illustration of the general truth expressed by the conceit. Thus the hero delights in the partial view of the campanile whose radiant Angel, though a mere detail of a whole town, nonetheless announces a bright world without. The narrator who has already taught the reader this lesson in connection with childhood experiences in Combray, reminds him of it by juxtaposing the radiant tower of Saint-Hilaire to the campanile of Venice.

The sensory impression of light is at the base of this analogy, as is clear from the visual imagery depicting the two towers, and the metaphorical imagery of the conceit based on the sundial. The conceit places the light imagery in relief by confronting us with a "sundial" that works in reverse: not by casting a shadow but by reflecting sunlight. This modified sundial corresponds to the Combray-Venice imagery: the radiant tiles of Saint-Hilaire and the

---

[18] See I, 64-65 where we are told how the partial view of the Saint-Hilaire tower on a sunny Sunday morning evokes for the hero the particular aspect of the village square on similar Sunday mornings.

golden Angel are both sunny segments of the world whose particular aspect tells the hero what the world looks like in the light of a specific hour. The narrator supplies the exact hour in each case: the particular light impression is thus directly related to the hour of day, a notion communicated by the conceit of the sundial, a time piece regulated by the sun.[19]

The full meaning of another brief conceit can only be determined by taking into consideration the preceding images evocative of a particular time and place. In this instance, the narrator recalls a particular aspect of Madame Swann's apartment, namely the dark-painted walls and the color effect of the chrysanthemums during the crepuscular hour in November.[20] After this brief recall of the representative image of the time when the hero frequented the Swanns (which is an anticipation, for the hero does not visit Madame Swann until the following book, "Autour de Madame Swann"),[21] the narrator takes the reader to the present moment by introducing descriptive details characterizing the modern apartment.[22] The narrator's emotional outcry, "hélas," interpolated between the two contrasted sketches, reinforces their opposition, the narrative break emphasizing the descriptive and temporal break. The abrupt juxtaposition of the contrasting descriptive details sets

---

[19] Nine o'clock in Combray (I, 64); ten o'clock in Venice (III, 623).
Proust uses the image of the sundial in another temporal context to express the close conceptual relationship between sensory impression and time of day. The sundial conceit again refers to a fragmentary view, in this instance a single image that has become symbolic of a whole period within the hero-narrator's memory (I, 641): "le plaisir que j'éprouve, chaque fois que je veux lire, en une sorte de cadran solaire, les minutes qu'il y a entre midi un quart et une heure, au mois de mai, à me revoir causant ainsi avec Mme Swann, sous son ombrelle, comme sous le reflet d'un berceau de glycines."

[20] The image of the chrysanthemums will actually be recalled several times during *A la recherche*; the flowers thus become symbolic, in the sense that they are the hero's private symbol representing for him a particular time and place. See I, 595-596; 607; 634; III, 166. The process of the flower's symbolization through repetition and emphasis is discussed *infra*, pp. 61-63.

[21] The reader is made aware of the chronology: "l'année d'après celle où se termine la première partie de ce récit" (I, 426). The juxtaposition of the two contrasting images is thus explicitly prepared.

[22] The advent of the anticipation is clearly indicated in I, 421. The narrator explicitly juxtaposes his present point of view ("cette année") to the narration of the past. He further specifies the present moment by referring us to a particular season: "un des premiers matins de ce mois de novembre."

in relief the gulf between the two periods. The narrator, who for a brief moment had hoped to relive the past by searching for and recreating a familiar past setting within present reality — thus overcoming the gulf between the two eras — conveys his inability to do so by focusing on an irretrievable element of the past. The metaphors within this passage underline the notion of separation from the past:

> Je voulais les [ces instants] retrouver tels que je me les rappelais. Hélas! il n'y avait plus que des appartements Louis XVI tout blancs, émaillés d'hortensias bleus. D'ailleurs, on ne revenait plus à Paris que très tard. Mme Swann m'eût répondu d'un château qu'elle ne rentrerait qu'en février, bien après le temps des chrysanthèmes, si je lui avais demandé de reconstituer pour moi les éléments de ce souvenir que je sentais attaché à une année lointaine, à un / millésime vers lequel il ne m'était pas permis de remonter, / les éléments de ce désir devenu lui-même inaccessible comme le plaisir qu'il avait jadis vainement poursuivi. (I, 426-427)

The utter impossibility of recreating the past, in this case Madame Swann's former salon, is set in relief by the hypothetical sentence preceding the conceit, for it shows that not even one of the conditions can be met.[23] We know from the previous imagery that the chrysanthemums are an essential part of this setting, in fact, the very symbol, from the narrator's personal point of view, of a particular time and place: the November tea hour at Mme Swann's. Her absence until February would make it impossible to recreate the unique atmosphere associated with November afternoons.

The notion of temporal isolation from the past already implied by this context is now concisely restated by the metaphor *millésime*, reinforced by the verb *remonter* with which it forms a brief conceit. The exact time aspect of *millésime* is prepared for and determined by the stereotype metaphor *année lointaine*, which overtly defines the image in a syntactical relationship of identity implied by the

---

[23] The importance of recalling this setting — which is an essential component of the era the narrator is trying to recall — is clear from the preceding context where he explicitly points out that remembrance relies on a person's ability to recall everything that constituted an experience (I, 426).

apposition. The reader's attention centers on *millésime,* a temporal expression of restricted usage (year of coinage, and by extension year of vintage or of manufacture), which forms a renewed cliché in connection with *remonter,* a verb frequently used within a temporal context.

Within the present context, the metaphor's connotation of "unique date" (year of coinage, vintage) stresses the fact that the mental and sensory impressions associated with a certain era have become emblems of the past. As a year of coinage or vintage identifies an item, so the unique impressions associated with an era serve as symbols of recognition within the hero's memory.

The reference to a unique period re-emphasizes the notion of "compartmentalized" time whose conceptual demarcation was already conveyed by the previous descriptive details contrasting two periods.[24] The contrasting descriptive details and the metaphor *millésime* thus both emphasize the notion of complete separation between one era and the next, a notion central to the passage in question.

The temporal notion is further set in relief through the addition of a symbolic tableau within the same paragraph. The narrator continues to write from the present perspective, which allows him to introduce a shocking anticipation, the description of the now-aged women whom, however, the hero has yet to meet as young women in "Autour de Mme Swann." The vast anticipation of this final paragraph of *Du côté de chez Swann* is the first and most

---

[24] The notion of discontinuity between two periods is expressed by another brief conceit whose precise conceptual image insists on the aspect of separation: "cette nuit qui lui avait semblé presque surnaturelle et qui en effet... appartenait bien à un monde mystérieux où on ne peut jamais revenir quand les portes s'en sont refermées" (I, 346-347). See also I, 537 where a similar conceit expresses an even more drastic notion of temporal discontinuity, this time between two contiguous states of being: "Et la pensée ne peut même pas reconstituer l'état ancien pour le confronter au nouveau, car elle n'a plus le champs libre: la connaissance que nous avons faite, le souvenir des premières minutes inespérées, les propos que nous avons entendus, sont là qui / obstruent l'entrée de notre conscience...." /

Proust also uses the spatial metaphor of passageways to convey the opposite notion, the hero's sudden discovery of temporal continuity: "Des portes de communication depuis longtemps condamnées se rouvraient dans mon cerveau" (III, 25). See p. 217 of the Conclusion for cross references to other metaphors expressing an aspect of conceptual discontinuity between one moment and the next, between one era and the next.

powerful prefiguration of old age before the final section of *Le Temps retrouvé*, the "Matinée Guermantes."

As in the descriptive imagery above, the tableau depicting the actual present is ushered in by the narrator's emotional outcry "Hélas!" This outcry, which suddenly introduces a strong emotional content and a break into the narration, focuses the reader's attention on the contrasting imagery.

In this instance the images are not descriptive, literal images symbolic of a particular period, but rather a transposition into the realm of mythology whose specific implications communicate a temporal notion in exaggerated terms:

> Hélas! dans l'avenue des Acacias — l'allée de Myrtes — j'en revis quelques-unes, vieilles, et qui n'étaient plus que les ombres terribles de ce qu'elles avaient été, errant, cherchant désespérément on ne sait quoi dans les bosquets virgiliens. (I, 427)

By placing the women within a well-known setting of the underworld, the narrator emphasizes both the enormous time lapse and his subjective notion of the different world he has entered. The mention of "l'allée de Myrtes" and "bosquets virgiliens," in alluding to Aeneas' visit to the Fields of Mourning, links the suffering of old age and the suffering inflicted by the cruelties of past loves. And we are reminded that the aged women were great beauties and lovers in their youth.[25] The "Jardin élyséen de la Femme," as he calls this present universe, conveys the same insurmountable separation and drastic difference expressed by *millésime* and the contrasting descriptions of the two apartments. The epoch-defining descriptive details, the brief conceit and the mythological tableau all work together in conveying the same notion of temporal discontinuity. The combined imagery focuses the reader's attention on the temporal notion thus set in relief within the narrative context.

In one passage a brief conceit stands at the beginning of a four-page explanatory narrative describing the complexity of the hero's

---

[25] A previous passage introduces the analogy between the "allée des Acacias" and the "allée des Myrtes de *l'Enéide*," and tells us that they were frequented by "celebrated beauties" (I, 417-418). This passage is a considerable anticipation, as the reader has yet to meet the most famous of these Beauties, Madame Swann, described in the following book.

inner reality (I, 84-88). It functions as a conceptual model translating the complex temporal notion into a single image. The imaginal résumé focuses the reader's attention on the notion under discussion and guides his understanding of it. The metaphors' conceptual implications are pointed to by the literal reinforcement accompanying the image:

> Dans / l'espèce d'écran diapré d'états différents que, tandis que je lisais, déployait simultanément ma conscience, / et qui allaient des aspirations les plus profondément cachées en moi-même jusqu'à la vision tout extérieure de l'horizon que j'avais, au bout du jardin, sous les yeux.... (I, 84)

Our attention is focused on the metaphorical transposition by the cautionary *espèce de* announcing the approximate nature of the image. The explicit nature of Proust's time imagery becomes apparent once more when the initial metaphor *écran diapré* is immediately followed by the genitive link pointing to the literal content underlying the metaphor. The temporal indication "tandis que je lisais," and the adverb *simultanément* reinforce and specify in literal terms the temporal aspect of the imagery. *Déployait* lengthens the code introduced by *écran diapré* and particularizes it. Modified by *simultanément, déployait* transmits this temporal specification to its object *écran* and finally to its abstract subject *conscience,* which receives the full impact of the metaphorical action by standing at the end of the sentence.

The relative clause, whose plural verb refers us to the plural noun of the genitive link, is a literal qualifying statement commenting further on *états différents*: "et qui allaient des aspirations les plus profondément cachées en moi-même jusqu'à la vision tout extérieure de l'horizon." While this statement recalls the complexity of the hero's awareness and distinguishes between inner feelings and outer perceptions, the metaphor *écran diapré* translates the simultaneous impact of the various perceptions into a single image.

The inclusion of the conceptual breakdown specifying the very content of *états différents* reveals the author's concern to be explicit when dealing with a temporal notion, since his style unites the poetic and discursive. This tendency towards the discursive is further obvious when the narrator continues to describe the hero's inner complexity in literal terms, by speaking separately of his mental state, his emotions, and finally his sense impressions.[26]

---

[26] Further on within the same context the narrator introduces a second metaphorical image to concretize the notion of simultaneity (I, 84). Like *écran diapré, jet d'eau irisé* — the metaphor in question — translates the narrator's notion of conceptual complexity into concrete terms: the image of multiple colors helps us to grasp the multiple conceptual impact due to the hero's simultaneous awareness of various sensations, emotional and mental reactions. These metaphors are our only direct contact with a mimesis of simultaneity, since the literal account of this state of being presents the components of the complexity one by one.

Chapter III

THE CONTINUED METAPHOR

The continued metaphor is a conceit of more elaborate structure than those studied in Chapter II. While the basic conceit was made up of two (occasionally more) metaphors working together within the same syntactic unit to establish a single code, the continued metaphor consists of an initial metaphor extended by two or more successive metaphors that illustrate or develop its various implications. The relationship to the initial metaphor of those that follow is therefore one of subordination: they explain, qualify, or repeat in altered words the sense of the initial metaphor, and thus extend an already established code.

Textually, continued metaphors may be confined to a single sentence — often a very long sentence in Proust's novel — or they may branch out into several sentences, even paragraphs, related, however, by being within the same descriptive or narrative framework conveying the temporal concept.

The extended structure of the continued metaphor allows for more precision. It specifies the code and gives us further insight into the concept at hand, since it clarifies the semantic relationships between tenor and vehicle.[1]

---

[1] See Michael Riffaterre, "La Métaphore filée dans la poésie surréaliste," *Langue Française* (September 1969), pp. 48-49, for a more detailed presentation of the interrelationship between the verbal sequence constituting tenor and vehicle.

A. Aphoristic Conceit Extended For Illustration

In the following brief extension consisting of four metaphors, an initial predicate adjective sets up the code, which is then extended by three verb metaphors, each illustrating a particular aspect of the original notion:

> Le temps dont nous disposons chaque jour est / élastique; / les passions que nous ressentons le / dilatent, / celles que nous inspirons le / rétrécissent, / et l'habitude le / remplit. / (I, 612)

The initial metaphor focuses the reader's attention on an aspect of time, since the word *élastique* is explicitly linked to the noun *temps* through the copula *est,* and since it appears within a declarative sentence whose tone is authoritative. The second sentence is an illustration of the notion of temporal "elasticity": the three metaphorical verbs each take up one of the implications of elasticity, thereby jointly arguing that the pliability of time is dependent on particular circumstances. Our attention is focused on these verbs, since each one stands at the end of a clause preceded by the anaphora *le,* which introduces a triple parallelism into the sentence, and closely joins each verb to its direct object: time. In particular the identical syntactical structure of the first two clauses — each amplified by a relative clause — calls special attention to the changed elements, the antithetical verb metaphors.

The conceit of temporal "elasticity" closes an account of the hero's various emotional states with a general observation that elevates a subjective experience to a universal truth. The musing narrator thus draws a philosophical conclusion based on his personal discovery that man's subjective notion of time is based on his emotional state. The lack of syntactical and semantic links between the generalizing metaphorical statement and the preceding context, and the abrupt change of tone from personal narration to objective aphorism draw the reader's attention to the temporal concept thus thrown into relief. Both the declarative tone of the sentence and the authoritative nature of the metaphorical transposition through the copula give us the impression of reading an aphorism. The careful breakdown of the implications of the initial metaphor into three qualifying metaphors further reinforces the explanatory nature, hence cognitive function, of the imagery.

Another continued metaphor is similar to the example just studied and fulfills the same function of confronting the reader with a general truth derived from personal experience. The initial metaphor, a predicate adjective, establishes the code within the framework of a general, aphoristic statement, while the following three verb metaphors specify its content:

> Je sais que je prononçai alors le mot "mort" comme si Albertine allait mourir. Il semble que les événements soient plus / vastes / que le moment où ils ont lieu et / ne peuvent y tenir tout entiers. / Certes, ils /débordent / sur l'avenir par la mémoire que nous en gardons, mais / ils demandent une place / aussi au temps qui les précède. Certes, on dira que nous ne les voyons pas alors tels qu'ils seront, mais dans le souvenir ne sont-ils pas aussi modifiés? (III, 401)

The tone of the general statement is cautious: the verb *sembler* carefully warns us that what follows belongs to the realm of subjective interpretation, and the subjunctive copula *soient* reinforces this note of circumspection. The hesitant tone is called for by the narrative context, for both the initial sentence and the general statement are anticipations. The reader still lacks the narrative reinforcement of the hero's subsequent experience.

The three verb metaphors (*ne peuvent tenir, débordent, demandent une place*) reinforce each other and confer a specific meaning on *vastes*. In fact, it is their particular impact that determines the code. They bring out the concrete meaning of *vastes,* which otherwise might be taken abstractly, and they animate their subject *événements*. The temporal implications of the passage are clear from the prepositional phrase qualifying each verb, thereby closely linking the metaphorical domain and the literal subject under discussion: *sur l'avenir, au temps qui les précède,* and *y* — replacing *le moment où ils ont lieu.*

The aphorism plays the same role as that in the previous example: it serves to clarify the hero's particular experience by finding in it a general truth. The general statement again closes the narration of a particular experience by juxtaposing two different points of view: one presenting the hero's viewpoint contemporary with the given experience, the other revealing the broader perspective of the narrator familiar with events still to come.

B. Extensions Clarifying the Semantic Domain

The code established by a brief conceit may be particularized by metaphors that extend it. In one instance, the initial conceit is extended by two additional ones, which confine it to a specific semantic domain:

> Alors, dès le lendemain (ou attendant une fête s'il y en avait une prochaine, un anniversaire, le nouvel an peut-être, un de ces jours qui ne sont pas pareils aux autres, où le temps recommence / sur de nouveaux frais en rejetant l'héritage du passé, en n'acceptant pas le legs de ses tristesses) / je demandais à Gilberte de renoncer à notre amitié ancienne et de jeter les bases d'une nouvelle amitié. (I, 412-413)

The prepositional phrase *sur de nouveaux frais* introduces the code and forms the initial conceit with the verb *recommencer*. The direct syntactical link between the metaphors and *temps* reveals the conceptual link between imagery and temporal subject. The following two conceits, grammatically linked to the first as verbal qualifying phrases, specify and emphasize the implications of *nouveaux frais*. In each case, a noun metaphor particularizes the code: *l'héritage du passé* and *legs de tristesses*. The parallel syntactical structure of the two conceits, and the synonymic repetition of the verbs (*rejeter, ne pas accepter*) and the noun metaphors (*héritage, legs*) focus the reader's attention on the different elements of the genitive links (*passé* and *tristesses*). Such textual emphasis functions as an effective recall of the subject under discussion, the hero's sadness caused by Gilberte's past indifference.

The insistence, through the three related conceits, on the idea of emotional rebirth, in turn stresses his subjective conception of existence within time: he intends to cut himself off from the past by abruptly denying Gilberte's indifference, the cause of his sadness.

These continued metaphors are part of a parenthetical remark that introduces a long, explanatory disjunction into the narrative framework. In this continued metaphor the reader's attention is focused on the metaphorical details, forcing him to deduce the notion of temporal discontinuity that each conceit states hyperbolically through the verb-noun interaction: *recommence* reinforces *nouveaux frais,* whereas *rejetant* and *n'acceptant pas* forcefully act upon and negate *héritage* and *legs,* both archetypes of continuity. The function of this extended metaphor is one of emphasis: the narrative, when resumed, takes on a note of urgency.

C. Metaphorical Tableau

The semantic relationship between a series of metaphors may be less evident than in the passages just examined. I have found one example where several metaphors suggest a visual image without limiting it to a definite representation. The passage describes the narrator's conception of the various perspectives from which he has viewed Albertine over the years, with the important discovery that these mental images are so distinctive because they are separated by long time intervals:

> Je la voyais aux différentes années de ma vie, occupant par rapport à moi / des positions différentes qui me faisaient sentir la beauté des espaces interférés, ce long temps révolu où j'étais resté sans la voir, et sur la diaphane profondeur duquel la rose personne que j'avais devant moi se modelait avec de mystérieuses ombres et un puissant relief. / (III, 69)

The reader's interpretation of the visual tableau is assured through literal reinforcement and syntactical links carefully joining the various imaginal details: the imagery is preceded by a literal clause that explicitly relates the temporal indication *aux différentes années de ma vie* to the following tropes. The metaphor *espaces interférés* brings out the spatial content of *positions différentes* and forms with it the initial conceit. The temporal implications of *espaces interférés* are revealed by the literal explanatory statement in apposition. The metaphor *diaphane profondeur,* whose genitive link *duquel* explicitly points back to *temps révolu,* also refers back to *espaces interférés,* closely linked to *temps révolu* by apposition.[2] *Rose personne* is the non-metaphoric detail drawn into the tableau.

The synecdochic reduction of Albertine to *rose personne* reinforces the tableau's imaginal content: the pictorial opposition to *ombres,* reinforced by the descriptive detail *puissant relief,* confronts the reader with a striking visual contrast that impresses upon him the notion of contrast in regard to temporal perspective.

This perspective is reduced by the imagery to two basic viewpoints: *rose personne* is a metonymic résumé of Albertine observed over the years, and *espaces interférés, diaphane profondeur,* and *mystérieuses ombres* are the pictorial equivalents of the times Albertine was not observed, as the explanatory apposition to *espaces interférés* explicitly states. The visual ambiguity of *espaces interférés* and *diaphane profondeur,* reinforced by the adjective *mystérieuses,* conveys the undefinable perspective of the years when the hero did not see Albertine. Against this vaguely defined background, the pictorial precision of *rose personne,* whose concrete aspect is reinforced through *modelait* and *puissant relief,* stands out emphatically.[3] The imagery thus functions as a concrete, visual translation of the narrator's perception of Albertine over the years.

D. Continued Metaphors Within A Symbolic Context

The repetition of a descriptive detail or image associated with a particular experience points to its symbolic significance. When such a motif or image appears within the metaphors' surrounding context, its special implications must be taken into account in determining the metaphors' meaning.

---

[2] The editors of the Pléiade edition refer us to another manuscript version which reads *diaphane profondeur desquels*: the genitive link of *profondeur* thus directly points back to *espaces interférés,* lengthening the spatial code established by *espaces.* See III, 1069, footnote 1 to page 68.

[3] The visual contrast emphasized by this imagery may explain the presence of the term *interférés,* which is given only a technical definition in the nineteenth-century Littré: "une suite de bandes alternativement brillantes et obscures" (IV, 1088). Cf. I, 642 where the same word is used in a more abstract context, calling on its figurative implications. See *supra,* pp. 30-31 for a discussion of the passage.

In one example, the conceit's surrounding context includes the image of an actual setting gradually becoming symbolic through repetition. In the hero's eyes, Madame Swann's chrysanthemums have become representative of a particular season, time and setting.[4] Yet the flowers' acquired significance and, by association, the importance of the particular time and place they symbolize is questioned in the present passage. The metaphorical extension throws this notion into relief:

> Et moi aussi, il fallait que je rentrasse, avant d'avoir goûté à ces plaisirs de l'hiver, desquels les chrysanthèmes m'avaient semblé être l'enveloppe éclatante. Ces plaisirs n'étaient pas venus et cependant Mme Swann n'avait pas l'air d'attendre encore quelque chose... Je sentais que j'aurais pu rester sans rencontrer ces plaisirs inconnus, et que ma tristesse n'était pas seule à m'avoir privé d'eux. / Ne se trouvaient-ils donc pas situés sur cette route battue des heures qui mènent toujours si vite à l'instant du départ, mais plutôt sur quelque chemin de traverse inconnu de moi et par où il eût fallu bifurquer? / (I, 607)

The significant question entrusted to the metaphorical transposition is of capital importance: it alludes to a central aspect of the major theme of time, namely, how to salvage *le temps perdu,* both wasted and lost. The graphic image sketched by the metaphors translates this notion into concrete terms, which help us to conceptualize it.

Route battue des heures accomplishes the metaphorical transposition and forms the basic conceit in conjunction with the verbal structure se *trouvaient... situés.* The verb *mènent,* whose plural refers us to the abstract noun *heures,* does not, grammatically speaking, reinforce *route.*[5] Yet the entire relative clause within

---

[4] Several pages before the present passage the narrator explicitly points to the symbolic content of these flowers: "ils m'invitaient, ces chrysanthèmes, et malgré toute ma tristesse, à goûter avidement pendant cette heure du thé les plaisirs si courts de novembre dont ils faisaient flamboyer près de moi la splendeur intime et mystérieuse" (I, 596). Cf. also *supra,* pp. 50-51.

See I, 426 where the narrator longingly evokes the beauty of the chrysanthemums through a visual image followed by a remark anticipating his future disappointment. The fact that the narrator recalls this particular image as symbolic of a specific time, prefigures its future significance within the hero's life.

[5] In an earlier version, the 1918 edition, the verb appears in the singular; *mène* would here have to be considered as part of the basic conceit, since it refers us to *route.* See I, 971, footnote 3 to page 607.

which the verb appears further clarifies the temporal aspect of *heures,* its antecedent, and in turn influences the imagery to which *heure* is equated through the genitive link. The metaphor *chemin de traverse* extends the basic conceit of *route battue.* The semantic opposition between the metaphor of the "beaten track" and that of the "short cut" helps us conceptualize the hero's abstract notion of misguided choice, of wasting his time. The extension of the same image through "par où il eût fallu bifurquer" adds further emphasis to the impression of misguided choice. The notion of uncertainty so emphatically stressed by this image is reinforced through the hypothetical verbal mood of the statement, and the indefinite adjective *quelque* modifying *chemin de traverse.* Thus image, verbal mood, and modifying elements all emphasize the key concept.

As in many of Proust's time images, the temporal aspect of the semantic transposition is explicitly pointed to here by a genitive link metaphor. The metaphorical expression responsible for the initial transposition, *route battue des heures,* establishes the code and fulfills a guiding function, as the temporal aspect is syntactically linked to the metaphorical transposition. *Route battue,* a familiar cliché denoting that which is habitual or humdrum, confers these implications upon the description of the whole setting, to which it is closely linked through the syntax. The essential significance of the time and place being described is thus seriously being questioned. While the metaphorical image emphasizes and concretizes an abstract notion, the image itself is significantly reinforced in its cognitive mission through clear syntactical links to the literal domain, which direct our decoding through the semantic equation of tenor and vehicle.

E. Continued Metaphors Within A Context Associating Similar Temporal Experiences

The narrator occasionally relates several experiences within the same narrative framework in order to point to the special significance they have in common, and to imply a general truth. In one instance, the temporal notion expressed by continued metaphors is illustrated by the textual juxtaposition of three different experiences.

In this passage, the metaphorical transposition is interpolated into the narrative for explanatory purposes, and is carefully prepared for. The metaphors are introduced by a literal observation, elevating the hero's personal experience to a general truth:

> Nous ne profitons guère de notre vie, nous laissons inachevées dans les crépuscules d'été ou les nuits précoces d'hiver les heures où il nous avait semblé qu'eût pu pourtant être enfermé un peu de paix ou de plaisir. Mais ces heures ne sont pas absolument perdues. / Quand chantent à leur tour de nouveaux moments de plaisir qui passeraient de même, aussi grêles et linéaires, elles viennent leur apporter le soubassement, la consistance d'une riche orchestration. / Elles s'étendent ainsi jusqu'à un de ces bonheurs types qu'on ne retrouve que de temps à autre mais qui continuent d'être.... (II, 396)

The temporal references *crépuscules d'été* and *nuits précoces d'hiver* metonymically refer to the privileged moments of life, which, as the surrounding context tells us, we ordinarily ignore, and lose forever. The phrase qualifying *heures* further elaborates on the special content of these moments. The literal remark, "Mais ces heures ne sont pas absolument perdues," serves as a transition, by announcing that there is another way of looking at our existence within time. The extended conceit is introduced to explain this new insight. It supplies us with a familiar analogy from the material world to illustrate the increasing complexity when one moves from a conception of chronological time — conceived as linear and one dimensional, since the present moment becomes the past and is forever lost — to a type of duration where past and present unite in a "timeless" moment. The metaphor *chantent,* in conjunction with *grêles* and *linéaires,* first refer us to chronological time, alluding to the initial statement that privileged moments pass imperceptibly and are lost to us. The extension of the image to *orchestration* translates the revised, more complex temporal notion into concrete terms. The opposition between musical simplicity and musical complexity sets the difference between the two temporal viewpoints in relief.

The double genitive link with *orchestration* insists on the main aspect of the transposition's most significant metaphor. Both *soubassement* and *consistance,* introduced into the established semantic domain through their syntactical link to *orchestration*, specifically emphasize the aspect of structural complexity which stands in direct opposition to the previous metaphors: the idea of reinforcement derived from *soubassement* stands in contrast to *grêles,* and the idea of solidity or volume conveyed by *consistance* stands directly opposed to *linéaires.* A distinction between the various metaphors is here necessary. Strictly speaking, only *chantent, grêles* and *orchestration* are continued metaphors of the same code. *Linéaires, soubassement,* and *consistance* are themselves metaphoric within the realm of musical terminology. Yet they are drawn into this domain by their close ties to the conceit's musical terms: *linéaires* is given as a complement to *grêles* — which is a metaphorical hyperbole of *linéaires,* thus a metaphor of a metaphor within this context — *soubassement* and *consistance* are closely tied to *orchestration* by the genitive link. In each case, their extensive semantic implications are given a particular connotation within this context.[6] It is significant that the reader has a concrete grasp on these terms, since *linéaires, soubassement* and *consistance* play a double role: their common usage within the material and abstract sense makes it possible for them to refer at once to music and time. *Linéaires* simultaneously expresses musical and temporal simplicity, whereas *soubassement* and *consistance* jointly express musical and temporal complexity. In their full sense, these words modify both the tenor and the vehicle.

The active verbs *chantent, passeraient* and *viennent ... apporter* command our attention since they personify an abstract notion (*nouveaux moments de plaisir*). The animation of time continues into the following sentence, without, however, extending the conceit: "Elles s'étendent ainsi jusqu'à un de ces bonheurs types." The abstract term *bonheurs types* stands as a résumé, as a general designation for the temporal experience just described metaphorically.[7]

---

[6] The same temporal notion is expressed by a set of continued metaphors each of which may be taken figuratively or literally. As accumulated metaphors referring to the same phenomenon, they mutually clarify each other and insist on the same salient characteristic: "en restant présents en celles de mes impressions d'aujourd'hui auxquelles ils peuvent se relier, ils [le côté de Méséglise et le côté de Guermantes] leur donnent / des assises, de la profondeur, une dimension de plus / qu'aux autres" (I, 186).

[7] There are several instances where the metaphorical rendering of a temporal notion is directly followed by an abstract expression referring to the

The function of the continued metaphors within this context is mainly explanatory: they are part of an aphoristic passage that introduces a general observation on time into the narrative, wherein the specific function of the metaphors is to illustrate in concrete terms, hence to render conceptually accessible a complex, abstract notion. The metaphorical passage is immediately followed by an illustration of *bonheur type* taken from the hero's present experience. The explicit link through *dans l'exemple présent* between metaphorical passage and the resumed narrative clearly indicates the tie between general rule and example. The illustration is significantly reinforced by its narrative juxtaposition with two different experiences, each revealing the same truth about time (II, 397).[8] One of these is the recollection of an incidence of sensory analogy drawn between Paris and Rivebelle, described a few pages earlier (II, 390); the other, a presently felt sensory analogy between Paris and Combray.

This triple narrative juxtaposition is significant to the metaphorical passage. It serves as a multiple illustration of the temporal notion under discussion, thus allowing the reader to deduce the element of similarity which links these three different experiences. A joint analysis reveals that each experience is based on a sensory analogy, which, in retrospect, adds a significant comment to the above metaphors and to *bonheurs type*. The metaphors, in turn, emphasize and prepare us for the specific temporal significance contained in the following illustrations. The continued metaphors thus function as a general illustration for similar temporal experiences recalled within the same narrative context.

---

same subject, conferring on it a "generic" designation, which functions as a conceptual résumé. See III, 26 and *supra*, p. 43.

[8] II, 397: "Si en descendant l'escalier je revivais les soirs de Doncières, quand nous fûmes arrivés dans la rue, brusquement, la nuit presque complète où le brouillard semblait avoir éteint les réverbères, qu'on ne distinguait, bien faibles, que de tout près, me ramena à je ne sais quelle arrivée, le soir, à Combray, quand la ville n'était encore éclairée que de loin en loin, et qu'on y tâtonnait dans une obscurité humide, tiède et sainte de crèche, à peine étoilée ça et là d'un lumignon qui ne brillait pas plus qu'un cierge."

Chapter IV

METAPHORICAL EXPANSION AND MULTIPLE SETS OF METAPHORS

In studying Proust's time metaphors we encounter certain passages where distinct metaphors interpenetrate and overlap. Such passages cannot be treated as examples of extended metaphor, because they contain vehicles from more than one domain, or vehicles from the same domain referring us, however, to separate images. Nor can they be separated for isolated study, since the overall meaning of the passage is a result of their interaction. Rather they must be treated as distinct phenomena, which I call "metaphorical expansion" within the same syntactical framework, and "multiple sets" when the vehicles form distinct images.

A. Metaphorical Expansion

The first two passages to be considered are borderline cases between the continued metaphor and the multiple structure. Although the metaphors share the same verbal domain, some of them expand the code by introducing a new aspect. In the first instance, a brief conceit determined by the mutual reinforcement of a verb and substantive metaphor functions as a conceptual model expressing an abstract notion concerning the hero's perception within time. The conceit is a conceptual constant repeatedly used by the narrator to express his notion of temporal discontinuity when looking back at his life or at Swann's: he conceives the various periods of life as separate time blocks.[1] In the present example, the narrator, who has drawn us into the midst of one time period — the Champs Elysées era of his childhood — suddenly interrupts his narrative to interpolate a long, parenthetical remark that forces us to step out of the narrated period and to look at it objectively from the double perspective of the hero's present point of view contrasted with the earlier one. Our attention focuses on Swann, who is an essential part of the present, but who also belongs to a particular period of the hero's past, namely, childhood vacation periods spent in Combray. The brief conceit first gives us a concrete grasp on the notion of temporal discontinuity, and is then expanded to add another aspect to the temporal notion under discussion:

> (Cela me rappela qu'il m'avait pourtant vu bien souvent à la campagne; souvenir que j'avais gardé, mais dans l'ombre, parce que depuis que j'avais revu Gilberte, pour moi Swann
> 1. était surtout son père, et non plus le Swann de Combray; / comme les idées sur lesquelles j'embranchais maintenant son nom étaient différentes des idées dans le réseau desquelles il était autrefois compris / et que je n'utilisais plus jamais quand j'avais à penser à lui, il était devenu un per-
> 2. sonnage nouveau; / je le rattachai pourtant par une ligne artificielle, secondaire et transversale / à notre invité d'autrefois.... (I, 407)

The verbal metaphor *embranchais,* linked to the prepositional phrase *sur lesquelles* (i.e. *idées*), which specifies its realm of action and closely joins the domains of tenor and vehicle, sets up the metaphorical transposition. Together with *réseau* — linked to *idées* through the genitive link *desquelles* (i.e. *idées*) thereby reinforcing the conceptual rapprochement between the two domains — it establishes the controlling conceit of this passage. *Réseau* particularizes *embrancher* by introducing a definite semantic domain. The image remains schematic, however, since it lacks any further pictorial detail. What matters is its double application, since the two "networks" illustrate the conceptual dichotomy between two separate periods, referred to by *maintenant* and *autrefois.* This schematic

---

[1] See I, 346, I, 720, and III, 1030 where the same metaphor is used. Among the many conceptual variants are the metaphors *assemblage* (I, 426), and *cohésion* (I, 539). See *supra,* pp. 45-47 for a discussion of a brief conceit based on *réseau.*

translation gives us a precise insight into the narrator's double temporal perspective and clarifies our conception of *personnage nouveau*. It is now clear that "new" refers to a subjective vision, and not to a drastic change in Swann's appearance.

The following metaphors grow out of the basic conceit without strictly staying within it. They develop it, adding another aspect to the temporal notion under discussion. This metaphorical expansion consists of the verb *rattachai* and the noun *ligne* to which it is linked through the prepositional phrase particularizing the mode of action.

The verb *rattachai* is reinforced in its metaphorical use by *ligne* with which it forms a secondary conceit. *Ligne,* which has a wide range of meanings, is here drawn into the semantic field called upon by the previous conceit. The term *ligne* is pliable enough to expand the image of whatever "network" the individual reader may have conceived. What matters is the emphatic insistence on the concept of separateness, which is underscored three times by the adjectives modifying *ligne*: *artificielle* and *secondaire* are discriminatory adjectives that both convey the idea of qualitative difference between the network and its appendage. *Transversale* reinforces this concept with a concrete pictorial detail and is mainly responsible for the expansion of the original schema. The development of the basic conceit is reinforced by a brief narrative digression that takes the reader into the hero's past, allowing him a small glimpse of the former viewpoint: the narrator mentions the "drame du coucher," which took place during Swann's visits at Combray. This brief reminder of a particular aspect of Combray is a narrative equivalent of the "ligne artificielle, secondaire et transversale," its brevity indicating that the former setting is now of little significance to the hero who can hardly conceive of the former Swann.[2] His and the reader's attention

---

[2] The same notion of temporal discontinuity is expressed through another conceit specifically referring to Swann. In fact, this conceit anticipates the passage just studied. It appears in "Combray" where the Swann known during the hero's childhood is in the foreground:

> j'ai l'impression de quitter une personne pour aller vers une autre qui en est distincte, quand, dans ma mémoire, du Swann que j'ai connu plus tard avec exactitude, je passe à ce premier Swann — à ce premier Swann dans lequel je retrouve les erreurs charmantes de ma jeunesse et qui d'ailleurs ressemble moins à l'autre qu'aux personnes que j'ai connues à la même époque, comme s'il en était de notre vie ainsi que d'un musée où tous les portraits d'un même temps ont un air de famille, une même tonalité.... (I, 19-20)

at once return to the interrupted account of the Champs Elysées period.

In the example just studied, the metaphorical imagery is part of a parenthetical passage interpolated into the narration. The initial conceit confronts the reader with a concise conceptual image, graphically representing the abstract notion. The imagery then becomes autonomous as it expands to a second conceit growing out of the first to which it is semantically related. This metaphorical expansion in turn calls forth a narrative aside that extends the parenthetical passage dealing with the notion of time, thereby further emphasizing this notion.

In the second example of imaginal expansion, an extended conceit of continued metaphors expands into a brief conceit that adds another aspect to the temporal notion. The additional conceit is closely related to the preceding metaphors through one of its terms; yet this same term, in connection with a second one, calls forth another domain:

> Certes, s'il s'agit uniquement de nos cœurs, le poète a eu raison de parler des "fils mystérieux" que la vie brise. Mais
> 1. il est encore plus vrai / qu'elle en tisse sans cesse entre les êtres, entre les événements, qu'elle entre-croise ces fils, qu'elle les redouble pour épaissir la trame, / si bien
> 2. qu'entre le moindre point de notre passé et tous les autres un riche réseau de souvenirs ne laisse que le choix des communications. / (III, 1030)

Fils mystérieux and *brise* establish the basic conceit on which the following continued metaphors will draw. By replacing *briser* with *tisser*, the image is reversed, since the antithetical concept of formation is substituted for that of destruction. The following verbs — all antonyms of *briser* — jointly convey the ever-increasing complexity of the interrelationships between people and events by focusing the reader's attention on the growing compositional complexity expressed by the verbs and their direct objects. *Tisser* is developed through *entrecroiser*, *redoubler*, and *épaissir*, whereas *fils* suddenly evolve to *trame*, the resulting formation. This accumulation of technical verbs from weaving all referring to the formation of a network, emphasizes the notion of complex interrelationships and illustrates it with an image from the material world.

The appended conceit, formed by *réseau* and *choix de communications,* introduces an additional aspect to the notion of complexity. The context calls on two different connotations of *réseau,* one directly related to the metaphors from weaving of the preceding conceit, the other called on by *choix de communications,* a combination that brings to mind networks of transportation and communication. This second schematic image reinforces the first, since they both present the reader with a conceptual model based on the idea of complexity.

Besides introducing a second image that insists on the notion of complexity, the final conceit brings out an additional aspect: the two genitive link metaphors *point de notre passé* and *réseau de souvenirs* anchor the image within the temporal context by explicitly linking time and memory, whose joint action alone can produce the complex "network" perceived by the aging narrator examining his life.[3]

This expanded conceit stands at the end of a long passage (III, 1029-30) recalling a number of the hero's experiences and illustrating various interrelationships. The metaphorical imagery is directly juxtaposed to this narrative enumeration, and illustrates a general truth derived from personal experience. Its considerable extent makes it autonomous, since the reader is allowed to become involved in it, losing sight for a moment of the actual narration at hand. Moreover, its elaboration and its important position at the end of the passage put all the emphasis on the general truth derived from personal experience.

B. Cumulative Series of Metaphors

The difference between the metaphorical expansion just studied and the following examples is found in the looser syntactical and semantic ties of the latter. For instance, the metaphors, although extended, may be separated textually by appearing within different syntactical frameworks, or they may share the same semantic domain without, however, contributing to the same image. Moreover,

---

[3] *Point,* which may be used abstractly or concretely, constitutes here part of the concrete detail of the final image.

they may belong to entirely different domains, though linked by syntax and content. The metaphors belonging to this structure share several characteristics: they enjoy textual proximity — they must appear close enough within the same passage to be jointly perceived by the reader — and they convey the same notion of time. Semantically they range from metaphors forming complementary but separate images derived from the same domain to metaphors constituting images derived from different realms of discourse. Structurally, their complexity does not exceed the formation of two sets of metaphors working together within the same passage. Each set may range from the basic structure of the simple conceit to the extended structure of continued metaphors.

1. Clarifying Function of Additional Transposition

In the first example, the initial sentence states a general truth about time in aphoristic terms. The two metaphors appearing within this context briefly convey the essence of this notion. After several sentences of descriptive narrative illustrating the maxim with a specific example just observed by the narrator, the aspect of time is once more formulated in metaphoric terms, through an extended conceit that anchors the image in a specific domain:

> Il faut cependant faire cette réserve que les mesures du temps lui-même peuvent être pour certaines personnes /
> 1. accélérées ou ralenties. / Par hasard, j'avais rencontré dans la rue, il y avait quatre ou cinq ans, la vicomtesse de Saint-
> 2. Fiacre. . . . Le Temps a ainsi / des trains express et spéciaux qui mènent vite à une vieillesse prématurée. Mais sur la voie parallèle circulent des trains de retour, presque aussi rapides. / Je pris M. de Courgivaux pour son fils, car il avait l'air plus jeune (il devait avoir dépassé la cinquantaine et semblait plus jeune qu'à trente ans). (III, 942-943)

The two predicate adjectives *accélérées* and *ralenties,* modifying *mesures du temps,* introduce the code of temporal speed on which the metaphors of the following extended conceit directly draw. Introduced by *ainsi* and immediately following the narration of a particular incident illustrating the general truth, the final conceit comes as a conclusive résumé, taking up once more the general tone of the initial aphorism. Now, however, the general truth is conveyed through a specific image personifying Time as the performer of a particular activity: Time, whose personification is emphasized by the capital "T," operates trains. The adjectival metaphors *express* and *spéciaux* take up the notion of speed already introduced by the previous metaphors *accélérées* and *ralenties,* and stress the aspect of acceleration. By specifying the main characteristic to be attributed to trains, these adjectives function as the conceit's principal metaphors. The verbal metaphor *mènent,* modified by *vite,* reinforces these adjectives by extending the speed code. The direct syntactical link between the metaphorical conceit and *vieillesse prématurée,* by joining the literal and metaphoric levels, introduces an explicit directing function into the imagery.

The conceit's second sentence extends the image by reinforcing its pictorial detail with *sur la voie parallèle,* and *trains de retour.* These additional details extend the underlying temporal message: physical movement in reverse translates the notion of time moving backward. The verb *circulent* activates the conceit's extension, whereas the modifying phrase *presque aussi rapides* defines the salient aspect of *trains de retour,* their speed.

While the conceit's first sentence functions as a conclusion drawn from the preceding descriptive tableau contrasting the once youthful but now decaying physiognomy of the vicomtesse de Saint-Fiacre, the second sentence introduces another temporal aspect not yet illustrated by the narrator. This antithetical concept of time speeding backward is, however, immediately followed by a specific example of "aging in reverse," a notion embodied in M. de Courgivaux.

The two metaphorical statements are thus both interpolated into the course of the descriptive narrative focusing on the physical appearance — here symbolic of aging — of those attending the "Matinée Guermantes." The change from literal narrative describing a specific setting to the metaphorical conceits of the aphoristic insertions focuses the reader's attention on the temporal message, and points to the symbolic implications of the entire setting.

The structure of the temporal metaphors may be called "cumulative" in this instance, because two sets of metaphors, textually separated, work together to convey the same message: the more general implications of the initial metaphors introduce the realm of discourse (speed), whereas the following conceit introduces a specific image into the semantic domain (*trains express*). The imagery autonomously extends itself to introduce another temporal aspect (aging in "reverse"), which, in turn, calls forth another narrative illustration from the realm of experience.

Why the narrator only describes "accelerated" aging is obvious from the narrative context of the "Matinée Guermantes": the hero did not witness the gradual aging of friends and acquaintances, since illness had removed him from the scene for a number of years. Moreover, the exaggerated description of the physical manifestations of time and the accelerated pace of narration through hiatus and anticipation shock the reader into an awareness of Time.

2. Syntactical Integration of Additional Metaphors

The relationship of two sets of metaphors is more evident when they are closely joined by syntax and are not separated by intervening narrative or descriptive remarks. The tropes' interrelationship is evident, for instance, when the second conceit is introduced into the verbal domain of the first set of metaphors, as in the following example: the combined metaphors appear within a lengthy passage dealing with the hero's personal association between seasons and places. The metaphors' immediate context deals with a specific seasonal stimulus that has the power to call forth a mental image of Florence, epitomizing Spring for the hero.[4]

A brief remark explaining that a Spring-like day may evoke Florence precedes the metaphorical imagery. The importance of this temporal notion is then emphasized by a series of metaphors personifying a unit of time, *un jour*. The animated tableau culminates in a brief conceit, adding a concise conceptual model:

---

[4] The mental image of Florence is a recurring image within the novel. It symbolizes the advent of Easter and evokes a floral setting within the hero's imagination. Each of these images translates his idealized conception of a place and setting. The original image appears in I, 387. Recurring images may be found in I, 389-392; II, 143 and 148; II, 348-349.

For a discussion of the hero-narrator's personal associations with place names, consult Gérard Genette, *Figures* II ("Proust et le langage indirect"), pp. 232-242.

Puis il arriva qu'une simple variation atmosphérique suffît à provoquer en moi cette modulation sans qu'il y eût besoin d'attendre le retour d'une saison. Car souvent dans
1. l'une / on trouve égaré un jour d'une autre, qui nous y fait vivre, en évoque aussitôt, en fait désirer les plaisirs particuliers et interrompt les rêves que nous étions en train
2. de faire, / en plaçant plus tôt ou plus tard qu'à son tour ce feuillet détaché d'un autre chapitre, dans le calendrier interpolé du Bonheur. / (I, 386-387)

The introductory statement explicitly announces the temporal notion (the specific implications of *modulation* are defined by a preceding conceit equating the musical term *changement de ton* with *sensibilité*), while the metaphors effecting the personification of time constitute an explanatory tableau. Their discursive nature is evident through *car*, which introduces the transposition. *Egaré*, applied to *jour*, sets up the process of personification, and *dans l'une* (i.e. *saison*) in conjunction with *une autre* and its various pronouns (y, en) specify the temporal cadre, the precise realm of action attributed to *jour*. The specific mention of *plaisirs particuliers* reveals what constitutes the sensory recall dramatized by the personifying verbs.

The participial phrase, "en plaçant plus tôt ou plus tard qu'à son tour ce feuillet détaché d'un autre chapitre," extends the metaphorical code by qualifying the action described by all of the previous active verbs and their objects. It introduces an additional set of metaphors forming their own brief conceit. They play a complex role by constituting at once part of the activity attributed to *jour*, and by introducing an additional image that functions as a conceptual model briefly recapturing the subject under discussion.

The conceit based on the metaphor of the book is a recurrent image in *A la recherche*.[5] The code is here set up by *feuillet détaché d'un autre chapitre*. The prepositional qualifying phrase attached to *chapitre* reinforces the code, especially since *calendrier* is the conceit's key metaphor, explicitly designating the model whose constituent parts we have already encountered. The accompanying adjective *interpolé* is all-important in reemphasizing the notion of anachronism previously stressed by the adverbial phrase modifying *plaçant* ("plus tôt ou plus tard qu'à son tour"), and the preceding

---
[5] See II, 756 and III, 989. A variant, *évangile*, appears in III, 26. See *supra*, pp. 42-43.

animated tableau. The genitive link *du Bonheur* refers us to the particular emotional state that characterizes the experience of temporal anachronism and recalls the previous mention of *plaisirs*.

The two sets of metaphors work together by bringing before the reader's eyes an animated tableau and a concrete, conceptual model, both translating a subtle intuition about temporal anachronism. Aside from a brief introductory statement, the task of conveying this notion is entirely assigned to the extended metaphors.

3. Juxtaposition of Antithetical Images

In some instances, two sets of metaphors participate in the same semantic domain, but form separate images. The related metaphors strikingly emphasize through contrasting images the opposition between two temporal notions.

In the first example, two distinct images expressing opposed viewpoints about the interrelationship of distance, time and space appear within the same syntactical framework and grow out of the same semantic domain. Earlier within the same passage, a brief aphorism announces the relationship between these three concepts: "Les distances ne sont que le rapport de l'espace au temps et varient avec lui" (II, 996). The metaphors then illustrate this law by juxtaposing the hero's former view of the distance-time relationship between two towns hitherto visited by carriage on separate days to his new experience of visiting them all by automobile in one afternoon:

> Douville et Quetteholme, Saint-Mars-le-Vieux et Saint-Mars-le-Vêtu, Gourville et Balbec-le-Vieux, Tourville et Féterne,
> 1. / prisonniers aussi hermétiquement enfermés jusque-là dans la cellule de jours distincts / que jadis Méséglise et Guermantes, et sur lesquels les mêmes yeux ne pouvaient se
> 2. poser dans un seul après-midi, / délivrés maintenant par le géant aux bottes de sept lieues, vinrent assembler autour de l'heure de notre goûter leurs clochers et leurs tours, leurs vieux jardins que le bois avoisinant s'empressait de découvrir. / (II, 997)

The textual juxtaposition of the antithetical images of enclosure and open space emphasizes the abrupt change in the hero's conception of time and space. The code established by *prisonniers, hermétiquement enfermés* and *cellule* is extended by *délivrés* and *vinrent assembler,* which translate the changed perspective into concrete, spatial terms. The personification that makes towns into prisoners, the animation and transformation of the automobile into a giant, and the insistence on concrete, pictorial images (*clochers, tours, vieux jardins,* as synecdochal references to towns) combine the two images into a drama of imprisonment and liberation that significantly emphasizes the subject under discussion.

The temporal aspect underlying the spatial code is carefully linked to the concrete imagery and guides our interpretation of the metaphors. The genitive link of the figure *cellule de jours distincts* explicitly anchors the image of the initial conceit to the temporal notion under consideration. The space-time relationship is further emphasized by the discursive remark "et sur lesquels les mêmes yeux ne pouvaient se poser dans un seul après-midi." The temporal concept to be derived from the initial conceit is further reinforced by the comparative structure that relates another temporal experience to the same image of enclosure.[6] The theme of time is stressed once more by the qualifying phrase "autour de l'heure de notre goûter," which specifies the verb's (*vinrent assembler*) realm of action. The reader is explicitly told that the temporal unit of *jours distincts* associated with the initial image has changed to *l'heure du goûter* in the second image. The syntax joins the spatial and temporal realms whose interdependence is doubly stressed through semantic and grammatical ties.

In another passage where two sets of metaphors related to the same domain are introduced to emphasize antithetical experiences through contrasting images, the second image, by recalling and modifying the first, sets the diametrically opposed aspects in relief.

---

[6] The analogy to Méséglise and Guermantes has a double function: by including it in the same image of enclosure, the reader is reminded of the identity of the two temporal experiences; moreover, this unique comparison from the narrator's personal experience brings to mind the particular conceit of enclosure applied to Méséglise and Guermantes, translating the young hero's conception of temporally and spatially divided worlds that were visited on separate days. We may recall that in the hero's eyes, the habit of seeing them only on different days "les enfermait pour ainsi dire loin l'un de l'autre, inconnaissables l'un à l'autre, dans les vases clos et sans communication entre eux d'après-midi différents" (I, 135).

The imagery is introduced as a general observation into the narrative of the hero's experiences with dreams. The passage deals with two distinct states of man's temporal and spatial awareness upon awakening, and relies on the imagery to objectify and emphasize the different perspectives. The first image translates the notion of temporal and spatial orientation, which is associated with regular sleep. The overwhelming disorientation translated by the second image is to be attributed to irregular sleep. The dynamic nature of this additional image stands in sharp contrast to the immobility of the previous image. The two images are separated by a brief account of unusual sleeping conditions — such as falling asleep over a book or in an armchair — which may result in a feeling of utter disorientation upon awakening. The continued metaphors of the second image appear at the end of the otherwise literal account of disorientation, and constitute part of the same syntactical framework:

1. Un homme qui dort / tient en cercle autour de lui le fil des heures, l'ordre des années et des mondes. Il les consulte d'instinct en s'éveillant et y lit en une seconde le point de la terre qu'il occupe, le temps qui s'est écoulé jusqu'à son réveil; mais leurs rangs peuvent se mêler, se rompre / .... Que s'il s'assoupit dans une position encore plus déplacée et divergente, par exemple après dîner assis
2. dans un fauteuil, / alors le bouleversement sera complet dans les mondes désorbités, le fauteuil magique le fera voyager à toute vitesse dans le temps et dans l'espace, / et au moment d'ouvrir les paupières, il se croira couché quelques mois plus tôt dans une autre contrée. (I, 5)

The initial metaphorical phrase *tient en cercle* presents the reader with a graphic conceptual framework that determines his mental image of *fil des heures* and *ordre des années*. Within this context, *fil* and *ordre* are drawn into the material realm as constituent parts of the archetype of orderly spatial disposition, the circle.[7] The simplicity and precision of this image linking man, time and space impresses upon us the main concept of the temporal notion. The concept is further clarified through the syntactical structure and

---

[7] The circular disposition of hours is a familiar image in Greek mythology, which Proust may have had in mind. Greek art and letters represent the Hours as dancing maidens, often in the formation of a circle, and charged with the activity of measuring time.

the presence of literal pointers: the genitive links of the figures *fil des heures* and *l'ordre des années et des mondes,* by explicitly joining the metaphorical and literal domains, fulfill the cognitive function of supplying a key for the imagery. The double genitive link of the syllepsis *l'ordre des années et des mondes* is particularly important, since the hero's orientation depends on the linkage between time and space.

The sentence "Il les consulte d'instinct en s'éveillant et y lit en une seconde le point de la terre qu'il occupe, le temps qui s'est écoulé jusqu'à son réveil" draws on the first image and extends it, the circle becoming a measuring device of spatial and temporal orientation. Whereas the verb *lire* insists on the concrete nature of the image, its component parts are recalled by the object pronouns *les* and *y,* both referring back to *fil* and *ordre* of the initial sentence. "Mais leurs rangs peuvent se mêler, se rompre" extends the code with a contrasting image announcing the antithesis of order and continuity: the verbs *mêler* and *rompre* applied to *rangs* — a semantic synonym of *fil* and *ordre* in the domain of spatial disposition — at once point to this contrast. After a brief introductory remark announcing the sleeper's transfer from bed to armchair, the resulting disorientation is conveyed through the dynamic metaphorical image of travel through space.[8] The sleeper's very armchair is drawn into the image by becoming the vehicle effecting the removal from the world of order to a universe of disorder.

---

[8] See II, 981 where a brief conceit expresses the same notion of temporal and spatial alienation by means of the voyage code: "Alors, sur le char du sommeil, on descend dans des profondeurs où le souvenir ne peut plus le rejoindre...." In this instance, the conceit triggers off an extended metaphorical tableau, which takes us from the actual subject at hand into the realm of the fantastic.

The disorienting nature of sleep is again expressed in terms of spatial travel in III, 121, where sleep, conceived as substance, is charged with locomotion:

> mais cette matière y est "traitée," malaxée de telle sorte — avec un étirement dû à ce qu'aucune des limites horaires de l'état de veille ne l'empêche de s'effiler à des hauteurs inouïes....

In the last book of the novel, time — or age — is repeatedly described in terms of height. Cf. III, 533-534 and III, 1046-1048 for images based on this metaphorical transfer. The image *hauteur de nos années* is also used in III, 870 and III, 940. A number of related images express a temporal notion in terms of vertical distance. For images based on *profondeur,* see I, 185; I, 311; III, 940 and III, 944. The variant metaphor *abîme* is used in I, 24; I, 311; II, 91-92; II, 398 and III, 926.

Bouleversement introduces the concept of disorder, which the initial and controlling metaphor *mondes désorbités* emphatically restates. As the antonym of *l'ordre des mondes, désorbités* echoes the "circularity" of order in the first image, while denying that order. The precise reason for this new disorientation of the universe is briefly stated by the "magic voyage" conceit of the sentence in apposition: "le fauteuil magique le fera voyager à toute vitesse dans le temps et dans l'espace." *Fauteuil magique* and *voyager,* reinforced by *à toute vitesse,* establish the basic code. As in the previous archetype of order, the conceptual relationship between space and time is again reflected in the syntactical structure of the syllepsis "voyager ... dans le temps et dans l'espace," which joins time and space in a single action.

The development of this image is similar to that of the previous one: after a brief sketch objectifying the type of sleep in concrete, schematic terms, the sleeper's relative temporal and spatial perspective is described. The vast disorientation conveyed by "quelques mois plus tôt dans une autre contrée" stands in striking contrast to the exact orientation expressed by *point de la terre* and *temps ... écoulé.* The peaceful sleeper of the first image consults his stable surroundings — symbolized by the circle — to orient himself, whereas the uprooted sleeper of the second image has lost all bearings as participant in the voyage. The combined temporal and spatial content of the resulting orientation or disorientation is made clear in each case by extending the image; the lengthening of the travel code ("quelques mois plus tôt dans une autre contrée") explicitly links time and space, as did the previous extension to the temporal-spatial measuring device.

The considerable extension of the imagery and its textual integration within the narrative command the reader's attention. The sudden change from the narrator's *je* to the impersonal third person (*l'homme; il*) gives the passage the impersonal cadre of aphorisms, thereby setting it off within the hero's account of personal experience. This narrative break is underscored by the typographical division, which introduces the passage as a new paragraph.[9]

---

[9] In the following pages the narrator occasionally introduces an isolated metaphor referring back to the travel code of the image on disorientation; for example (I, 5): "alors celui-ci [mon esprit] lâchait le plan du lieu où je

Images of spatial and temporal disorientation are important to the initial pages of "Combray" (I, 3-9), where the hero experiences such disorientation several times. The imagery focuses our attention on the phenomenon, and helps us to understand it. Moreover, the voyage conceit of the second image is important for an understanding of the novel's narrative development. The uprooted hero whom sleep has transplanted "quelques mois plus tôt dans une autre contrée" extends these fortuitous journeys into the past once he is awake. His conscious memory continues to recall other places and eras. He thus tells us about Combray, later to be followed by accounts of Balbec, Paris, Doncières and Venice, the other "worlds" of his past remembered whose narrative representation constitutes a significant part of *A la recherche*. [10]

4. Juxtaposition of Different Images

The relationship between the two sets of metaphors is less obvious when they are from different semantic domains. Their possible conceptual dependency and joint function is then disclosed by the context:

1. Mais surtout je mettais entre eux, bien plus que leurs distances kilométriques, / la distance qu'il y avait entre les deux parties de mon cerveau où je pensais à eux, une de ces distances dans l'esprit qui ne font pas qu'éloigner, qui séparent et mettent dans un autre plan. / Et cette démarcation était rendue plus absolue encore parce que cette habitude que nous avions de n'aller jamais vers les deux côtés un même jour, dans une seule promenade, mais une
2. fois du côté de Méséglise, une fois du côté de Guermantes, / les enfermait pour ainsi dire loin l'un de l'autre, inconnaissables l'un à l'autre, dans les vases clos et sans communication entre eux d'après-midi différents. / (I, 135)

In this passage the first image is based on a metaphoric use of the word *distance,* while the second image depends upon a metaphoric

---

m'étais endormi"; (I, 6): "ma pensée qui hésitait au seuil des temps et des formes"; (I, 8): "mon corps avait viré une dernière fois."

[10] I, 9: "je passais la plus grande partie de la nuit à me rappeler notre vie d'autrefois à Combray chez ma grand' tante, à Balbec, à Paris, à Doncières, à Venise, ailleurs encore, à me rappeler les lieux, les personnes que j'y avais connues, ce que j'avais vu d'elles, ce qu'on m'en avait raconté."

use of the word *vase*. Since these two words, taken literally, are from entirely different semantic domains, why should they be studied together? The answer lies in the half-sentence that stands as transition between the two images: "Et cette démarcation était rendue plus absolue encore parce que cette habitude que nous avions de n'aller jamais vers les deux côtés un même jour, dans une seule promenade, mais une fois du côté de Méséglise, une fois du côté de Guermantes." The key term here is *démarcation*, which links the metaphorical meaning of the term *distance* to that of the term *vases*, by stating the concept that underlies the metaphorical transposition of both images. Thus the first image translates the idea of "mental distance" into an absolute dichotomy made concrete by an anatomical analogy (*les deux parties de mon cerveau*), and reinforced by *séparent et mettent dans un autre plan*. The second image repeats the sense of absolute separation implicit in *démarcation* by rendering it in the form of sealed vases, between which no communication is possible. The narrator's mildly apologetic *pour ainsi dire*, which might seem to excuse the image as a flight of poetic fancy, actually calls the reader's attention to it.

With the completion of the second image, *dans les vases clos et sans communication entre eux d'après-midi différents,* the temporal implications of the word *démarcation* are at last explicit: the separation between Méséglise and Guermantes, is, finally, a separation in *time*. To the reader who does not know the rest of the novel, the narrator's insistence on the absolute temporal separation between Méséglise and Guermantes may seem exaggerated, for the full implications of this separation emerge only as the novel progresses. Thus is produced one of Proust's many anticipations of the future course of the narrative, in which Méséglise and Guermantes are to become symbolic of separate eras in the hero's life, between which no communication exists until time is recaptured. The narrative structure of the novel echoes this mental separation between the two localities. The two destinations for Sunday walks are taken up separately (Méséglise: I, 135-165; Guermantes: I, 165-183), and the narrative accounts of *Du côté de chez Swann* and *Le Côté de Guermantes* are separated by several books.[11]

---

[11] See Georges Poulet, *L'Espace proustien*, where the relationship between temporal and spatial concepts and the composition of the novel is repeatedly stressed. For a study of narrative anachronisms of *A la recherche* see J. P.

METAPHORICAL EXPANSION   83

In another example, two conceits from different domains are juxtaposed and closely linked within the same syntactical framework, presenting the reader with two widely different images, though their message is tautological.[12] Both images deal with the exclusive importance of the most recent impression in determining a person's present perspective. A long, literal remark giving a general explanation to a particular instance of "present perspective" precedes the double metaphorical transposition:

> Pour n'importe laquelle de mes amies de la petite bande, comment le dernier visage que je lui avais vu n'eût-il pas été le seul que je me rappelasse, puisque, de nos souvenirs relatifs à une personne, l'intelligence élimine tout ce qui ne concourt pas à l'utilité immédiate de nos rela-
> 1. tions quotidiennes.... / Elle laisse filer la chaîne des jours passés, n'en garde fortement que le dernier bout, souvent d'un tout autre métal que les chaînons disparus dans la
> 2. nuit, / et dans le voyage que nous faisons à travers la vie, ne tient pour réel que le pays où nous sommes présentement. / (I, 949)

The two images, though based on two distinctly different conceits, are closely linked syntactically by the co-ordinating conjunction *et*, guiding the reader from one image to the next. These images reinforce each other by jointly conveying the same idea that perspective is ruled by time.

The first conceit is extended and insists on precise pictorial details: days become metal links forming a chain. The descriptive details *dernier bout* and *tout autre métal* insist on the transposition to the concrete, which is further enhanced by *chaînons disparus dans*

Houston, "Temporal Patterns in *A la recherche du temps perdu*," and Hans Robert Jauss, *op. cit.*, pp. 106-127.

[12] A similar example of image juxtaposition occurs in a context where the narrator speaks of his temporal confinement in the present because of the overpowering effect of alcohol: "j'étais enfermé dans le présent, comme les héros, comme les ivrognes; momentanément éclipsé, mon passé ne projetait plus devant moi cette ombre de lui-même que nous appelons notre avenir" (I, 815). Here the single metaphor *enfermé* alone effects the metaphorical transposition, the following comparison merely drawing heroes and drunkards into the same image of incarceration. The second image, by extending into a conceit, adds the precise pictorial details that enable the reader to grasp the notion. The image is especially striking, since it presents a well-known visual phenomenon in reverse, for light is here replaced by shadow.

la nuit, thus emphasizing a conceptual distinction in terms of visual contrast. The active verb *filer* gives motion to the whole image and emphasizes the disappearance of the past. In the light of the preceding descriptive details, *laisse filer la chaîne* suggests the nautical use of the verb *filer* and may evoke the visual image of the links of an anchor chain disappearing one by one into dark waters.

The second, much briefer conceit equating man's lifetime to a voyage and the concept of present perspective to the material realm of *pays où nous sommes présentement,* further stresses the temporal notion and impresses the conceptual relationship between time and perspective upon the reader. The two conceits work together within the same syntactical unit to convey the same temporal notion through different transpositions. The emphatic differentiation between past and present perspectives through the graphic model of the chain, and the extension of the abstract concept into material terms through the voyage conceit focus the reader's attention on the temporal aspect under discussion, and divert it from the narrative account of the hero's personal experience.

The imagery is followed by a specific illustration from the hero's personal experience within time. Written from the retrospective viewpoint of the narrator, the illustration consists of the hero's two contrasting perspectives, one past, one present, in regard to the young girls at Balbec. Within this context of personal narrative, the metaphorical imagery, due to its extent and precision, is autonomous and draws the reader's attention to the general truth to be derived from such an experience. The shift of emphasis from the personal to the general is further apparent from the substitution of the first person plural for the first person singular.

CHAPTER V

ACCUMULATED METAPHORS

A special type of metaphorical extension I call "accumulation" of time metaphors; it differs from the continued metaphor in that its constituent metaphors all have the same grammatical relationship to a particular "pivotal" element of the sentence or phrase within which they appear.[1] In almost all of these accumulations, the constituent elements are juxtaposed and are of the same part of speech and morphological structure. A study of the various examples reveals that this syntactical and grammatical disposition emphasizes the metaphors' combined effort to express the same temporal notion.

---

[1] I am here borrowing Yvette Louria's term, put forth in her book *La Convergence stylistique chez Proust* (Geneva: Librairie E. Droz, 1957) where she refers to the common syntactical link as "pivot" (p. 9). Miss Louria uses the term "convergence" to designate the phenomenon of accumulation, for, in her words, "les éléments de la 'convergence', reliés chacun à un centre commun par la même fonction grammaticale, font 'converger' l'attention du lecteur sur ce centre" (p. 4). I do not feel, however, that the term applies as well to what the author calls "convergence voilée" (p. 17), for the reader's attention can hardly be said to converge on the various elements of the accumulation, which may be placed "à une distance plus ou moins grande les uns des autres" (p. 17).
Within the present study, there is no need for the distinction between "convergence évidente" and "voilée," as the metaphorical accumulations are closely juxtaposed, hence quite evident. For my purposes, it does not appear necessary to break down these accumulations into the various grammatical parts of speech. I shall concentrate on their relative extension and structure.
I should like to refer the reader to the more encompassing definition of accumulation as given by Michael Riffaterre in *Le Style des Pléiades de Gobineau*, pp. 133-143. See also Jean Mouton, *Style de Proust*, pp. 145-172 for a psychological analysis of the phenomenon of accumulation, and R. A. Sayce, *Style in French Prose*, pp. 75-77.

The concept to be conveyed by these metaphorical accumulations is usually complex; the accumulated metaphors break this complex idea down into its component elements while their close syntactical and grammatical ties fuse these elements into a conceptual whole. Such accumulated metaphors reflect the hero's complex inner reality, by conveying multiple impressions or sensations experienced simultaneously.

Accumulated metaphors vary widely in number and complexity. I shall first examine the simple structure of two or more metaphors joined to the same pivotal element. The more complex structures of a second accumulation growing out of the first — either by juxtaposition to or insertion within the first — or of two or more separate sets working together within the same syntactical framework will be taken up later within this section.

Proust's accumulated metaphors are carefully integrated into the text and are accompanied by explicit semantic or syntactic indications linking them to a literal statement concerning time. In some instances, the pivotal element itself may be a temporal expression (*passé, année, heure, jour*). When the pivotal element is a time metaphor, a genitive link, usually directly attached to the group of metaphors, refers the reader to the aspect of time under discussion.

Accumulated metaphors are seldom from the same domain, yet they are closely related within the same cognitive sphere — not a universal one, but rather the hero's private, subjective one. Each element within an accumulation, although it is metaphoric in relation to the concept of time it expresses, may be a synecdoche, metonymy or metaphor in relation to one or more of the elements within the same group.[2] The accumulated metaphors seldom extend the same code.

---

[2] Stephen Ullmann distinguishes between metaphor and metonymy by quoting examples from *A la recherche* in his article "L'Image littéraire — quelques questions de méthode" in *Langue et Littérature,* Actes du VIIIe Congrès de FILLM, 1961. He defines metonymy as "basée sur une association par contiguïté" (p. 44), and cites as an example the image "la surface azurée du silence." Besides constituting a metonymy, I feel that this image is also metaphoric, as becomes evident when one examines the surrounding context within which the figure is an integral part of an extended image composed of a series of continued time metaphors. See *A la recherche,* I, 88, and *infra,* pp. 110-115. Cf. also Ullmann, *Style in the French Novel,* p. 197. Gérard Genette follows Ullmann's definition of metonymy in his excellent

A. Simple Structures

1. Accumulated Metaphors from the Same Semantic Domain

Within the basic structure of several metaphors joined to the same pivotal element, three or more metaphors usually work together. The exception is the binary structure whose brief transposition can give the reader only a glimpse at the temporal aspect, whereas Proust's predilection, when touching upon the theme of time, is to be more elaborate. Yet even the briefest of accumulations is carefully interpolated into the text, and guides the reader's interpretation of the temporal message. For instance, in the following example, the pivotal element of the metaphorical group is closely linked to the preceding context through the genitive link:

> Et, plus débile encore dans le silence de la grève sur laquelle la mer montait, et comme une voix qui aurait traduit et accru / le vague énervant de cette heure inquiète et fausse, / un petit orgue de Barbarie arrêté devant l'hôtel jouait des valses viennoises. (II, 787)

The close grammatical link and syntactical juxtaposition of the pivotal element, the adjectival group and the preceding ambiguous expression *vague énervant* clarify the temporal message: *vague énervant* is directly attributed to *heure*, whose nature is specified through the two personifying adjectives. The particular temporal impression is further clarified through the explicitly stated mental contiguity between the auditory stimulus — "orgue de Barbarie" — and a specific hour and place, as revealed by the surrounding context.[3]

---

article "Métonymie chez Proust, ou la naissance du Récit," *Poétique*, pp. 156-173. Genette's important contribution consists in showing how metonymy and metaphor are sometimes related in a Proustian figure of speech.

[3] Two other examples of accumulated metaphors belong to the binary structure: see III, 487 where a double genitive link modifies a metaphorical expression translating a particular temporal impression: "le titre sans alliage d'or fixe et d'indestructible azur." The salient sensory impressions that determine this specific mode of being are revealed through the double accumulation *d'or fixe* and *d'indestructible azur*, both metonymies referring to the visual impressions of sunny summer skies.

See also II, 398 where the accumulation consisting of a double genitive link expresses the narrator's different impressions of two distinct periods of

The accumulation of three adjectives grammatically linked to the same noun is the predominant type of triadic structure. As in the previous example, the adjectives within the next passage modify a temporal expression, *grise journée*: "Lasse, résignée, occupée pour plusieurs heures encore à sa tâche immémoriale, la grise journée filait sa passementerie de nacre..." (II, 350).[4] The adjectival group stands in relief because of its extended structure and its syntactical position at the head of the sentence, where it precedes the modified noun. The reader's attention is drawn to the conspicuous adjectives and the delayed noun. The metaphorical accumulation establishes the code that personifies time, an aspect further particularized by *filait sa passementerie de nacre* and the following metaphorical extension to an animated tableau.[5]

2. Accumulated Metaphors from Different Semantic Domains

Unlike the examples studied in the previous section, most of Proust's accumulated metaphors are from different semantic domains. Since their relationship in conveying the temporal notion is then less obvious, they are reinforced by the surrounding context, disclosing one or several aspects of the conceptual complexity, as in the following passage from *Le Temps retrouvé*. It describes how the hero is suddenly transported to his childhood while travelling through old, familiar streets. The context preceding the metaphorical accumulation announces the temporal journey ("je m'élevais lentement vers les hauteurs silencieuses du souvenir") and prepares our understanding of the metaphorical passage: "Dans Paris, ces rues-là se détacheront toujours pour moi en une autre matière que les autres." The figurative implications of *matière* are clear from the preceding context, explaining that the sudden change from a

---

his life: "l'incompatibilité de deux qualités incomparables d'atmosphère respirée et de colorations ambiantes."

[4] See *infra*, p. 123 for further analysis of this passage.

[5] See I, 830 where a series of animating adjectives modifies *journées*: "ces journées oisives et lumineuses qu'on passe sur la plage. Elles sont alors, et par là, bien que désœuvrées, alertes comme des journées de travail, aiguillées, aimantées, soulevées légèrement vers un instant prochain...."

bumpy to a smooth ride is not due to a change in the pavement, but is brought about by the hero's sudden remembrance of former rides along the same streets (II, 858). Hence the change in the conditions of the journey is not material, but mental:

> Quand j'arrivai au coin de la rue Royale où était jadis le marchand en plein vent des photographies aimées de Françoise, il me sembla que la voiture, entraînée par des centaines de tours anciens, ne pourrait pas faire autrement que de tourner d'elle-même. Je ne traversais pas les mêmes rues que les promeneurs qui étaient dehors ce jour-là, mais / un passé glissant, triste, et doux. / Il était d'ailleurs fait de tant de passés différents qu'il m'était difficile de reconnaître la cause de ma mélancolie.... (III, 858-859)

The reader's attention is drawn to the metaphorical transposition thrown into relief at the end of a passage announcing the temporal notion. The modifying phrase attached to *voiture* ("entraînée par des centaines de tours anciens") recalls the temporal dimension introduced into the scene. The intrusion of the past is closely linked to the tableau through the syntactical relationship of *rues* and *passé,* both sharing the verb *traversais,* which performs a double function by being at once literal (in relation to its object *rues*) and metaphorical (in relation to its second object *passé*). The close syntactical ties between the literal and figurative domains verbally translate the hero's sudden shift from actual journey to a journey into the past. The nature of the metaphorical journey is particularized by the three modifying adjectives attached to *passé* (*glissant, triste, et doux*). These adjectives convey the complexity of the temporal notion by modifying *passé* with terms referring to different semantic domains. The semantic opposition is especially keen between the adjective *glissant* derived from an active verb and the affective adjectives *triste* and *doux.*

Although the accumulation in itself is rather ambiguous, the surrounding context allows us further insight into the meaning of the three adjectives. The preceding context prepares us for the otherwise unusual adjective *glissant* as a modifier of *passé*: "entraînée par des centaines de tours anciens" points to the temporal aspect of the carriage ride, whereas "Le sol de lui-même savait où il devait aller; sa résistance était vaincue" emphasizes the specific nature of the metaphorical journey, the smooth progress of remembrance.

Glissant may partly be explained by these details from the preceding street tableau whose content is at once literal — describing a voyage in the material world — and retrospectively symbolic of the temporal journey, thereby anchoring the abstract temporal notion in the material realm. Thus the streets' *résistance vaincue* prepares the specific content of *glissant* whose literal meaning fits into the same semantic domain, whereas the hyperbole "centaines de tours anciens" significantly emphasizes the temporal aspect of the setting — *centaines* exaggerates the multitemporal content of the experience — as well as the dynamic activity of *entraînée*.

In view of this particular textual preparation anchoring *glissant* in the concrete, material realm, the direct juxtaposition of *triste* and *doux* seems especially abrupt. Nothing in the preceding context points to their coming. The following context, however, explains their presence as part of the same inner reality, for the narrator explicitly speaks of his melancholy. The personifying adjective *triste* transfers the hero's emotional state to *passé*, an anthropomorphizing process in which *doux* participates. *Tant de passés* recalls *centaines de tours anciens* and the multi-temporal implications conferred onto *glissant*. The multiple aspect of the evoked past and the indefinite content of *mélancolie* are specifically illustrated by the following textual juxtaposition of three past experiences (I, 859), all from different periods of the hero's past, and associated with the same place and emotional state.

The metaphorical accumulation modifying *passé*, reinforced by the surrounding context, sets the dominant traits in relief, each representative of the complexity of the hero's inner reality at a specific moment in time. This complexity is communicated to the reader through each additional adjective, referring us to the hero's mental association between sensory and emotional domains.[6]

---

[6] A similar example of three adjectives from different domains all modifying the same noun is found in a simile, which translates the hero's temporal conception about remnants of the past within the present: "telle légende... demeure au milieu du présent comme une émanation plus dense, immémoriale et stable" (II, 418). Here the ambiguous metaphorical transposition composed of the pivotal element *émanation* and its three modifiers is prepared for by the preceding metaphorical aphorism "Le passé n'est pas fugace, il reste sur place." *N'être pas fugace* and *rester sur place*, reinforced by various illustrations of past remnants within the present material world, prepare the static image evoked by the adjectival group.

Proust increases the number of elements in a metaphorical accumulation as the temporal notion itself becomes more complex. Not only does the greater number of accumulated metaphors help the reader better to understand, but the very length of the accumulation draws his attention to the importance of the idea presented. The emphasis becomes especially obvious when each element of the group is preceded by the repetition of the same auxiliary word: "Une heure n'est pas qu'une heure, c'est un vase rempli de parfums, de sons, de projets et de climats" (III, 889). The repetition of *de* introduces a noticeable parallelism and rhythm into the accumulation, underlining the nouns' identical grammatical function in regard to their common link *rempli*. It also emphasizes their close relationship within the same cognitive sphere, their close syntactical tie to the image *vase rempli* stressing their mental contiguity. The direct link to *heure* through the copula *être* at once clarifies the temporal implications of the metaphorical transposition. The nouns, although from entirely different domains — the various sensory appeals of *parfums, sons, climats* and the abstract noun *projets* — are presented as component parts of the same conceptual ensemble through their close structural links and common pivotal image *vase*. The image of the sealed vase supplies us with an obvious conceptual model illustrating the abstract notion of concurrent impressions.

Our comprehension of the metaphors is aided by the preceding narrative account where two examples from the hero's personal experience illustrate the metaphorical statement, which thus introduces a general rule as derived from the hero's individual experience (III, 889). Whereas the aphorism generalizes by pointing to the common law to be derived from the two experiences, these in turn

---

I have found one more example belonging to the structure of the triple adjectival accumulation. There three metaphorical adjectives, besides working together to modify *année,* are drawn together by the following temporal comparison whose hyperbolic analogy applies to each one of them: "cette année finale ... m'apparaissait remplie, diverse, vaste comme un siècle" (III, 485). The analogy to *siècle* merely exaggerates the content of the adjectives; it does not introduce an analogy drawn from another domain, since it shares that of *année.*

illustrate the rule and give the reader a particular insight into a specific experience.[7]

B. Complex Structures

To express complex ideas, Proust uses accumulations of metaphors even more complicated than those already discussed. When an element of a metaphorical accumulation extends itself to form a second accumulation, which may either be inserted within the first or directly follow it, we have one type of complex structure. A second type is the juxtaposition of two syntactically dependent groups, each modifying the other, such as a double genitive link modifying the various elements of an accumulation. These complex structures are able to convey to an even greater extent intricate conceptual relationships.

1. Extension to an Additional Accumulation

In the following contiguous accumulation, the second element of a binary group is in turn extended by five adjectives that focus the reader's attention on the various characteristics attributed to the temporal journey into the past.[8] A close tie exists between all the adjectival elements of both accumulations, since each one is preceded by the anaphora *plus*. The repeated auxiliary term underlines the essence of each element, since it joins them all within the same comparative framework, stressing the fact that the presently described temporal journey is more successful than the previous one in recapturing the past. Besides reinforcing the metaphors' essential

---

[7] Cf. III, 885 and the corresponding footnote 1 (pp. 1135-1136) where the same two experiences, stated in slightly different terms, are followed by almost the same metaphorical aphorism, here extended, however, to an accumulation of five nouns: "une heure est un vase rempli de parfums, de sons, de moments; d'humeurs variées, de climats" (III, 1136).

[8] In a "contiguous accumulation," the contiguity in question is a syntactical one. In this particular combination of two accumulations, the first element of the second series constitutes the last element of the first. The second accumulation grows directly out of the first, since its pivotal element — the last member of the initial group — participates in both series. See Yvette Louria, pp. 48-49, where this structure is discussed, though no distinction is made between literal and metaphorical accumulations.

message, the descriptive parallelism through the repetition of the same term emphasizes the double accumulation:

> Mais on verra combien certaines impressions fugitives et fortuites ramènent bien mieux encore vers le passé, / avec une précision plus fine, d'un vol plus léger, plus immatériel, plus vertigineux, plus infaillible, plus immortel, / que ces dislocations organiques. (II, 92)

The two contiguous prepositional phrases modifying the action of *ramènent* constitute the first accumulation ("avec une précision plus fine, d'un vol plus léger"). The initial accumulation is closely tied to the temporal notion it describes, since its grammatical link to the verb of action (*ramènent*) brings it in contact with the scene of action, *le passé*. The second accumulation grows out of the first, its pivotal element being the noun of the second element, whose modifying adjective is at once part of both accumulations. The far more noticeable extension of the second group focuses all our attention on the particular nature of the flight into the past, and puts all the emphasis on the metaphorical transposition. The various traits attributed to the flight into the past are again from different domains: *léger, immatériel* and *vertigineux* appeal to our sensory experience, whereas *infaillible* and *immortel* are abstract modifiers that remain a mystery to the reader until he actually reads the detailed analyses of the hero's various encounters with involuntary memory in *Le Temps retrouvé*.[9] The adjectives thus retain part of the mystery announced by this anticipatory passage, which was specifically introduced as such by the initial words "mais on verra."

The second component of the comparative structure ("que ces dislocations organiques") stands out at the end of the sentence, where it is especially noticeable after the long disjunction of the double accumulation. It recalls another type of voyage into the past, an experience described in the passage immediately preceding the present quotation.

---

[9] The phenomenon of involuntary memory is here alluded to by "impressions fugitives et fortuites."

2. Juxtaposition of Two Syntactically Dependent Groups

One of the most tightly knit structures joining two juxtaposed accumulations occurs when the two groups are syntactically interdependent through the genitive link. In the following example, an accumulation of three nouns is joined by a double genitive link to a second accumulation:

> De sorte que ces quelques années n'imposaient pas seulement au souvenir d'Albertine, qui les rendait si douloureuses, / les couleurs successives, les modalités différentes, la cendre / de leurs saisons ou de leurs heures, / des fins d'après-midi de juin aux soirs d'hiver, des clairs de lune sur la mer à l'aube en rentrant à la maison, de la neige de Paris aux feuilles mortes de Saint-Cloud, mais encore de l'idée particulière que je me faisais successivement d'Albertine.... (III, 487)

Both of the terms of the binary accumulation *de leurs saisons, de leurs heures* modify each of the nouns in the first accumulation, so that *couleurs, modalités,* and *cendre* are all made metaphorically descriptive of certain time periods — seasons and hours. Whereas the binary group consists of two literal time expressions, the three elements of the preceding accumulation are metaphoric within this context. Although *couleurs, modalités,* and *cendre* refer us to the same conceptual ensemble, their semantic domains differ. In the case of the first two nouns, the modifying adjective attributes a salient characteristic to the noun: *successives* stresses the aspect of change within time, whereas *différentes* emphasizes the concept of variety. The parallelism of the first two elements is not shared by the third, whose noun is not modified by an adjective, since it immediately expands into the genitive link (*cendre de leurs saisons ou de leurs heures*). The resulting change of rhythm and structure draws our attention to this element. *Cendre* is semantically quite different from the two previous terms, which are metonymic in the sense that they represent two essential characteristics of what constitutes the hero's awareness of existence within time. As an ambivalent poetic image suggesting the notion of radical reduction, *cendre* fulfills an expressive function within this context.[10] It makes a striking comment on the hero's emotional state regarding the nature of his memories about time spent with Albertine.

The metaphorical transposition and its genitive link are immediately followed by the direct juxtaposition of three descriptive phrases whose particular details illustrate the nature and content of the hero's memories. These details give the reader a specific glimpse of the hero's memories, which the previous metaphors described in its chief characteristics of change, variety and reduction. The aspect of change and variety expressed by each phrase is set in relief by the parallel structure: two distinct details conveying a different temporal or seasonal aspect are juxtaposed in each phrase, the first always preceded by *de,* and the second by *à,* prepositions that underline the opposition between the two images. The structural identity of these descriptive phrases stresses the fact that they closely work together in illustrating the notion expressed by the previous metaphorical accumulation. As an archetype of a particular season or hour, each image evokes or alludes to a different mode of being: thus *fins d'après-midi de juin* is contrasted with *soirs d'hiver, clair de lune* with *aube, neige de Paris* with *feuilles mortes de Saint-Cloud.* These selected details representing temporal and seasonal changes and varieties also comment on the highly schematic nature of remembrances, for they merely retain the essence of an hour or season, or of a place become representative of a particular moment. This descriptive process retrospectively clarifies the meaning of *cendre,* since the evocative details are symbols of the essence to which a period has been reduced within the narrator's mind. They are a descriptive mimesis of *couleurs successives* and *modalités différentes.*

In the next example, two contiguous accumulations — again closely linked by the genitive structure — are part of a descriptive passage contrasting two different conceptions of the nature of man's temporal existence: the one viewing it as a series of drastic changes,

---

[10] My concept of "expressive" or "emotive" function follows Roman Jakobson's definition as put forth in "Linguistics and Poetics": "The so-called EMOTIVE or 'expressive' function, focused on the ADDRESSER, aims a direct expression of the speaker's attitude toward what he is speaking about. It tends to produce an impression of a certain emotion whether true or feigned..." (p. 354).

the other momentarily regarding it as static, unchangeable. The double metaphorical accumulation focuses on the static aspect of existence as communicated by the special atmosphere of the theatre. The two contrasted viewpoints are the hero-narrator's:

> les loges ... composaient un panorama éphémère que les morts, les scandales, les maladies, les brouilles modifieraient bientôt, mais qui en ce moment était immobilisé par l'attention, la chaleur, le vertige, la poussière, l'élégance et l'ennui, / dans cette espèce d'instant éternel et tragique / d'inconsciente attente et de calme engourdissement / qui, rétrospectivement, semble avoir précédé l'explosion d'une bombe ou la première flamme d'un incendie. (II, 54-55)

The literal elaboration preceding the metaphorical transposition enumerates the various aspects of existence that render it ephemeral, and juxtaposes them to a second enumeration explaining why existence momentarily seems static at the theatre.

The temporal implications of the double accumulation are clear from the two adjectives of the first one and the two genitive links of the second, all modifying *instant*: "instant éternel et tragique d'inconsciente attente et de calme engourdissement." The adjectives reveal the two salient characteristics attributed to this temporal experience by the narrator: *éternel* stresses the notion of stability and stands in sharp contrast to *instant,* the hyperbole of the ephemeral within the same semantic domain. The temporal code of the oxymoron *instant éternel* is not continued by the second adjective: *tragique* adds another dimension to this state of being within time. It is an anthropomorphic metaphor, which confers the narrator's emotional disposition onto *instant*.

The double genitive link that follows recalls the previous enumeration of what constitutes the particular state of being at the theatre. *Inconsciente attente* and *calme engourdissement* refer us especially to the audience's complete unawareness that life is ephemeral, since they are totally immersed in the present. The tragic aspect of this instant is strikingly illustrated by the following literal elaboration, stating the ephemerality in exaggerated terms by means of two dramatic instances of unexpected disaster: the explosion of a bomb and the start of a fire. The exaggerated statement of the metaphorical transposition reinforced by the dramatic illustrations and the anticipation of the knowing narrator predicting the ephemeral nature of life, health and social relations all point to the symbolic significance of the tableau depicting the theatre. The more general implications of the context take the reader from the momentary, particular experience to a common truth applying to the world at large. This passage also anticipates the future narrative development of *Le Temps retrouvé,* where we are repeatedly reminded of this truth.

Another type of accumulation closely knit through syntax occurs when a second accumulation is inserted between two elements of the first.[11] In the next example, a second accumulation expands the first by adding a second modifier to one of three accumulated nouns. The binary adjectival group introduces a structural incongruity into the nominal accumulation whose other elements are modified by only one adjective each. This lack of structural parallelism results in a less obvious accumulation. The passage describes the hero's recent discovery of the ordinary nature of the New Year's Day whose special importance within the conventional calendar had misled him into believing the very essence of this day to be different from that of ordinary days:

> je sentais qu'il ne savait pas qu'on l'appelât le jour de l'an, qu'il finissait dans le crépuscule d'une façon qui ne m'était pas nouvelle: dans le vent doux qui soufflait autour de la colonne d'affiches, j'avais reconnu, j'avais senti reparaître / la matière / éternelle et commune, / l'humidité familière, l'ignorante fluidité des anciens jours. / (I, 488)

The context preceding the metaphorical accumulation announces the new temporal discovery in vague terms: "il [le jour de l'an] finissait dans le crépuscule d'une façon qui ne m'était pas nouvelle." The descriptive details of both accumulations each take up a particular aspect of what constitutes the familiar essence of former days. The very sensory experience underlying this new temporal awareness is clear from *dans le vent doux,* which modifies the double verbal structure *j'avais reconnu, j'avais senti reparaître.* The two verbs constitute the pivotal element to which the three follow-

---

[11] Yvette Louria discusses this type of syntactical relationship under "combinaison emboîtée," pp. 49-52.

ing noun metaphors of the main accumulation are grammatically linked. *Reconnu* and *reparaître* both stress the idea of recurrence that is central to this experience. The key aspect of continuity and uniformity is expressed by the binary adjectival group modifying *matière,* which constitutes the accumulation within the accumulation. *L'humidité familière* recalls and particularizes the sensory stimulus underlying the temporal notion. While the adjective *familière* reveals the observer's point of view, *ignorante* personifies time. The process of personification, already introduced at the start through "il ne savait pas" further commands the reader's attention. The main temporal content is made explicit through the addition of the genitive link *des anciens jours,* which once more stresses the notion of continuity and recurrence, and attributes the component parts of the accumulation to the temporal domain. The various accumulated elements thus translate the hero's mental contiguity at a specific moment in time.

3. Combined Accumulations

The constituent parts of an accumulation may appear within successive phrases or clauses, textually separated from each other by intervening material. In the following example, the framework of the accumulation is extended syntactically because each of the three nouns composing this group is modified by a rather extensive clause. In addition, two of these clauses contain their own accumulation. This more extended and complex structure may be called a "combined accumulation," since the secondary groups appearing within the framework of the main accumulation elaborate on the notion conveyed by the main element, which in turn shares this content with the other main elements bound by the same structure. In the first example of this structure, each descriptive detail of the three accumulations discloses another aspect of the hero's sensory impressions and special sensitivity within a given duration. The setting is the hotel room at Balbec. The importance accorded this passage and the surrounding descriptive imagery of metaphors and similes reflect the narrator's insistence on this particular temporal notion:

1. cette chambre, que je traversais un moment avant de m'habiller pour la promenade, avait l'air / d'un prisme où se décomposaient les couleurs de la lumière du dehors, d'une ruche où les sucs de la journée que j'allais goûter étaient /
2. dissociés, épars, enivrants et visibles, / d'un jardin de l'es-
3. pérance qui se dissolvait en une palpitation / de rayons d'argent et de pétales de rose. / (I, 704-705)

The main accumulation's three nouns are grammatically linked to the pivotal element *avait l'air de,* which announces the metaphorical transposition. This hesitant transitional element between the literal and metaphoric introduces a structure close to the simile, and puts the reader on his guard by emphasizing the semantic shift. The three nouns bound to this pivotal element all work together to express the complexity of the hero's concurrent perceptions associated with a definite place and time. Although from different domains, the three nouns may all be said to be conceptual models conveying the same notion of sensory complexity associated with the multiple sensory appeals experienced within the room. *Prisme* and its modifying clause emphasize the multiple light effects of the setting: "prisme où se décomposaient les couleurs de la lumière du dehors." This light impression constitutes the principal sensory appeal, as already stressed by the preceding descriptive imagery, and further insisted upon by the following elements and their modifiers. The fact that the room exhibits "les couleurs de la lumière du dehors" is already plausible to the reader from the initial sentence initiating the room's description: "Et à cette heure où des rayons venus d'expositions et comme d'heures différentes, brisaient les angles du mur" (704). The different gradations of light are here explicitly linked to time: "comme d'heures différentes."

The second noun *ruche* is again particularized through a modifying clause: "une ruche où les sucs de la journée que j'allais goûter étaient dissociés, épars, enivrants et visibles." It introduces a different sensorial domain, which, however, is closely related to the first through the accumulation of four adjectives modifying *sucs*: *dissociés* and *épars* again stress the multiple content of the room's sensorial impressions, whereas *visible* refers us back to the visual realm, without, however, revealing the nature of this visual transformation. The affective attribute *enivrants* introduces the observer's personal reaction into the picture. The genitive link attached to *sucs* (*de la journée*) reveals the domain to which the various sensory impressions are conceptually related. The third noun is ambiguous; although the concept of *jardin* may evoke the notion of visual and compositional variety, the modifying genitive link *de l'espérance* primarily appeals to our imagination, and discloses the hero's particular emotional state. The relative clause modifying *jardin de l'espérance* further particularizes the unique conception of this experience: *dissolvait* again stresses the concept of sensorial interpenetration previously expressed by *décomposaient, dissociés* and *épars,* whereas the prepositional phrase "en une palpitation de rayons d'argent et de pétales de rose" recalls the room's special atmosphere through two metonymic visual images.

The two visual details *rayons d'argent* and *pétales de rose* constitute the third accumulation which closes the metaphorical passage with a poetic image appealing to the reader's aesthetic sensibility, while recalling to him the very essence of this sensory experience: *rayons d'argent* is a poetic résumé for the light impressions that underlie the imagery of the entire description, whereas *pétales de rose* is a poetic reduction of the room's floral aspect insisted upon by the descriptive tableau preceding the metaphorical accumulation — in particular the *fleurs roses* of the armchairs. *Palpitations* underlines the animistic aspect of the setting caused by the variety of light and color, an aspect previously referred to by the metaphorical transposition animating light: "les ailes repliées, tremblantes et tièdes d'une clarté prête à reprendre son vol."

The metaphorical images of the three accumulations work together to express a visual and conceptual ensemble. Whereas the descriptive details preceding the present passage allow the reader to "see" the room's color and light effects (as, for instance, the visual details *des fauteuils brodés de filigranes métalliques et de fleurs roses*), the metaphors *prisme, ruche,* and *jardin d'espérance* translate the perceptual complexity into images from other domains, each of which typefies, hence symbolizes, the notion of sensory complexity. Each perceptual image is in turn particularized by a modifying phrase. The two genitive links *de la lumière du dehors* and *de la journée* supply the figurative description with a key revealing the association between light impression and temporal notion. It is thus clear to the reader that the room's particular atmosphere during the morning hours evokes for the hero the various

ACCUMULATED METAPHORS 101

aspects of the outside world, and the day's various pleasures yet before him. The room becomes symbolic of a larger setting and time span, a private association based primarily on the hero's sensitivity to light.[12] This particular sensitivity and the spatial and temporal notion associated with it are conveyed by the metaphorical accumulation whose various details jointly communicate the perceptual complexity.

In a second example, three accumulations combine to convey the idea that concurrent sensory impressions (the special atmosphere of Sunday afternoons) and activities (the hero reading a book) will always be remembered together.

A literal statement introduces the subject. It also sets the tone for the whole passage, which begins with a lyrical apostrophe to the very time span in question, sunny Sunday afternoons:

> Beaux après-midi du dimanche sous le marronnier du jardin de Combray ... vous m'évoquez encore cette vie quand je pense à vous et vous la contenez en effet pour l'avoir peu
> 1. à peu / contournée et enclose — / tandis que je progressais dans ma lecture et que tombait la chaleur du jour —
> 2. dans / le cristal successif, lentement changeant et traversé
> 3. de feuillages / de vos heures / silencieuses, sonores, odorantes et limpides. / (I, 88)

The lyrical tone of the passage and the direct address to sunny Sunday afternoons underline the importance the narrator attaches to this experience. The precise reference to the time, day and place establishes the uniqueness of this experience and insists on the conceptual relationship between the particular setting and certain sensory impressions. The observation "vous m'évoquez encore cette vie quand je pense à vous" announces the conceptual dependency. To communicate the essence of this experience, the narrator changes

---

[12] Cf. I, 926 where a similar notion is expressed. The narrator refers to his room at Balbec as "la cuve des beaux jours, semblable à une piscine à mi-hauteur de laquelle ils faisaient miroiter un azur mouillé de lumière, que recouvrait un moment, impalpable et blanche comme une émanation de la chaleur, une voile reflétée et fuyante." Again a particular visual impression is at the base of this private association, namely, the room's glass-fronted book case so often mentioned by the narrator as reflecting the ocean. The room becomes symbolic of the world without on sunny days. See I, 383 for the earliest explicit statement.

from literal to figurative language. The verb *contenez* is semantically the pivotal element between the literal and metaphorical domains. It announces and participates in the metaphorical code of the first accumulation, *contournée* and *enclose,* both participles of *avoir.* Since these verb forms are from the same code, they reinforce each other and point towards the materialization of the abstract that begins to take shape. The repetition of the direct object pronoun referring to *vie* clearly indicates the recipient of the metaphorical action expressed by these verbs.

The second metaphorical accumulation is withheld for a moment by the syntactical disjunction of the parenthetical, literal remark "tandis que je progressais dans ma lecture et que tombait la chaleur du jour." This discursive interpolation briefly recalls the hero's concurrent activity and suggests that time is passing — *progressais* and *tombait la chaleur* both imply an activity extended over a time span — alerting the reader to the temporal aspect to be kept in mind while reading the following metaphors depicting the unique experience.

The second accumulation's pivotal element is *cristal,* which works in conjunction with the verbal metaphors of the first group whose image sphere it expands. The expected "container" is about to take shape when we reach *cristal,* but then expands with each adjective and those conferred onto it by the four adjectives of the genitive link with *heures,* which constitute the third accumulation: "le cristal successif, lentement changeant et traversé de feuillages de vos heures silencieuses, sonores, odorantes et limpides." These accumulated adjectives do not facilitate our interpretation of *cristal,* since they are drawn from different domains, and hence do not extend an established code to illustrate or develop its various implications.

Cristal is the crowning ambiguity of the entire passage, giving free range to our imagination. Yet the meaning and function of each adjective modifying *cristal* and *heures* are clear from the context at hand: each refers back to a particular impression registered by the hero. *Successif* — within the temporal context specified by *de vos heures* — and *lentement changeant* refer to the passing of time and the ensuing change of atmosphere, especially if we recall the previous literal indication implying the passage of time and referring to the concurrent atmospheric change: "tandis que je pro-

ACCUMULATED METAPHORS 103

gressais dans ma lecture et que tombait la chaleur du jour." *Traversé de feuillages* is a descriptive metonymy, referring to a specific sensory impression closely associated with this experience. The syntactical contiguity (i.e. juxtaposition through grammatical co-ordination) and the joint grammatical link to *cristal* reinforce the statement of perceptual simultaneity to be conveyed by these adjectives: [13] the tree under which the narrator is reading constitutes part of the special atmosphere of sunny Sunday afternoons. He is probably aware visually of the chestnut tree through the changing light and shade pattern cast about him by its leaves. That the chestnut tree is an important element of these particular sessions in the garden has already been underlined by the repeated mention of this tree, and especially by its inclusion in the initial sentence of the apostrophe: "Beaux après-midi du dimanche sous le marronnier." The tree's presence is echoed once more in the metaphorical accumulation of adjectives modifying *heures*: "de vos heures silencieuses, sonores, odorantes et limpides." This third and final accumulation is closely tied to the previous group through the genitive link *de vos heures*, which refers us to the tenor, revealing that the image of the "crystal container" is to be attributed to *heures*. [14] The syntactical juxtaposition of these final adjectives recalling the various sen-

---

[13] For a discussion of syntactical contiguity consult Roman Jakobson and Morris Halle, *Fundamentals of Language*, pp. 71-72.

[14] The genitive complement through *de* signals a relationship of dependency between tenor and vehicle, and usually provides the reader with an obvious key to the metaphorical image. In her discussion of the genitive link, Christine Brooke-Rose explains this conceptual relationship: "the noun metaphor is linked sometimes to its proper term and sometimes to a third term which gives the provenance of the metaphoric term: B *is part of*, or *derives from*, or *belongs to*, or *is attributed to*, or *is found in* C, from which relationship we can guess A, the proper term ..." (p. 198).

Besides providing explicit references, some genitive links give us indirect hints, as in the following passage describing the hero's impression of the hours he spends travelling on dark, unfrequented country roads leading to the luxurious dinners at La Raspelière, where brightly-lit, elegant rooms stand in sharp contrast to the dark, rustic countryside he has just left: "un dîner rutilant de clarté comme un véritable dîner en ville et qu'entourait seulement, changeant par là son caractère, la double écharpe sombre et singulière qu'avaient tissée ... les heures nocturnes, champêtres et marines de l'aller et du retour" (II, 1096). Besides specifying that the particular traits attributed to *heures* refer to the sensory impressions registered during the trip to and from la Raspelière, the genitive link also clarifies the adjective *double* of the metaphorical image *double écharpe sombre et singulière*.

sory appeals — their relationship is metonymic, for each one refers to a particular aspect of this experience — and their common grammatical function underline their joint message, namely, how closely concurrent sensory impressions are related in the hero's mind.

The metaphorical accumulations at the end of this passage on time semantically and syntactically translates the complex essence of the atmosphere on sunny Sunday afternoons. The narrator is able to bring everything together in a final image by basing it strictly on the information previously given the reader. We understand that these hours may be both "silent" and "sonorous."[15] Out of context, these antonymous adjectives would seem paradoxical; yet the descriptive context that precedes the metaphors in question has informed the reader that silence and sound are closely related in the narrator's mind: the peals of the bell — the sonorous content of these afternoons — sets in relief the following silence that would otherwise not have been noticed. Sound and silence are likewise associated with the concurrent pleasure of the lovely fragrance coming from the chestnut tree, which explains why *odorantes* is joined to *silencieuses* and *sonores* within the same mental framework.

The adjective *limpide* translates the hero's overall impression of these afternoons, including the pure brilliance of the atmosphere on a sunny day. While this and other adjectives modifying *cristal* and *heures* all refer to a specific aspect of the hero's reading sessions, the metaphor *cristal* is not a direct reference to this experience. It has no mimetic function, but rather a conceptual one: as a model of enclosure, the "crystal container" dramatizes the notion that things related to the same experience will be remembered together: the hero's readings will always be associated with the particular atmosphere in which they took place. While the metaphorical imagery of the three accumulations stresses this conceptual relationship through syntactical correlations, the metaphor *cristal*, as an archetype of all that is precious, underlines the special importance the narrator attaches to this unique experience.

---

[15] See I, 87 where the narrator describes his awareness of the successive strokes of the church bells as contrasted with the following silence and the peculiar visual association called forth by these auditory impressions.

C. Multiple Structures

Accumulations appearing within the same passage are not always bound by the same grammatical and syntactical structure. In the following descriptive passage, three accumulations appear within successive clauses of a long descriptive sentence. Though not interdependent grammatically, they are closely related in content since they jointly express a specific notion of time. The passage conveys the hero's particular sensitivity to the varying aspects of an aquatic flowerbed observed within a certain hour. The gradual change in light and atmosphere, as reflected by the flowers' aquatic milieu, is at the base of the temporal notion:

> il [le parterre d'eau] donnait aux fleurs un sol d'une couleur plus précieuse, plus émouvante que la couleur des fleurs elles-mêmes; et, soit que pendant l'après-midi il fît
> 1. étinceler sous les nymphéas / le kaléidoscope d'un bonheur attentif, silencieux et mobile, / ou qu'il s'emplît vers le
> 2. soir, comme quelque port lointain, / du rose et de la rêverie du couchant, / changeant sans cesse pour rester toujours
> 3. en accord, autour des corolles de teintes plus fixes, / avec ce qu'il y a de plus profond, de plus fugitif, de plus mystérieux — avec ce qu'il y a d'infini — dans l'heure, / il semblait les avoir fait fleurir en plein ciel. (I, 170)

The initial accumulation of the three adjectives modifying the metaphorical expression *kaléidoscope d'un bonheur* refers us to the hero's complex awareness of what characterizes this special duration: *attentif* reinforces *bonheur* in communicating the onlooker's subjective attitude and emotional state, while *silencieux* and *mobile* recall the peaceful atmosphere and the constantly changing visual impression. The visual impression is illustrated and emphasized by the analogy to the kaleidoscope, specifically referring us to visual variety and change. The relationship of dependency between *kaléidoscope* and *bonheur* through the preposition *de* discloses the conceptual relationship between visual impression and emotional state.

The temporal implications of the passage are explicitly stated: the metaphorical image of the kaleidoscope is linked to a specific time of day, the afternoon, while the second image is attributed to the evening, at sundown: "il s'emplît vers le soir, comme quelque port lointain, du rose et de la rêverie du couchant." The accompanying simile, which expands this image, reinforces it in its water context and appeals to the reader's imagination. The binary accumulation *du rose et de la rêverie,* linked to the pivotal element *s'emplît,* constitutes a syllepsis, which translates the concurrent existence of a visual impression and a subjective mode of being.[16] The verb *s'emplît* fulfills a double semantic function: it is to be taken in its concrete, literal sense in conjunction with *rose,* and in the figurative sense in its link with *rêverie.* The close verbal relationship of two different semantic levels through the syllepsis translates the mental contiguity between sensory impression and a certain frame of mind.

The literal descriptive phrase "changeant sans cesse pour rester toujours en accord, autour des corolles de teintes plus fixes" reemphasizes the main aspect of the visual phenomenon, the constant change, which the following extended accumulation explicitly attributes to time. Each accumulated element adds an additional complement to "pour rester toujours en accord avec ce qu'il y a," which they all jointly modify. That these accumulated descriptive details apply to time is clear from the prepositional complement *dans*

---

[16] My definition of the term "syllepsis" is basically the same as the one given by Huntington Brown in the *Princeton Encyclopedia of Poetry and Poetics,* who describes the device as the "use of any part of speech comparably related to two other words or phrases, correctly with respect to each taken separately, as to both syntax and meaning, but in different ways..." (p. 832). The *Encyclopedia's* definition then calls for "a witty effect," which, in my opinion, is not universally the case. Whereas the humorous syllepsis derives its effect primarily from the abrupt juxtaposition of two different domains whose close syntactical relationship through the figure is usually unexpected and seems semantically incongruous, the serious syllepsis is called for by the context, as it constitutes part of the same mental framework. Thus the apparent semantic antithesis is resolved by the conceptual relationship. See *supra,* pp. 26, 46, 79 and 80 for further examples of "serious syllepsis" conveying such a conceptual relationship.

The nineteenth-century Littré gives a more comprehensive definition, which more appropriately applies to the present example: "Figure par laquelle un mot est employé à la fois au propre et au figuré" (VII, 647). This type of syllepsis as used by Proust is discussed by Justin O'Brien in his article "Proust's Use of Syllepsis," 743-744. The article supplies also a useful distinction between "zeugma" and "syllepsis" in pointing out that "syllepsis does no violence to grammar, whereas the single word in zeugma makes sense with but one of its pair, forcing us to supply a cognate word" (p. 741).

l'heure. The temporal indication is retrospectively conferred onto the previous imagery to which this final accumulation is linked by syntax.

The special characteristics finally attributed to *heure* are emphasized through the repetition of *de plus* before each accumulated adjective: "avec ce qu'il y a de plus profond, de plus fugitif, de plus mystérieux — avec ce qu'il y a d'infini — dans l'heure." While *fugitif* recalls the ephemeral nature of the experience, *fugitif, profond,* and *mystérieux* together are now defined as corresponding to *infini*. As a hyperbole of the boundless, *infini* stresses the richness and complexity of this duration.

Chapter VI

METAPHORICAL EXTENSIONS TO SYMBOLIC TABLEAU

Several types of metaphorical images are determined by their context in such a way that they carry a more general meaning than the type of metaphor that is introduced to convey an incidental impression or notion. For instance, some metaphors acquire added significance when they are repeatedly used to convey the same temporal notion. Through repetition, the image becomes an emblem of the particular notion that it carries with it within the novel's context. Other metaphorical passages are given added significance through veiled or discursive remarks that lend more universal, far-reaching implications to the specific instance. I shall describe a metaphorical image as "symbolic" when such additional implications are attached to it.

The metaphorical extensions to be studied within the first section — synaesthetic metaphors — acquire added significance when we realize that they are not mere poetic embroidery to enhance a descriptive passage, but rather that they are a verbal mimesis of a unique experience of synaesthesia, described step by step through the extension of the metaphors to a tableau. Repetition of the same or related metaphors associated with the identical sensory impression makes it quite clear that the tropes are verbal emblems designating a unique *type* of sensorial response attributed to the novel's hero.

A. Synaesthetic Metaphors Symbolic of Mental Contiguity

When Proust describes one sensory perception in terms of another, he is using synaesthetic metaphors.[1] Whether they exist merely on the level of description or whether they translate the hero's experience of synaesthesia can usually be learned from the context within which they appear. From the description of the temporal passages to be studied in this section it becomes obvious that the provenance and presence of the synaesthetic analogies can be explained by the fact that they "reproduce" verbally a close conceptual relationship between various sensory impressions experienced simultaneously.[2] Recurrence of the same phenomenon reinforces our impression that we are actually dealing with one of the hero's typical experiences.[3] The synaesthetic metaphors then gradually become symbolic of the sensory experience they repeatedly convey. The reader begins to associate these concurrent impressions, since he is allowed to witness the simultaneous translation of one sense perception into another sense modality within a descriptive context that points to the contiguity between the senses.

---

[1] It is important here to distinguish between the description of an experience of synaesthesia and the verbal mimesis of this experience. Only in the latter case are we dealing with synaesthetic metaphor. For further discussion, see W. B. Stanford, "Synaesthetic Metaphor," pp. 27-28, and Stephen Ullmann, *Principles of Semantics,* p. 225.

The most elaborate and comprehensive study of synaesthesia, distinguishing between various types, is that of Ludwig Schrader, *Sinne und Sinnesverknüpfungen* (Heidelberg: Carl Winter, 1969), pp. 49-54.

For a more general study of Proust's use of synaesthesia, consult Stephen Ullmann, *Style in the French Novel,* Chapter V: "Transposition of Sensations in Proust's Imagery."

[2] Stephen Ullmann labels synaesthesia that is based on simultaneous sense impressions "pseudo-synaesthesia" (*Principles of Semantics,* p. 233 and p. 267).

[3] In his recent study "Métonymie chez Proust, ou la naissance du Récit," Gérard Genette studies the role of metonymy in several types of Proustian metaphor. He points out that in the case of synaesthetic metaphors, the sensorial transfer may actually be explained as a transfer of cause to effect, as in the "tintement ovale et doré de la clochette du jardin" where the particular shape and color of the bell are most likely responsible for the figure of speech. While the reader sees in this a semantic transfer and understands it as a synaesthetic metaphor, the figure grows out of a metonymic relationship of things existing within the same mental framework.

The passages to be examined within this category are related in that they all have their origin within the same perceptual phenomenon: the hourly chime of the Saint-Hilaire bell tower. The metaphors convey how the chimes spontaneously call forth certain visual images within the hero's consciousness. The repetition of this particular sensory transfer associated with a specific place, atmosphere and stimulus reveals that the metaphors are emblematic of a genuine sensory transfer, that they refer to a certain *type* of experience repeatedly encountered by the hero and remembered as such by the narrator.

The most elaborate metaphorical statement within this category presents the reader with a precise visual emblem gradually created before his eyes by a series of metaphors, all of which are closely related through imagery, as they contribute to the pictorial detail of the same visual phenomenon. Furthermore, they are closely related within the same sensory realm, since each one of them springs forth from the same auditory stimulus, the hourly strokes from the Saint-Hilaire belfry.[4]

The unexpected introduction of the synaesthetic metaphors into the midst of a discursive, literal description stylistically translates the suddenness and spontaneity of this sensory experience:

> Enfin, en continuant à suivre du dedans au dehors les états simultanément juxtaposés dans ma conscience, et avant d'arriver jusqu'à l'horizon réel qui les enveloppait, je trouve des plaisirs d'un autre genre, celui d'être bien assis, de sentir la bonne odeur de l'air, de ne pas être dérangé par une visite et, quand une heure sonnait au clocher de Saint-
> 1. Hilaire, / de voir tomber morceau par morceau ce qui de l'après-midi était déjà consommé, / jusqu'à ce que j'entendisse le dernier coup qui me permettait de faire le total
> 2. et après lequel / le long silence qui le suivait semblait faire commencer, dans le ciel bleu, toute la partie qui m'était encore concédée pour lire / jusqu'au bon dîner....

---

[4] The same sensory phenomenon, in fact attributed to the same time and place — sunny Sunday afternoons in the garden of Combray — was already described by the accumulated metaphors analyzed above on pp. 101-104. The previous set of metaphors appears within the same descriptive passage as the present one (I, 88), where it functions as an all-encompassing résumé of an extensive metaphorical description depicting the hero's concurrent impressions within a certain duration.

Et à chaque heure il me semblait que c'était quelques instants seulement auparavant que la précédente avait sonné;
3. / la plus récente venait s'inscrire tout près de l'autre dans le ciel et je ne pouvais croire que soixante minutes eussent tenu dans ce petit arc bleu qui était compris entre leurs deux marques d'or. / Quelquefois même cette heure prématurée sonnait deux coups de plus que la dernière; il y en avait donc une que je n'avais pas entendue, quelque chose qui avait eu lieu n'avait pas eu lieu pour moi; l'intérêt de la lecture, magique comme un profond sommeil,
4. avait donné le change à mes oreilles hallucinées et / effacé la cloche d'or sur la surface azurée du silence. / (I, 87-88)

After the straightforward mention of these "plaisirs d'un autre genre," all of which are simple pleasures of physical comfort and well-being, the level of communication changes abruptly, because the reader cannot take literally the statement "voir tomber morceau par morceau." The sudden intrusion of the concrete, visual representation of something auditory and invisible — the sounds coming from the belfry — immediately draws the reader into the transposition of the senses. The ground of the metaphorical transfer is neither prepared for nor stated, and since the metaphorical apparatus is hidden, the vehicle *morceau,* reinforced by the active verb *tomber,* comes as a shock, especially since *morceau* implies something tangible, visible, yet does not allow us to make the necessary mental jump to actually picture these *morceaux de l'après-midi.* The only clue is the simultaneity of each stroke of the bell and the *morceau qui tombe,* revealing that the hero visualizes each chime of the church clock. The code of the synaesthetic imagery (the metaphorical transfer from the auditory to the visual realm) is pursued and extended as the absence of sound, silence evokes another visual image: silence, which, we are told, signifies the "part" of the afternoon still left for reading ("la partie que m'était encore concédée pour lire"), is linked to the blue sky.

The following literal remark ("Et à chaque heure il me semblait que c'était quelques instants seulement auparavant que la précédente avait sonné") reveals that the hero feels freed from the passage of time, for the narrator explicitly tells us that an hour feels like moments, and that two hours might pass without him being aware of the hourly chime. The imagery is then extended to express the particular sensation experienced by the hero during this duration. This second image consists of synaesthetic metaphors that include and expand the previous, visually unfulfilled imagery of *morceau* and *partie*: "la plus récente venait s'inscrire tout près de l'autre." The verb phrase *venait s'inscrire* animates the abstract noun *heure,* and aids in the transposition from one sense modality to another, while the prepositional phrases *tout près de l'autre* and *dans le ciel* specify the realm of action by continuing the code and by reinforcing its visual message. Finally, the addition of precise, visual details to the same image enables the reader to see each hour as part of an emblematic image gradually taking shape in the sky. The details in question, which make us *see* the past hour as the clock strikes, are the *petit arc bleu,* and *deux marques d'or*. The vague image *s'inscrire dans le ciel* thus becomes clear, because we are given a precise visual equivalent of *l'heure qui sonne,* namely, *marque d'or*. Furthermore, the fixed pattern of inscription of each "golden dot" becomes apparent when *tout près de l'autre* is reinforced by "ce petit arc bleu qui était compris entre leurs deux marques d'or." The precise geometric shape evoked by *arc bleu* determines the physical shape of the visual image in the sky. Since consecutive hours add a number of "blue arcs" and "golden dots," each representing sixty minutes (the temporal equivalency explicitly given by the context), and each continuing the same curved line (insisted upon by "tout près de l'autre"), the reader, who has been given all the necessary details for this visual transposition, realizes that a half circle gradually takes shape as the afternoon progresses. And since this partial dial, marked by equidistant golden dots, is here directly related to time (the hourly chime, which calls forth the image, signifies the passage of time), the reader automatically makes the mental transition from the emblem in the sky to the specific dial of the face of a clock. He is able to follow the narrator's visual representation of his sensory experience and to grasp its symbolic implications, for the notion of time passing has found an archetypal image in the clock which has been telling time, through dial and sound, for centuries.

By translating his notion of time into an emblem, the narrator conveys both the hero's sense of freedom from time and his occasional awareness of time through the hourly recall. Time has been symbolized by an exterior object whose physical removal to the sky states in obvious visual terms the hero's experience of being outside the realm of time during his peaceful, solitary reading sessions in the garden at Combray.

The description of this particular duration is reinforced by another metaphorical image directly based on the preceding imagery. A literal statement informs us that the hero, engrossed in his reading, would sometimes fail to hear the hourly chime. The narrator then communicates this durational experience through the visual image "effacé la cloche d'or sur la surface azurée du silence." The verb *effacé* points back to the metaphorical code of *s'inscrire*, thereby linking the two images. *Cloche d'or* extends the image of *marque d'or*, yet it is far more elliptical and bold. It is comprehensible only because it follows a synaesthetic metaphor in which sound was made visible, since otherwise one would take *cloche d'or* as merely a visual image, without realizing that *cloche* is also a metonymy of sound. Proust's synthesis of the various sense impressions is complete in this image, for it recalls at once the origin of the sound and its synaesthetic conversion, where the sound of the bell *is* golden.[5] The narrator thus recalls the visual manifestation of sound before it disappears from "la surface azurée du silence." Since the reader has been allowed to visualize fully the metaphorical transposition, he immediately grasps the meaning of *surface azurée* in relation to the golden image which he has seen inscribed in the sky. The metaphoric complement *du silence,* directly joined to *sur-*

---

[5] An earlier version of this passage also suggests a metonymic reference to the sun. Instead of *cloche d'or* it reads *les rayons de la cloche* (First Typescript, Volume 23, p. 130 of the bound Proust collection at the Bibliothèque Nationale.

A similar, more explicit synaesthetic image appears in "Journées de lecture," reprinted in *Pastiches et mélanges*: "alors plus aucun bruit; seul de temps en temps le son d'or des cloches qui au loin, par delà des plaines, semblait tinter derrière le ciel bleu" (237). The repeated association between the golden sound (*son d'or, cloche d'or*) and the blue sky (*ciel bleu; la surface azurée*) points to a synaesthetic transfer based on sensory contiguity: the fact that the sky is blue presupposes the simultaneous presence of the sun, to which *or* refers us metonymically.

In the larger context describing the sunny Sunday afternoons of Combray the presence of the sun as an integral part of the overall atmosphere is repeatedly mentioned. Particularly the description of the sun's reflection from the Saint Hilaire tower, figuratively described as *soleil noir* and *doré et cuit comme une plus grande brioche bénie* (I, 64-65), suggests a metonymic relationship between the hourly chime coming from the belfry and its "golden appearance" on sunny days. For a reference to further images linking the same auditory impression to a visual one, see *infra*, p. 114 (footnote 6), and p. 115.

face azurée, extends and clarifies the previously established time image, by emphasizing the close relationship between visual image, auditory perception and being in time: the absence of the hourly chime results in an absence of sensory conversion. Total silence is synonymous with a clear blue sky, for the *surface azurée* is unmarked. This visual contrast, based on the previous imagery, thus translates in concrete terms the hero's notion of removal from time, since time no longer exists for him, neither within his inner consciousness, nor as an emblem on the periphery of consciousness. The reader participates in this removal from the realm of time by *seeing* the emblem of time disappear in the sky. This obliviousness to time, here suggested visually, is reinforced by the preceding literal remark comparing the hero's state while reading to a "profound sleep."

The immediate translation of the sound of the church bell into specific visual terms is a metaphoric constant in "Combray." Repetition of the same sensorial phenomenon lends symbolic significance to the hourly chimes, and gives us the impression that we are dealing with a genuine sensory impression. These images are not to be taken for mere poetic embroidery, for they convey the very essence of the hero's unique inner life.[6]

The fact that all these experiences are described within a context of sunny days may explain the recurrent use of the color gold in each visual image, constituting a metonymic reference to the sun. Since sunshine, the hourly chime and a particular sensorial experience are all linked to a similar mode of being and repeated by similar imagery, we may infer that these impressions are concurrent within the narrator's mental context.[7] Through repetition and elab-

---

[6] Another image depicting the synaesthetic conversion of sound materialized appears in I, 166: the chime gives rise to the concurrent sensory impression of sound and visual image, in this case, *gouttes d'or.*

To what extent concurrent auditory and visual impressions are remembered as part of the same mental context is evident from a passage in II, 780. The hero, resting in his Balbec hotel room, with the shades pulled, participates in the bright world without, since he "pictures" the sunny beach from the sounds penetrating his room. Besides calling forth visual images, the sounds evoke a whole state of being, the emotional and mental impressions linked to this experience.

[7] The hero's multi-sensorial perception of the chimes of the church bell as heard from afar is described in another image towards the end of "Combray" (I, 170): "sur l'herbe où parvenaient jusqu'à nous, horizontaux, affaiblis, mais

oration the narrator allows the reader to grasp the significance of certain images that had become symbolic within his private universe, because of the identity of certain experiences.

The same sensory experience of perceiving "golden sound" is described in another synaesthetic image explicitly linked to a sunny weather context. The setting is Paris, yet it is not only the identical image of "son doré des cloches" that reminds us of the earlier experience described in "Combray," but also the narrator's explicit mention of Combray within this passage.

The context of this later image from *La Prisonnière* is much more discursive than the earlier images dealing with the same phenomenon in "Combray." Besides referring explicitly to sunny weather, the present passage actually defines the various sensory impressions contiguous in the hero's mind with the auditory perception. The narrator further elaborates on the hero's particular sensibility to the link between sound and weather by generalizing the image to include both sunny and rainy days. Finally, the passage ends in an explanation of the image, which is then generalized by an aphorism:

> Mais je n'y étais plus le même sous un ciel sans nuages; /
> 1. le son doré des cloches ne contenait pas seulement, comme le miel, de la lumière, / mais la sensation de la lumière (et aussi la saveur fade des confitures, parce qu'à Combray il s'était souvent attardé comme une guêpe sur notre table desservie) ... Il y avait des jours où le bruit d'une cloche
> 2. qui sonnait l'heure / portait sur la sphère de sa sonorité une plaque si fraîche, si puissamment étalée de mouillé ou de lumière, / que c'était comme une traduction pour aveugles ou, si l'on veut, comme une traduction musicale du charme de la pluie ou du charme du soleil. Si bien qu'à ce moment-là, les yeux fermés, dans mon lit, je me disais que tout peut se transposer et qu'un univers seulement audible pourrait être aussi varié que l'autre. (III, 83-84)

The literal remark "sous un ciel sans nuages" explicitly states the weather conditions irrevocably linked to the synaesthetic experience of "son doré des cloches." The discursive note introduced by the

---

denses et métalliques encore, des sons de la cloche de Saint-Hilaire qui ne s'étaient pas mélangés à l'air qu'ils traversaient depuis si longtemps et, côtelés par la palpitation successive de toutes leurs lignes sonores, vibraient en rasant les fleurs, à nos pieds."

verb *contenait* sets up a conceptual equation between "son doré des cloches" and the following explanatory details. The explicitly stated association between *lumière, sensation de la lumière,* and *son doré* renders the sensorial contiguity between sound and visual content obvious. The mental contiguity between the light impressions and the gustatory sensation is likewise evident from the close syntactical structure: the various sensations are all direct objects of *contenait,* and the coordinating conjunction *et* directly links the parenthetical remark to the preceding context. The explanatory nature of the passage is further obvious when the narrator explains the intrusion of the gustatory sensation within this context ("parce qu'à Combray il s'était souvent attardé comme une guêpe sur notre table desservie").[8] Yet it is up to the reader to remember that the Saint-Hilaire chimes constituted part of this setting as described in "Combray" (I, 71).

That the visual translation of sound is once more attributed to the auditory stimulus of bells is clear from "le bruit d'une cloche qui sonnait l'heure." After this literal preparatory statement, the synaesthetic conversion is directly introduced into the same syntactical framework through the imagery "portait sur la sphère de sa sonorité une plaque si fraîche, si puissamment étalée de mouillé ou de lumière." The phrase *de sa sonorité* emphasizes once more the image's auditory content to which the concurrent visual transformation is then immediately juxtaposed. The ambiguous materialization of the hourly chime into *plaque si fraîche* is particularized through the descriptive extension "étalée de mouillé ou de lumière," which may suggest an analogy to photographic plates, since their surfaces, covered with an emulsion sensitive to light, could account for *mouillé* and *lumière,* though the author is probably referring us to a less technical and more general connotation of *plaque,* such as *tache* ("spot"). The substantival complements *de mouillé, de lumière,* alluding to antithetical weather conditions — as explicitly stated by the following discursive comparison referring us to "rain" and "sunshine" — introduce a more general context into the syn-

---

[8] The similes *comme le miel* and *comme une guêpe* are suggestive rather than explanatory. While the comparison with honey is based on a visual analogy within the context of *son doré* and *lumière,* the animation of *son doré* through the analogy to the wasp unexpectedly materializes the close association between the sweet desserts and the sound from the belfry.

aesthetic image, informing the reader that the sensory conversion takes place, although with different visual content, during various atmospheric conditions.[9] *Puissamment* underlines the strong sensory impact of this perceptual experience.

The discursive structure of the two comparisons adds a double explanatory comment to the preceding synaesthetic imagery. This tendency towards the discursive, elaborating upon or explaining the metaphorical statements regarding a temporal notion, becomes increasingly evident as we progress through *A la Recherche*. The frequency and extent of this tendency is most evident in the last three books, *La Prisonnière, La Fugitive,* and *Le Temps retrouvé,* and may be explained by the fact that the narrator's range of experience within time has significantly increased, while the reader is better able to participate in such explanations and generalizations after witnessing the hero's journey through time.

The aphoristic observation regarding the possible visual content of auditory perceptions again reveals the narrator's tendency to derive a general law from a particular experience. It is here interpolated into the description, both literal and metaphoric, of a particular sensory experience, which the narrator takes up again in the context immediately following the aphorism. The reader thus reenters the private world of personal experience, as he witnesses the hero's reverie recalling past experiences in sunny weather (III, 84).

The more far-reaching significance of simultaneous sensory impressions symbolic of a particular experience becomes evident in *Le Temps retrouvé,* in a passage dealing with the importance of "metaphor" in art. Proust uses the term "metaphor" to designate the analogical process in general. He illustrates the importance of sensory impressions within this context by recalling two instances of

---

[9] In the previous paragraph, the narrator already described the intrusion of external atmospheric conditions into his very room through the sound of bells. This passage reveals the hero's mental association between differences in sound and changes in atmospheric conditions: "D'autres fois encore, aux premières cloches d'un couvent voisin, rares comme les dévotes matinales, blanchissant à peine le ciel sombre de leurs giboulées incertaines que fondait et dispersait le vent tiède, j'avais discerné une de ces journées tempétueuses, désordonnées et douces...." (III, 82). The metaphorical translation of the auditory sensation into weather vocabulary — "blanchissant à peine le ciel sombre de leurs giboulées incertaines" — recreates verbally the close association between sound and weather conditions.

perceptual analogy, one of which specifically reminds us of the Saint-Hilaire chimes, now irrevocably linked to the Combray setting:

> la vérité ne commencera qu'au moment où l'écrivain prendra deux objets différents, posera leur rapport... et les enfermera dans les anneaux nécessaires d'un beau style; même, ainsi que la vie, quand, en rapprochant une qualité commune à deux sensations, il dégagera leur essence commune en les réunissant l'une et l'autre pour les soustraire aux contingences du temps, dans une métaphore. La nature ne m'avait-[elle] pas mis elle-même, à ce point de vue, sur la voie de l'art, n'était-elle pas commencement d'art elle-même, elle qui ne m'avait permis de connaître, souvent, la beauté d'une chose que dans une autre, midi à Combray que dans le bruit de ses cloches, les matinées de Doncières que dans les hoquets de notre calorifère à eau? Le rapport peut être peu intéressant, les objets médiocres, le style mauvais, mais tant qu'il n'y a pas eu cela, il n'y a rien. (III, 889-890)

Within the narrator's memory, a specific auditory stimulus has become symbolic of a particular place and time. He has discovered that it contains the essence of the former experience, which can be recalled in its entirety — since the mental contiguity between the specific sensory impression and other concurrent impressions recreates the multi-sensorial impact of the experience — when the same sensory experience recurs.[10]

B. Metaphors Animating Abstractions

1. Duration

On a number of occasions, the narrator uses the process of personification to convey a highly original temporal impression. In all of these passages, the transposition from the abstract realm of the hero's personal sensibility to the concrete image of an animated

---

[10] The full implications of this passage emerge from the larger context in which the narrator explains the phenomenon of "involuntary memory" as based on sensory analogy between a present and a past experience (see especially III, 866-917). The mental contiguity between the multi-sensorial impacts of an experience is repeatedly described — in both literal and metaphorical terms — in *A la recherche*. See I, 345-346, 407, 426, 539, 720; III, 876, 1030.

tableau is unprepared, since it is not announced by transitional remarks or reinforced by explanatory comments. In each instance, an auditory perception calls forth a visual image in the hero's imagination.

The earliest passage describing the personification of the Saint-Hilaire chimes is suddenly introduced into the midst of a literal narration:

> Mais (surtout à partir du moment où les beaux jours s'installaient à Combray) il y avait bien longtemps que / l'heure altière de midi, descendue de la tour de Saint-Hilaire qu'elle armoriait des douze fleurons momentanés de sa couronne sonore, avait retenti autour de notre table, / auprès du pain bénit venu lui aussi familièrement en sortant de l'église, quand nous étions encore assis.... (I, 70-71)

The narrator once again specifies weather conditions before translating his subjective impression into imagery. The precise temporal content is clear from the genitive link *de midi* qualifying *heure altière*. This temporal specification is important in understanding the following visual image, the translation of sound to *fleuron,* from which it is evident that each stroke of the bell is transformed into a visual equivalent.[11] The temporal duration of this phenomenon is revealed through *momentanés,* transferring the momentary nature of each sound onto *douze fleurons*. The following genitive complement *de sa couronne sonore* reinforces the image, for it at once recalls the transformation of sound into matter and particularizes the personification of the noon hour by alluding to a specific social stratum, whose elevated status retrospectively accounts for the qualifying adjective *altière*.

The special significance that the narrator attributes to this hour is conveyed through the various aspects of the imagery: the personification of the hour as a royal personage is enhanced by the animation brought into the picture through the two verbal forms

---

[11] The present visual rendition of an auditory sensation is here to be taken as a metaphorical description rather than an intersensorial transfer experienced by the hero himself. Nevertheless, in the light of other passages describing the same phenomenon in synaesthetic terms (I, 87-88, III, 83-84), the reader may suspect that a genuine experience of synaesthesia underlies the personification of the noon hour.

descendue and *armoriait*. The personifying metaphors, in translating the hero's peculiar subjective reaction to the twelve o'clock chime into visual terms, significantly emphasize the mental contiguity between auditory perception, sunny weather and a particular setting.

The visual rendition and personification of the two o'clock bell in the next passage is preceded by the personification of the sun. The simultaneous animation of both nature and sensory perception conveys the hero's very personal mode of being within a special duration. His inner state of being is projected onto the material world:

> Après le déjeuner, le soleil, conscient que c'était samedi, flânait une heure de plus au haut du ciel, et quand quelqu'un, pensant qu'on était en retard pour la promenade, disait: "Comment, seulement deux heures?" / en voyant passer les deux coups du clocher de Saint-Hilaire (qui ont l'habitude de ne rencontrer encore personne dans les chemins désertés à cause du repas de midi ou de la sieste, le long de la rivière vive et blanche que le pêcheur même a abandonnée, et passent solitaires dans le ciel vacant où ne restent que quelques nuages paresseux) /.... (I, 111)

The passage expresses the hero's subjective awareness of a special type of duration: the "expansion" of time and a state of relaxation in a deserted setting experienced on Saturday afternoons. The temporal implications underlying this particular state of being are disclosed by the descriptive context: instead of directly stating his temporal awareness, the narrator attributes it to the sun in a personification: "le soleil, conscient que c'était samedi, flânait une heure de plus au haut du ciel."

The unexpected and unannounced change from metaphorical imagery to literal description within the same syntactical framework abruptly takes the reader from one mode of discourse to another. Thus the literal exclamation about time ("Comment, seulement deux heures?") is directly followed by the personification of the two chimes: "en voyant passer les deux coups du clocher de Saint-Hilaire," which modifies the verb *disait* of the preceding literal statement.

The sudden personification of a natural object — the sun — and the repetition of the same process through the unusual animation and materialization of an auditory perception add a humorous note to this passage. Thus the sun is not only portrayed as "conscious," but is also endowed with a particular human activity (*flânait*); and the two strokes of the bell are not only depicted as passersby, but are described within an otherwise realistic setting whose prosaic elements stand in sharp contrast to the unusual personification intruding upon the scene. The narrator's matter-of-fact description devoid of transitional remarks preparing the unusual imagery, increases our surprise at the descriptive incongruity.

That the hero spontaneously translates the auditory perception into a visual image is clear from the present participle *voyant*. The transition from literal to metaphorical description thus comes as a shock, since the personified element is directly introduced into the actual Combray setting of deserted roads and river. *Nuages paresseux* introduces another anthropomorphic element into the setting, reflecting the narrator's sensibility to this particular duration of Saturday afternoons at Combray.

The unexpected transition from literal narration to metaphorical imagery within the same syntactical framework occurs in another Combray passage depicting the hero's peculiar sensory reaction to the Saint-Hilaire chimes. The auditory perception is once more translated into concrete terms through the process of personification and materialization:

> On gagnait le mail entre les arbres duquel apparaissait le clocher de Saint-Hilaire. Et j'aurais voulu pouvoir m'asseoir là et rester toute la journée à lire en écoutant les cloches; car il faisait si beau et si tranquille que, quand sonnait l'heure, on aurait dit non qu'elle rompait le calme du jour, mais qu'elle le débarrassait de ce qu'il contenait et que le clocher, avec l'exactitude indolente et soigneuse d'une personne qui n'a rien d'autre à faire, venait seulement — pour exprimer et laisser tomber les quelques gouttes d'or que la chaleur y avait lentement et naturellement amassées — de presser, au moment voulu, la plénitude du silence. (I, 166)

As in the previous examples, the auditory stimulus that gives rise to the imagery is directly attributed to the Saint-Hilaire bells, and the fine weather and state of tranquillity is insisted upon by the context. In this passage, however, the transposition from literal to metaphoric language is announced by the conditional expression "on aurait dit," which warns the reader of the transition into the realm of subjective impressions.

The animation of the present tableau is largely due to the active verbs *débarrassait, venait de presser, exprimer* and *laisser tomber,* which personify *heure* or its metonymy *clocher*. The prepositional qualifying phrase "avec l'exactitude indolente et soigneuse d'une personne qui n'a rien d'autre à faire" reinforces the process of personification of the tower through the direct attribution of personal characteristics. The genitive link *d'une personne* underlines the fact that the psychological characteristics conferred on the hourly chime are human traits.

The subsequent additional metaphorical details constitute a descriptive elaboration of the notion already touched upon by *débarrassait* [le calme du jour], an action that now materializes in front of our eyes, as the auditory impression is converted into visual imagery: "pour exprimer et laisser tomber les quelques gouttes d'or que la chaleur y avait lentement et naturellement amassées." This surprising metaphorical statement is given further emphasis by being set off with a dash, signifying that a disjunctive element has been introduced into the sentence. The synaesthetic conversion of sound into a visual image is reinforced by the verbs *exprimer, laisser tomber* and *presser*, which extend the same image. The relative clause modifying *gouttes d'or* recalls the specific atmospheric conditions associated in the hero's mind with the synaesthetic conversion. The verb *presser* transfers the preceding image onto its direct object *plénitude*. *Plénitude du silence* thus combines the two elements of the concurrent sensory impression: *plénitude* is syntactically and imaginally linked to the visual image *gouttes d'or,* whereas *silence* recalls the auditory perception.

The repeated association between the weather and the narrator's subjective impressions of auditory stimuli seems to point to a genuine sensory contiguity between concurrent auditory and visual impressions. The descriptive context provides us with a key to the hero's inner sensibility in revealing the salient aspects of the setting responsible for the particular sensory impressions. For instance, the reference to sunny weather accounts for the repetition of the color "gold" (I, 71; 88; 166; III, 83-84), whereas the extended personifications convey the hero's awareness of the tranquil, deserted setting and his sensitivity to atmospheric pressure (I, 111; 166).

The close relationship between an outside stimulus and the narrator's subjective sensibility — which, in turn, he conveys by projecting his emotions onto the exterior phenomenon — is again evident in the following image.[12] The metaphorical tableau shows the hero's feeling of abandonment and melancholy on a lonely afternoon that, for him, passes ever so slowly, since it is devoid of any distraction.[13] An extended personification of the gray, eventless day turns the weather into an animated presence:

> Lasse, résignée, occupée pour plusieurs heures encore à sa tâche immémoriale, la grise journée filait sa passementerie de nacre et je m'attristais de penser que j'allais rester seul en tête à tête avec elle qui ne me connaissait pas plus qu'une ouvrière qui s'est installée près de la fenêtre pour voir plus clair en faisant sa besogne et ne s'occupe pas de la personne présente dans la chambre. (II, 350)

As personifying adjectives of *grise journée, lasse* and *résignée* reinforce the aspect of old age suggested by *grise,* a metonymy of old age. At the same time, these characteristics translate the hero's emotional state within this uneventful, seemingly endless duration of the rainy day. The third personifying adjective *occupée,* modified by the prepositional phrase "pour plusieurs heures encore à sa tâche immémoriale," emphasizes the temporal aspect underlying the imaginal transposition. The slow passage of time and the feeling of monotony — already suggested by the attributes of lassitude and resignation (*lasse, résignée*) — are conveyed through the incorporation of a particular monotonous, time-consuming activity within this personification: *filait sa passementerie de nacre.* The slow activity of weaving translates the slow passage of time into concrete terms. The image also recalls the actual visual impression that is at the base of the personification: the fine drops of rain.[14]

---

[12] The same metaphorical process is discussed in a more general study of Proust's use of imagery in *A la recherche*: Irma Tiedtke's *Symbole und Bilder im Werke Marcel Prousts,* pp. 41-47.

[13] The paragraph preceding the passage under discussion already touches upon the temporal notion in describing the endless aspect of a lonely duration: "Mais si nous sommes seuls, la préoccupation, en ramenant devant nous le moment encore éloigné, et sans cesse attendu, avec la fréquence et l'uniformité d'un tic-tac, divise ou plutôt multiplie les heures par toutes les minutes qu'entre amis nous n'aurions pas comptées" (p. 350).

[14] A similar image and the inclusion of the visual stimulus underlying the metaphorical transposition already appeared in a previous paragraph: "La

The hero's feeling of loneliness, directly stated in "je m'attristais de penser que j'allais rester seul en tête à tête avec elle," is dramatized through the tableau of the preoccupied woman working by the window, too busy to notice him. By personifying the gray day — a concrete representation of an abstraction — the narrator allows the reader to witness the hero's inner state.[15]

The narrator's particular sensibility to a special duration, the twilight hour preceding his trips to Rivebelle, is conveyed to the reader through the animation of this hour. His awareness of time as closely dependant on the dwindling daylight is communicated through the emphasis of the visual imagery. Repetition of the same image referring to the same duration points to the symbolic significance of this particular impression within the hero's mental context.[16] The first description of this subjective notion appears in I, 806:

> Au-dessus d'eux, je voyais de mon lit la raie de clarté qui y restait encore, s'assombrissant, s'amincissant progressivement, mais c'est sans m'attrister et sans lui donner de regret que je laissais ainsi mourir au haut des rideaux l'heure où d'habitude j'étais à table, car je savais que ce jour-ci était d'une autre sorte que les autres, plus long comme

---

brume avait disparu. Le jour gris, tombant comme une pluie fine, tissait sans arrêt de transparents filets dans lesquels les promeneurs dominicaux semblaient s'argenter" (II, 347).

[15] Other passages where personifying characteristics are attributed to a unit of time (hour, day) may be found in III, 487 ("le jour indiscret du printemps") and III, 762 ("journée qui s'attardait"). In both of these passages, the personification of time is an anthropomorphizing process, which reveals the hero's particular sensibility to a mode of being within a certain duration.

See also the animation of time in II, 350, already discussed *supra*, p. 88 under the structure of continued metaphors.

[16] How a light impression becomes symbolic of the particular time and place in which it was experienced is illustrated by a recurring image recalling the sunny setting of the Balbec dining room during late afternoon at the height of summer. Cf. I, 798-799; II, 153, 734; III, 874.

The close mental contiguity between another visual impression and a specific era is revealed in III, 166, recalling once more the famous chrysanthemums that have become symbolic of Madame Swann's tea hour: "Notre voiture descendait vite les boulevards, les avenues, dont les hôtels en rangée, rose congélation de soleil et de froid, me rappelaient mes visites chez Mme Swann doucement éclairées par les chrytanthèmes en attendant l'heure des lampes." The syllepsis *rose congélation de soleil et de froid* translates the mental contiguity between visual and tactile impressions.

ceux du pôle que la nuit interrompt seulement quelques minutes; je savais que de la chrysalide de ce crépuscule se préparait à sortir, par une radieuse métamorphose, la lumière éclatante du restaurant de Rivebelle.

The conceptual relationship between *raie de clarté* and *heure* becomes obvious when we realize from the description that *raie de clarté* is the only visual impression from which the hero infers that the hour is "dying," a relationship syntactically reproduced for the reader by *ainsi,* which links the two animated images of "light ray" and "hour." The personification of "hour" through the death code and the mention of sadness recall the hero's previous emotional reaction to the twilight hour. The literal remark "où d'habitude j'étais à table" underlines the fact that this is an exceptional day, and the explanatory elaboration, introduced by *car,* tells the reader what is special about it. The comparison "plus long comme ceux du pôle que la nuit interrompt seulement quelques minutes" further clarifies and underlines the temporal aspect that it throws into relief. The author's tendency to reinforce his images discursively accounts for the tautological character of this passage, in which parallel structures ("je savais que . . . je savais que") introduce both the literal and the metaphorical statements.

The descriptive tableau allows the reader a direct insight into the hero-narrator's mental context, for it reveals the subjective contiguity between sensory impression and mental framework: "je savais que de la chrysalide de ce crépuscule se préparait à sortir, par une radieuse métamorphose, la lumière éclatante du restaurant de Rivebelle." The animation of *lumière éclatante* stresses the importance of the light content within this temporal experience. The metaphors *chrysalide de ce crépuscule* and *radieuse métamorphose* both emphasize the notion of imminent change. *Radieuse* extends the image of the light metaphors, while the genitive link *de ce crépuscule* recalls the previous light impression associated with the sunset. The notion of metamorphosis introduced through *chrysalide* and visually depicted by the following metaphors concretizes the specific notion underlying the hero's subjective impression of this duration. The imagery thus reveals that the longer duration attributed to those days is a subjective notion contiguous in the hero's mind with a particular activity to which a specific sensory impression is irrevocably linked. The narrator's exclusive emphasis on the light aspect as representative of a particular duration lends symbolic significance to this sensory impression.

The symbolic significance of the light impression is enhanced by the repetition of the same sensory stimulus and the narrative recall of the Balbec experience within the following Paris setting:

> Au-dessus des rideaux, il n'y avait plus qu'un mince liséré de jour qui allait s'obscurcissant. Je reconnaissais cette heure inutile, vestibule profond du plaisir, et dont j'avais appris à Balbec à connaître le vide sombre et délicieux, quand, seul dans ma chambre comme maintenant, pendant que tous les autres étaient à dîner, je voyais sans tristesse le jour mourir au-dessus des rideaux, sachant que, bientôt, après une nuit aussi courte que les nuits du pôle, il allait ressusciter plus éclatant dans le flamboiement de Rivebelle. (II, 390)

The mention of his stay at Balbec, explicitly recalled as a similar durational experience ("Je reconnaissais cette heure inutile"), emphasizes the fact that we are confronted with the repetition of a temporal experience. The use of partly similar, partly identical images depicting this special hour further insists on the similarity between the two experiences. Thus the image *liséré de jour*, extended through *s'obscurcissant*, is synonymous with the previous image *raie de clarté* and *s'assombrissant*. The adjective *mince* modifying *liséré de jour* echoes the verbal form *s'amincissant* of the earlier tableau. The narrator again establishes the same conceptual relationship between light impression and crepuscular hour. In this instance, however, the reader is given some additional information: the metaphoric apposition equating "cette heure inutile" to "vestibule profond du plaisir" at once reveals the narrator's subjective conception of this hour whose particular atmosphere is related within his mind to the expected pleasure of going out. The mental contiguity between nightfall and the anticipated pleasure is verbally reproduced by the metaphorical metonymy *vide sombre et délicieux*. The explicit nature of the equation between the particular hour and its significance within the hero's mental context reveals the symbolic content of this hour as represented by the band of light.

The conceptual relationship between the two experiences is further stressed by the repetition of two additional images, that of the personified "hour" ("je voyais ... le jour mourir"), and that of the comparison to polar nights — within a context that is a paraphrase of the earlier passage. The extension, within the present passage, of *mourir* to *ressusciter* expresses more strikingly and directly the idea of temporal continuity, previously expressed by *chrysalide* and *métamorphose*.

A few general remarks regarding the symbolic content of the two types of extended images studied so far — the synaesthetic metaphors and the personifications — may help us to focus on their essential characteristic. As the reader follows the images step by step, he realizes that they are not simply poetic devices, but that they have a mimetic function: they play an essential role in telling the story, since they initiate us into the hero's unique sensory impressions, feelings, and thoughts. Through elaboration and recurrence, these images become symbolic for the reader, for they begin to stand for the "type" of experience with which they are repeatedly associated.

2. The "Self"

Proust repeatedly describes his awareness of constantly changing emotions and beliefs by personifying and multiplying the "self." He thus speaks of "les moi," "les moi successifs," or "les moi qui changent, qui meurent." The frequent recurrence of this conceit throughout *A la recherche* constitutes one of the novel's leitmotifs, symbolic of our ever-changing existence within time. But as we follow the hero's experience, the narrator reveals a complementary notion that significantly modifies the impression of constant flux. A second series of images dealing with the "revival" of a former "I" is introduced into the novel. The complementary relationship of these two temporal aspects within the narrator's conception of time is communicated to the reader through the repetition of the same conceit, the personification of the "moi" within the context of death and rebirth.

Most of the "moi" personifications are introduced into the narrative context as brief conceits that call our attention to the nature of existence within time. This conceit usually appears without introductory comments or explanatory remarks.[17] The first time the

---

[17] For an example of the sudden introduction of this brief conceit into the narrative context, see II, 113 where the narrator says "l'être que j'étais

"moi" conceit occurs, however, it is accompanied by explanatory remarks and is extended by continued metaphors. Thereafter the narrator may revive the conceit briefly without being obscure, since the reader is already familiar with it.

The earliest personification of the "moi" within a discursive context appears in *A l'ombre des jeunes filles en fleurs*. The subject is first treated literally: "alors notre moi serait changé" (I, 671), a notion that is further elaborated upon as the narrator tries to imagine what implications this new type of existence entails.[18] The conceit is then introduced into the literal context and extended by a number of additional metaphors from the same domain:

> ce serait donc une vraie mort de nous-même, mort suivie, il est vrai, de résurrection, mais en un moi différent et jusqu'à l'amour duquel ne peuvent s'élever les parties de l'ancien moi condamnées à mourir. Ce sont elles — même les plus chétives, comme les obscurs attachements aux dimensions, à l'atmosphère d'une chambre — qui s'effarent et refusent, en des rébellions où il faut voir un mode secret, partiel, tangible et vrai de la résistance à la mort, de la longue résistance désespérée et quotidienne à la mort fragmentaire et successive telle qu'elle s'insère dans toute la durée de notre vie, détachant de nous à chaque moment des lambeaux de nous-mêmes sur la mortification desquels des cellules nouvelles multiplieront. (I, 671-672)

---

encore en ce moment n'était peut-être pas voué à une destruction prochaine." *L'être* is here used as a variant of *moi*. See III, 1037 and 603 where *être* is again used within the same context.

In III, 897 the "moi" conceit is briefly interpolated into a philosophical passage on love where the narrator recalls "les moi divers qui meurent successivement."

In III, 971 the narrator reintroduces the conceit to explain his different impressions of the same person, clearly linking the multiplicity of the self to the passage of time: "je finissais par trouver des images d'une même personne séparées par un intervalle de temps si long, conservées par des moi si distincts...."

[18] Another example of the same conceit within a discursive context may be found in III, 594-595 where it is extended over two pages.

The earliest use of the "moi" conceit conveying the notion of inner change appears within a context describing Swann's changed feelings: "son moi ancien, parvenu à l'extrême décrépitude, agissait encore machinalement, selon des préoccupations abolies..." (I, 524). The narrator already touched upon the theme of the multiplicity of the self in I, 376 by introducing an aphoristic observation into the private account of Swann's love for Odette. He thus speaks of "amours successifs" and "jalousies différentes" without, however, introducing the "moi" conceit.

The transitional remark between the literal and metaphoric ("ce serait donc") explicitly introduces the personification as a conclusion to be drawn from the experience described above. The personification of the abstract notion becomes evident when the indefinite article is applied to "moi," and when the particular adjectives used as modifiers (*différent, ancien*) reveal the multiplication into individual animated entities of man's personality. The process of personification, and the hyperbolic death code, which conveys the aspect of change in dramatic, extreme terms, set this notion into relief within the narrative context. The emphasis is continued through the extension of the process of personification to particular sensory impressions, and the continuation of the death code through *résistance à la mort*. The specific focus on the aspect of "resistance" and "death" through the accumulation of adjectives introduces a pathetic note into the narrative. The pathetic tone begins to color the entire passage when it is maintained throughout the phrase modifying *mort* ("détachant de nous à chaque moment des lambeaux de nous-mêmes sur la mortification desquels des cellules nouvelles multiplieront"), and taken up again in a later phrase continuing the process of personification ("la plainte des plus humbles éléments du moi qui vont disparaître").

Besides focusing our attention on the aspect of change, the above-quoted passage contains a brief remark indicating the precise temporal notion to be derived from this context: the metaphoric conceit "la mort fragmentaire et successive" is directly commented upon by the accompanying explanatory phrase "telle qu'elle s'insère dans toute la durée de notre vie." [19]

---

[19] A far more discursive context accompanies the same conceit of the "moi" personification in III, 943: "J'avais bien considéré toujours notre individu ... dans la durée de la vie, comme une suite de moi juxtaposés mais distincts qui mourraient les uns après les autres ou même alterneraient entre eux, comme ceux qui à Combray prenaient pour moi la place l'un de l'autre quand venait le soir." The direct time reference "dans la durée de la vie" points out the temporal aspect before introducing the imagery. Whereas the narrator of *Le Temps retrouvé* uses the "moi" conceit to refer to both the "successive" and "alternate" states of being, earlier books use the abstract and less striking paraphrase "états qui se succèdent en moi" to refer to the experience of abruptly changing moods; for example (I, 183): "Et de la sorte c'est du côté de Guermantes que j'ai appris à distinguer ces états qui se succèdent en moi, pendant certaines périodes, et vont jusqu'à se partager chaque journée, l'un revenant chasser l'autre...." "Etats qui se succèdent en moi" takes here

The narrator reintroduces the same conceit to describe the life-long duration of a particular aspect of his sensibility, or to refer to the sudden rediscovery of a former self through the experience of involuntary memory. To communicate this new discovery about man's existence within time, the author frequently extends the previous image of death to the death-rebirth cycle. Through repetition, this conceit becomes a motif symbolic of a particular experience within time. Proust was not the first or only author to use this conceit, yet, to my knowledge, he was the only one who used it as a major motif within his work. [20]

The personification of the "self" to emphasize a permanent aspect of man's existence falls thematically into two categories. The first series of images appears within a context describing the duration of an aspect of man's inner reality as revealed through the phenomenon of sensory analogy. Though the second series of images appearing within the context of involuntary memory is likewise based on an experience of sensory analogy, the two temporal notions may be distinguished as follows: the first is based on the intuition that

---

the place of the conceit "moi successifs" which has not yet been introduced into *La Recherche*. The same experience is once more referred to in I, 857, where the narrator uses the terms "deux grands modes," and "alternance de deux états."

See III, 696 where the conceit of the "moi successifs" is introduced into a context which has just mentioned the temporal notion of "duration."

[20] Other authors speak of "le moi" to refer to the permanent aspect of man's inner being. Bergson attributes our awareness of our inner self to intuition: "Il y a une réalité au moins que nous saisissons tous du dedans, par intuition et non par simple analyse. C'est notre propre personne.... C'est notre moi qui dure" (*La Pensée et le mouvant*, VI).

Writers before Proust have used the "moi" conceit to refer to the rediscovery and identification of one's inner self through memory. For instance, Bonnet writes in his *Contemplations naturelles*: "Ce n'est qu'en comparant le sentiment de son état présent avec le souvenir de ses états passés, que l'être pensant juge qu'il est la même personne ou le même moi; je veux dire que le moi qui éprouve actuellement une telle perception sent qu'il est le même qui avait éprouvé autrefois cette même perception." This observation is remarkably similar to Proust's conception of involuntary memory as expressed in *Le Temps retrouvé*. In *Emile*, Rousseau also stresses the importance of memory in identifying the self: "Ce que je sais bien c'est que l'identité du moi ne se prolonge que par la mémoire, et que pour être le même en effet, il faut que je me souvienne d'avoir été."

Like Proust, Lamartine used the "moi" conceit to express the notion of constant change within man's inner being: "De ce moi qui n'est plus d'autres moi vont renaître" (*Méditations* II, "Réflexions").

one has "reentered" a familiar mode of being, which, in *A la recherche,* is primarily based on the hero's keen perception of similar light impressions and atmospheric conditions. The other experience of sensory analogy, described within the context of involuntary memory, suddenly evokes a specific incidence of the past based on the same sensory stimulus as the presently felt impression.

The narrator usually elaborates on the hero's rediscovery of a former self through sensory analogy. Within these passages the "moi" conceit, which is often rather brief, constitutes only part of the imagery. For instance, within the long description of the hero's discovery of a former mode of being based on a particular light impression (III, 11-12; 25-26), the aspect of duration has already been clarified by both literal context and imagery before the "moi" conceit is introduced. The narrator thus speaks of the rediscovery of "un jeune homme plus ancien" (III, 11), and "le petit personnage intérieur" (III, 12) before introducing the conceit: "En revanche, je crois bien qu'à mon agonie, quand tous mes autres 'moi' seront morts, s'il vient à briller un rayon de soleil tandis que je pousserai mes derniers soupirs, le petit personnage barométrique se sentira bien aise, et ôtera son capuchon pour chanter: 'Ah! enfin, il fait beau.' " (III, 12) [21] The previous mention of "petit personnage intérieur" modified by the apposition "salueur chantant du soleil" introduces the personification of the particular sensation, which the conceit takes up again as "petit personnage barométrique." Within this context, the personification of the "moi" is more vivid and striking through the extension of the process of animation to a particular "moi" endowed with human emotions and gestures: "le petit personnage barométrique se sentira bien aise, et ôtera son capuchon pour chanter: 'Ah! enfin, il fait beau.' ".

The notion of the rediscovery of a former self is stated even more emphatically when the narrator describes it in terms of "rebirth": [22]

---

[21] The special emphasis placed on the term "moi" through the use of quotation marks is infrequent in *La Recherche.* A more conspicuous use of the term through capitalization appears in II, 82: "ce 'Moi' que je ne retrouvais qu'à des années d'intervalles."

[22] See III, 478 where the narrator uses the metaphor *renaissance* to emphasize a similar temporal notion. In III, 642 he uses the same code to dramatically express the death of his former being: j'aurais été incapable de

> Quelque geste incantateur ayant suscité, pendant que je passais mon smoking, le moi alerte et frivole qui était le mien quand j'allais avec Saint-Loup dîner à Rivebelle et le soir où j'avais cru emmener Mlle de Stermaria dîner dans l'île du Bois, je fredonnais inconsciemment le même air qu'alors; et c'est seulement en m'en apercevant qu'à la chanson je reconnaissais le chanteur intermittent.... (II, 1035)

The adjectival modifiers *alerte* and *frivole* reinforce the personification of "le moi," which is further emphasized through *chanteur intermittent,* the animation of the particular sensory analogy responsible for the rediscovery of a former experience. The verb *suscité* dramatizes the temporal notion by underlining the sudden and miraculous aspect of this experience. The notion is significantly reinforced through the textual juxtaposition of three particular experiences from different periods, all related through the same sensory experience.

In another passage describing an experience of sensory analogy in terms of "rebirth" within time, the aspect of renascence is further emphasized through the additional image "monde nouveau." The context within which this imagery appears is rather discursive and treats the subject at length. Thus the brief metaphorical conceit "je venais de renaître" is immediately followed by an explanatory remark that explicitly introduces the additional metaphor "monde nouveau," in turn explained by: "or un changement de temps suffit à recréer le monde et nous-mêmes" (II, 345-346).[23] Through the emphasis of personification, elaboration, and repetition the reader begins to realize that this is one of the key temporal notions described in *A la recherche*.

The reintroduction of the same conceit within the context of involuntary memory further insists on the duration of the self within man's existence. The opposition between "death" and "rebirth" within the following passage sets this notion into relief: "notre

---

ressusciter Albertine parce que je l'étais de me ressusciter moi-même, de ressusciter mon moi d'alors."

The notion of renascence of the self through sensory analogy was already conveyed through an extended "moi" conceit in II, 757.

[23] See III, 404 for the description of a similar durational experience set in relief through the metaphors *région du printemps* and *univers nouveau* contrasted to *l'ancien monde*.

vrai moi qui, parfois depuis longtemps semblait mort, mais ne l'était pas entièrement, s'éveille, s'anime en recevant la céleste nourriture qui lui est apportée" (III, 873). The aspect of animation and rebirth is accentuated through the double action expressed by *s'éveille* and *s'anime,* whereas the qualifying phrase "en recevant la céleste nourriture" suggests the miraculous aspect of this experience. The precise temporal notion to be derived from this experience is revealed by the aphoristic observation following the above-quoted passage: "Une minute affranchie de l'ordre du temps a recréé en nous, pour la sentir, l'homme affranchi de l'ordre du temps." [24]

C. Metaphorical Extensions Within the Symbolic Portrayal of the Novel's Characters

1. Dehumanization

Most of the symbolic tableaux connected with the theme of time appear within descriptive passages depicting a scene or event that constitutes part of the novel's "story." A recurrent device is the dehumanizing description of characters, which points to an underlying, symbolic significance. Particular emphasis through certain details reveals the narrator's viewpoint, and guides the reader's interpretation. In most instances, the imagery based on the physical appearance of the novel's characters is supplemented by exterior analogies that are primarily responsible for the process of dehumanization. Many of these analogies announce the transition from "reality" to "appearance," since the narrator uses such obvious links as *sembler, avoir l'air de* and *être pareil à* to warn the reader of

---

[24] The narrator uses two variant conceits of the "rebirth" imagery. One appears within the narrative account of involuntary memory and points to the temporal implications of these experiences: "De sorte que ce que l'être par trois et quatre fois ressuscité en moi venait de goûter, c'était peut-être bien des fragments d'existence soustraits au temps, mais cette contemplation, quoique d'éternité, était fugitive" (III, 875). The animation of *être* through *ressuscité* is a variant of the previous "rebirth" imagery personifying the "moi." See III, 884 where the narrator applies the same code to another variant expression of "moi," *l'étranger*: "Cet étranger, c'était moi-même, c'était l'enfant que j'étais alors, que le livre venait de susciter en moi...." In this instance, the term *étranger,* by emphasizing the notion of unfamiliarity with the former self, insists on the aspet of change within time.

the change in focus from objective representation to the subjective realm of illusion. Whereas the underlying basis for comparison of the two domains is not directly revealed, the type of imagery used and various textual indications point to the symbolic significance. The particular image introduced by the dehumanizing analogies sets the symbolic content of the "actual" setting into relief and lends considerable expressiveness to the tableau. The imagery's forceful impact on the reader guides his interpretation of the description.

The fact that many of Proust's symbolic images grow directly out of the "actual" description of a particular setting is in itself significant. As we follow the hero-narrator in his journey through time lost and recaptured, we repeatedly are told or led to infer that general truth is learned from the particular, individual experiences in life. This credo, which pervades the entire novel, is also reflected in the author's use of imagery connected with the theme of time.

The hero of "Combray" makes an important observation regarding the use of symbol in art while describing Giotto's Virtues and Vices (I, 82).[25] The artistic beauty and meaningfulness here attributed to Giotto's symbolic figures because they seem so "real," reflects Proust's attitude towards the use of symbolism in literature, as more explicitly stated in the *Revue Blanche* of 15 July, 1896:

> Qu'il me soit permis de dire encore du symbolisme, dont en somme il s'agit surtout ici, qu'en prétendant négliger "les accidents de temps et d'espace" pour ne nous montrer que des vérités éternelles, il méconnaît une autre loi de la vie, qui est de réaliser l'universel ou l'eternel, mais seulement dans des individus.
>
> Les œuvres purement symboliques risquent donc de manquer de vie et par là de profondeur. Si, de plus, au lieu de toucher l'esprit leurs "princesses" et leurs "chevaliers" proposent un sens imprécis et difficile à sa perspicacité, les poèmes, qui devraient être de vivants symboles, ne sont plus que de froides allégories.[26]

---

[25] The passage in question reads: "l'étrangeté saisissante, la beauté spéciale de ces fresques tenait à la grande place que le symbole y occupait, et que le fait qu'il fût représenté, non comme un symbole puisque la pensée symbolisée n'était pas exprimée, mais comme réel, comme effectivement subi ou matériellement manié, donnait à la signification de l'œuvre quelque chose de plus littéral et de plus précis, à son enseignement quelque chose de plus concret et de plus frappant."

[26] "Contre l'obscurité," *Revue Blanche*, 11, No. 75, p. 72.

For Proust then, truth and profundity are to be found in the individual, concrete experience. And he particularly insists that the symbolic statement be clear and easily intelligible, as is obvious from the title of this essay: "Contre l'obscurité."

Within the present category of the symbolic tableau, obscurity is avoided through explanatory remarks or explicit indications pointing to the symbolic significance. Moreover, the symbolic content grows directly out of the concrete representation of the novel's characters and the milieu in which they move: the reader is gradually initiated into the symbolic process, as actual events, scenes and characters begin to convey a general truth.

A number of images symbolic of an aspect of time reduce man to stone or sculpture. They appear within a context describing aged people, wherein the process of dehumanization accentuates the extreme old age and enormous physical change wrought by time. In the following passage, the physical deterioration of three old society ladies is gradually conveyed through the descriptive analogy to stone and finally to weather-beaten statuary. This double reduction to the inanimate is introduced into the description by means of transitional links that are close to the comparative structure, since they explicitly announce the juxtaposition of another domain:

> Le coup d'Alix avait raté, elle se tut, resta debout et immobile. Des couches de poudre plâtrant son visage, celui-ci avait l'air d'un visage de pierre. Et comme le profil était noble, elle semblait, sur un socle triangulaire et moussu caché par le mantelet, la déesse effritée d'un parc. (II, 199)

The narrator's sudden change of focus from a description of Alix within the framework of the social gathering to the unexpected closeup of her that freezes a certain attitude and stance — her momentary silence and immobility — and that singles out two physical traits — her powdered face and her noble profile — is humorous in its insistence on the inanimate, an aspect that the analogy to crumbling statuary significantly exaggerates. The many layers of powder is the visual detail that gives rise to the dehumanizing image. While the metaphoric adjective *plâtrant* directly replaces an element of the literal description, the following transitional element *avait l'air* underlines the transition from reality to illusion before introducing the second metaphorical element, *visage de pierre,* which extends the same code.[27] The literal remark "comme le profil était noble" reveals again the actual, physical aspect underlying the analogy to statuary, which is introduced by the transitional element, *semblait*.[28] The pictorial elaboration of the final dehumanizing image emphasizes the inanimate, which now completely penetrates the physical description. *Socle triangulaire et moussu* imposes the image of the statue, which the analogy to *déesse effritée d'un parc* particularizes. This final image adds a forceful comment to the physical appearance of Alix, who is now entirely likened to the inanimate. The adjectives *moussu* and *effritée* are key modifiers of the tableau, since they reveal that the inanimate was not merely introduced to convey the lady's facial and physical immobility, but rather to express the aspect of decomposition and old age. The image of crumbling statuary — common in nineteenth-century literature to emphasize deserted settings symbolic of decay and transitoriness — enhances the process of dehumanization with an expressive image. The description of the aged, withered looks in terms of crumbling statuary introduces a striking archetype of the transitory, accentuating the symbolic significance recently discovered by the hero. One of the novel's "actual" characters thus turns into a symbolic figure in front of our eyes.[29] The intrusion of the imagery into the nar-

---

[27] One may consider this structure a "hybrid" between comparison and metaphor, as does Christine Brooke-Rose in her *Grammar of Metaphor*, pp. 127-128. Hermann Pongs, however, includes the German equivalent of "avoir l'air" and "sembler," namely, "scheinen," under the comparative structure. See *Das Bild in der Dichtung*, p. 157.

In an article entitled "Comparaison et métaphore," Danielle Bouverot points out that an image that semantically announces the analogy based on appearance through such pointers as *sembler* and *avoir l'air* may be considered an attenuated metaphor (*Le Français Moderne* [October 1969], pp. 305-306). She makes a primary distinction between analogies semantically based on comparison as opposed to relationships of identity (see *Le Français Moderne*, April, July and October 1969).

[28] In this instance, the anteposition of "sur un socle triangulaire et moussu caché par le mantelet," which delays the analogy announced by *sembler*, attenuates the cautionary transition by first confronting us with the statue.

[29] It should be briefly mentioned that the symbolic significance of Alix as old age incarnate is already prepared by several previous remarks referring to the three oldest society women, of whom she is one. The narrator refers to their former life, which he describes as being lost in "la nuit des temps" (II, 195). Twice he elevates them to mythological figures: "les trois divinités déchues" (II, 196), and "ces trois Parques à cheveux blancs, bleus ou roses avaient filé le mauvais coton d'un nombre incalculable de messieurs" (II, 197).

rative context reorients the reader's attention from the literal, descriptive level depicting the hero's observation of people attending a social gathering to the conceptual *niveau* were observation and mental reaction merge.

The physical metamorphosis symbolic of old age is again described in terms of the code reducing human physiognomy to stone:

> La Berma avait, comme dit le peuple, la mort sur le visage. Cette fois c'était bien d'un marbre de l'Erechtéion qu'elle avait l'air. Ses artères durcies étant déjà à demi pétrifiées, on voyait de longs rubans sculpturaux parcourir les joues, avec une rigidité minérale. Les yeux mourants vivaient relativement, par contraste avec ce terrible masque ossifié, et brillaient faiblement comme un serpent endormi au milieu des pierres. (III, 998)

The stereotype expression "la mort sur le visage" alludes to the symbolic content to be derived from the following imagery. As in the previous example, the analogy to the inanimate is explicitly introduced through *avait l'air*. *Marbre de l'Erechtéion* is thus presented as a visual illusion within the descriptive narrative of an "actual" setting. The following metaphors, however, which all extend the code of dehumanization, are directly integrated into the text without transitional pointers between the two semantic domains of tenor and vehicle. These metaphors all grow out of the descriptive detail *artères durcies*: as multiple metaphorical replacements from the mineral world, they emphasize the hyperbolic nature of the image based on arterial rigidity. The metaphoric attribute *pétrifiées* modifying *artères durcies* directly superimposes the mineral code onto the physical description, whereas the metaphor *rubans sculpturaux* further extends the semantic domain of the vehicle, while at the same time it is syntactically linked to the verbal sequence of the tenor, i.e., *les joues,* which refers the reader to the aspect of the physiognomy corresponding to the metaphorical image. The verbal modifying phrase "avec une rigidité minérale" reinforces the new code and reemphasizes the main characteristic underlying the metaphorical transposition, the arterial rigidity.

Whereas the previous metaphors all concentrate on a salient visual detail of the physiognomy, *masque ossifié* functions as a hyperbolic résumé, extending the aspect of lifelessness over the entire face. The reduction of the human face to an ossified mask, and the inclusion of *yeux mourants* as the only visual detail significantly emphasize the allusion to death previously stressed by the initial cliché "la mort sur le visage." This aspect is enhanced by the negative contrast between the relative liveliness of the "dying eyes" as opposed to the lifeless face. The final simile "comme un serpent endormi au milieu des pierres" illustrates the same notion through another image, thereby adding an emphatic comment to the general impression of immobility and lifelessness. The pictorial detail *pierres* recalls the previous mineral code applied to the description of La Berma's face. Through the exaggerated dehumanizing description, la Berma, like Alix, becomes a figure symbolic of old age and death.

In a passage depicting bedridden old people, several descriptive exaggerations and the analogy to funeral effigies set the tableau into relief within the narrative context and demand more than a literal reading:

> ces malades, depuis des années mourants, qui ne se lèvent plus, ne bougent plus, et, même au milieu de l'assiduité frivole de visiteurs attirés par une curiosité de touristes ou une confiance de pèlerins, les yeux clos, tenant leur chapelet, rejetant à demi leur drap déjà mortuaire, sont pareils à des gisants que le mal a sculptés jusqu'au squelette dans une chair rigide et blanche comme le marbre, et étendus sur leur tombeau. (III, 943)

The descriptive emphasis on dying ("depuis des années mourants"; "drap déjà mortuaire") and immobility ("qui ne se lèvent plus, ne bougent plus") hyperbolically depicts a state of illness in terms of the dying hour. This exaggerated portrayal sets the tone for the following analogy, which introduces an even more striking exaggeration by completely dehumanizing the very ill to funeral sculpture. The semantic link *sont pareils à* explicitly introduces the analogy. The relative clause elaborating upon the physical aspect of the "dying" continues the dehumanization to funeral sculpture by directly replacing the literal terms with metaphors extending the mineral image (*sculptés, tombeau*), and by inserting a brief simile ("comme le marbre"), which reintroduces an explicit analogy between the human and the mineral world.[30] These analogies between the human and mineral domains reduce the characters to the inanimate in an exaggerated manner. The discrepancy between the two domains and the narrator's insistence on the process of dehumanization introduce an element of humor into the description, while, at the same time, stressing the grim message.

The special significance to be attributed to this scene is thus conveyed through the very imagery chosen by the narrator. The descriptive exaggeration depicting the sick as dying, and the reduction of the still animate to the inanimate command the reader's attention and orient his viewpoint. The powerful intrusion of the figurative image, whose extended code allows the reader to enter the realm of funeral sculpture, emphasizes the shift in narrative focus from literal description to symbolic significance. The modifying phrase describing the activity of the bedside visitors as a "curiosité de touristes ou une confiance de pèlerins" already announces the gulf between the actual setting and the narrator's mental interpretation. This gulf becomes absolute when the "visitors" begin to move in the world of artistic mimesis where the human element has turned into a representation of human life, the *memento mori* of the funeral sculpture. The reader is thus allowed to participate in the hero's detached, interpretive viewpoint, as the deadly ill turn to artifacts.

In two instances the dehumanization of the novel's characters is followed up by explicit statements revealing the symbolic sig-

---

[30] An analogy reinforcing the metaphorical transposition actually presents us with a different semantic structure, which will be discussed in the chapter devoted to the interrelationships between metaphors and similes. Within the present passage, the above comparison and the "hybrid" structures *sembler* and *avoir l'air* all introduce the analogy between the animate and inanimate by juxtaposing the figurative image rather obviously to the literal description.

Other examples of dehumanization symbolic of old age that are introduced by the comparative structure are found in the following passages: II, 603 describes Charlus as "pâle comme un marbre"; III, 948 depicts a character "comme un petit fantôme qu'une main invisible promenait, diminué de taille, changé dans sa substance et ayant l'air d'une réduction en pierre ponce de lui-même." The character's drastic metamorphosis into a stone marionette is primarily humorous in this instance, as we are first struck by the funny and exaggerated nature of the image before concentrating on the actual implications to be inferred from this portrayal. In III, 1017 the Duc de Guermantes is compared to "un rocher dans la tempête."

nificance of the imagery. In the first example, the dehumanizing analogy to stone (which becomes an imaginal constant within the descriptive tableaux of old age in *Le Temps retrouvé*), from which the reader infers that Legrandin has aged, is explained a few lines further on by "c'était la vieillesse." As in the previous examples, the narrator first reveals the actual, physical trait responsible for the impression that men have aged. The reader infers the temporal notion from the combined message of the literal description and the analogy from the inanimate:

> La suppression du rose, que je n'avais jamais soupçonné artificiel, de ses lèvres et de ses joues donnait à sa figure l'apparence grisâtre et aussi la précision sculpturale de la pierre. (III, 934) [31]

The symbolic implications of this physical description are reinforced by the brief mention of Legrandin's changed behavior. In this instance, the unexpected analogy to the "dead" points to more than a literal description: "On s'étonnait de le voir si pâle, abattu, ne prononçant que de rares paroles qui avaient l'insignifiance de celles que disent les morts qu'on évoque." The satirical allusion to communication with spirits to stress the insignifiance of Legrandin's remarks is humorous; the analogy between a human trait and the behavior of spirits is funny in its exaggerated aspect — an aspect reinforced later on within the same passage by "pâle et triste fantôme" — and it is amusing since it is obviously satirical. The analogy to spirits, particularly introduced to modify *insignifiance,* pronounces a devastating judgment on mediumistic practices. The final sentence of the descriptive tableau briefly recalls the salient physical and behavioral aspects of Legrandin, which are then directly equated with old age: "Et on se disait que cette cause qui avait substitué au Legrandin coloré et rapide un pâle et triste fantôme de Legrandin, c'était la vieillesse." The direct textual juxtaposition of descriptive

---

[31] The editors' footnote to this passage reveals that the manuscript text was originally more extensive. They reproduce a non-deleted phrase that lengthens the above analogy to stone through an additional comparison to sculpture: "ses traits allongés et mornes comme ceux de certains dieux egyptiens" (p. 1141, footnote 3 to p. 934 of the main text). This imaginal extension is in keeping with Proust's tendency to elaborate on the imagery connected with the theme of time.

details referring to the former and present Legrandin reemphasizes the symbolic intention behind the description, which is then explicitly stated through the literal remark "c'était la vieillesse." The final sentence thus doubly stresses the tableau's symbolic content through imagery and explicit discursive comment.

The second example of a symbolic tableau whose temporal notion is directly explained by accompanying discursive remarks must be quoted at length to show how the various descriptive details and the insertion of revealing remarks convey the symbolic content. In this instance, one of the novel's characters, described in the midst of an actual setting, begins to stand for more than himself as he is progressively dehumanized. The scene is described from the viewpoint of the narrator presently writing the novel, which allows him to juxtapose several epochs, the time of the actual event and later developments related to it: [32]

> Je revois toute cette sortie, je revois, si ce n'est pas à tort que je le place sur cet escalier, portrait détaché de son cadre, le prince de Sagan, duquel ce dut être la dernière soirée mondaine, se découvrant pour présenter ses hommages à la duchesse, avec une si ample révolution du

---

[32] Other examples of dehumanization through the narrator's multiple perspective within time may be found in several passages depicting Albertine as a symbolic figure. The earliest example occurs in I, 829-830 where she is reduced to a silhouette. The dehumanizing aspect of this stylized portrayal is further set in relief when the narrator metaphorically "projects" this image onto a "screen": "C'est ainsi, faisant halte, les yeux brillants sous son 'polo', que je la revois encore maintenant, silhouettée sur l'écran que lui fait au fond, la mer, et séparée de moi par un espace transparent et azuré, le temps écoulé depuis lors..." (I, 829-830). The inclusion of the stereotype temporal expression *le temps écoulé* within the tableau, and the direct equation between the pictorial and the abstract introduced by this apposition, point to the symbolic content of the portrayal.

The recurrence of the symbolization of Albertine, as representative of a particular period within the hero's life, introduces a temporal leitmotif into the novel. For further references see II, 351-352, 354, 363, 365, 389, 645, 1021; III, 1069 (footnote to p. 68), 193, 360, 372, 386-387, 453, 915. See also *infra,* pp. 203-204.

Several articles have discussed the symbolic implications in Albertine's portrayal: Carl John Black, Jr., "Albertine as an Allegorical Figure of Time," *Romanic Review,* 54 (October, 1963), 171-186; Nicholas Kostis, "Albertine: Characterization through Image and Symbol," *PMLA,* 84, No. 1 (January, 1969), 125-135; and Charles N. Clark, "Love and Time: the Erotic Imagery of Marcel Proust," *Yale French Studies,* No. 11 (1953), pp. 80-90.

> chapeau haut de forme dans sa main gantée de blanc, qui répondait au gardénia de la boutonnière, qu'on s'étonnait que ce ne fût pas un feutre à plume de l'ancien régime, duquel plusieurs visages ancestraux étaient exactement reproduits dans celui de ce grand seigneur. Il ne resta qu'un peu de temps auprès d'elle, mais ses poses, même d'un instant, suffisaient à composer tout un tableau vivant et comme une scène historique. D'ailleurs, comme il est mort depuis, et que je ne l'avais de son vivant qu'aperçu, il est tellement devenu pour moi un personnage d'histoire, d'histoire mondaine du moins, qu'il m'arrive de m'étonner en pensant qu'une femme, qu'un homme que je connais sont sa sœur et son neveu. (II, 720)

The metamorphosis of an actual character into a symbolic figure is due to the dehumanizing description of the Prince seen as a portrait and historical figure, and to the narrative anticipation of his future death. Both the dehumanization and the narrative anticipation undermine the character's present individual existence.

The presentation of the Prince as a "portrait détaché de son cadre" immediately signals to the reader that more than a literal description is taking place. The feeling that we are dealing with more than one level of meaning is reinforced when the description of the Prince's hat is followed by the remark "on s'étonnait que ce ne fût pas un feutre à plume de l'ancien régime." That the *feutre à plume* represents another era is immediately evident from the modifying phrase *de l'ancien régime*. The following genitive complement attached to *ancien régime* comes as an explanatory remark, which gives us the key to the previous dehumanization and allusion to another era. The statement reveals why the Prince stands for more than himself: within the eyes of the beholder — in this case the hero-narrator of the novel — the close resemblance between the Prince and his ancestors calls forth images of another era as known through portraits. The illusion contaminates the actual perception, as the living Sagan is conceived as a portrait within the gallery of ancestors evoked in the hero's memory. The metaphor *tableau vivant* reinforces and recalls the previous reduction to "portrait détaché de son cadre," whereas the additional remark "comme une scène historique" again points to the tableau's symbolic content. The final sentence is entirely discursive, as the narrator explicitly reveals why he sees the Prince as a symbolic figure. By referring to him as "personnage d'histoire," by anticipating his future death, and by mentioning how difficult it is for him to believe that the Prince is related to living people, the narrator insists on his subjective impression that the Prince transcends physical reality.

The symbolic imagery of the examples studied within this section is thus part of the story depicting the novel's characters. The dehumanizing portrayal comes as a shock within the narrative account of a character's personal "history" and exploits. The striking nature of the imagery alerts the reader to a double level of reference. The temporal notion is thus thrown in relief, as the reader's attention is detached from the narrative level of the actual plot at hand to a mental evaluation and conceptualization thereof. The mention of the hero's mental or emotional reaction to the scene usually guides the reader's interpretation of the symbolic implications.

2. CHARACTERS FUNCTIONING AS SYMBOLIC FIGURES

Besides the process of dehumanization, Proust uses various other imaginal and narrative devices to invest the account of the characters' personal "history" with symbolic significance. Within *Le Temps retrouvé* we find a significant increase of such images, the majority of which grow out of the physical description of the novel's characters. The symbolic portrayal of the characters varies widely. Some are presented through realistic detail, whereas others are deliberately described from the naïve viewpoint of the hero's subjective illusion, taking, for instance, a social gathering for a costume ball or marionette performance.

The nature of the symbolic context varies from passages where the symbolic implications have to be inferred to others where they are discursively stated. Many symbolic passages must be studied not only in their immediate context but within the larger context of an entire section of the novel. This is especially true for images appearing within the narrative account of the "Matinée Guermantes," since the recurrence and insistence of some of them reinforces the symbolic message, and since the explanatory remarks accompanying others provide the key for similar images.

One of the predominant descriptive devices consists of investing an "actual" character with another level of meaning through insistence on the temporal notion conveyed by his physical aspect. Through emphasis on the abstract notion to be inferred from his physical presence, the character obviously begins to stand for more than himself: besides being engaged in the "action" of a personal "history" — on the level of the narrative "story" — he functions as a concrete emblem of an abstract idea. He is thus endowed with a double signification. The narrator conveys this to the reader by simultaneously developing the "Idea" as he depicts the character's physical appearance.[33]

One of the more explicit means used by the narrator to turn fictional "reality" into allegory is through the inclusion of obvious references to time.[34] For instance, the repeated inclusion and capitalization of the word *Temps* within the portrayal of Madame de Saint-Euverte overtly points to the abstract notion she embodies:

> Elle ne se rendait pas compte qu'elle donnait pour moi la naissance à un nouvel épanouissement de ce nom Saint-Euverte, qui, à tant d'intervalle, marquait la distance et la continuité du Temps. C'est le Temps qu'elle berçait dans cette nacelle où fleurissaient le nom de Saint-Euverte et le style Empire en soies de fuchsias rouges.... Mme de Saint-Euverte-La-Rochefoucauld ... était loin de soupçonner que son nom m'avait ravi, celui de son mari, non celui plus glorieux de ses parents, et que je lui voyais comme fonction, dans cette pièce pleine d'attributs, de bercer le Temps. (III, 1025)

The literal description of Mme de Saint-Euverte's Empire dress and her reclining position on a chaise longue, as well as a discussion of her family affiliation to the Saint-Euvertes formerly known by the narrator — and encountered by the reader in *Du côté de chez Swann* — precede the direct reference to time (III, 1024-25). The transition from the literal to the symbolic is clearly indicated by the narrator

---

[33] This descriptive approach of turning actual characters into "living symbols" reflects Proust's aesthetic theory as expressed in his article "Contre l'obscurité," and as echoed by the narrator of "Combray" while describing Giotto's Virtues and Vices (I, 82).
See *supra,* pp. 134-135.

[34] The term "allegory" is here used to refer to the repeated tendency of the narrative to superimpose another level of meaning — in this context, the narrator's discovery of the role of time within man's life — while portraying actual characters.

who reveals that it is the name "Saint-Euverte" that lends symbolic significance to the young woman. The symbolic implications are made more explicit through the temporal indications "à tant d'intervalle" and "la distance et la continuité du Temps." Mme de Saint-Euverte actually turns into an allegorical figure when she is endowed with symbolic action, as the narrator closely joins descriptive details referring to her physical appearance to the abstract concept of Time: "C'est le Temps qu'elle berçait dans cette nacelle où fleurissaient le nom de Saint-Euverte et le style Empire en soies de fuchsias rouges." The presence of the archaism *nacelle* within this context accentuates the temporal notion of the survival of the past within the present. Whereas the metaphorical conceit "berçait dans cette nacelle" recalls her reclining position on the sofa, the metonymical description "le style Empire en soies de fuchsias rouges" refers us to her dress whose floral pattern is already familiar to the reader.[35] The syllepsis "où fleurissaient le nom de Saint-Euverte et le style Empire," by closely joining two different semantic domains, once more alerts us to the fact that we are dealing with more than one level of meaning. Time thus enters the realm of physical reality in the guise of the young woman, whereas the young woman suddenly stands for more than herself, since she embodies an abstract notion.

The narrator insists on the symbolic portrayal by repeating it after an intervening passage of literal narrative. He again stresses the fact that the name "Saint-Euverte" is at the heart of this symbolic perception. Whereas the previous tableau syntactically linked the name and the physical appearance of Madame de Saint-Euverte through the syllepsis "où fleurissaient le nom de Saint-Euverte et le style Empire," the second tableau is preceded by a discursive literal comment that specifically stresses the importance of the name. By repeatedly attributing the function of "rocking time" to Madame de Saint-Euverte, the narrator significantly emphasizes her allegorical status within the setting of the "Matinée Guermantes."

The portrayal of Mlle de Saint-Loup as an allegorical figure embodying an aspect of time is conveyed through the double mean-

---

[35] The metaphorical conceit "berçait dans cette nacelle" is previously prepared for in III, 1024 where the chaise longue supporting Mme de Saint-Euverte is described as "une chaise longue, placée de façon rectiligne, mais à l'intérieur incurvée comme un berceau."

ing, one literal, one metaphoric, of the term *distance,* and the series of metaphors drawing time into the material realm: [36]

> je fus étonné de voir à côté d'elle une jeune fille d'environ seize ans, dont la taille élevée mesurait cette distance que je n'avais pas voulu voir. Le temps incolore et insaisissable s'était, pour que pour ainsi dire je puisse le voir et le toucher, matérialisé en elle, il l'avait pétrie comme un chef-d'œuvre, tandis que parallèlement sur moi, hélas! il n'avait fait que son œuvre. (III, 1031)

The demonstrative adjective modifying *distance,* and the accompanying relative clause "que je n'avais pas voulu voir" both command the reader's attention, for they both imply a special meaning over and above the literal connotation of physical height already introduced through *taille élevée.* The metaphorical implications of *distance* are revealed by the following personification of time due to the verbs *s'était matérialisé, avait pétrie* and *avait fait,* which turn time into an active agent, a sculptor working upon human beings. The symbolic implications conferred on the description of the characters' physical appearance are pointed to by the cautionary transitional remark *pour ainsi dire,* which attracts our attention to the manner of discourse, and the remark "pour que ... je puisse le voir et le toucher," which explicitly reveals the observer's symbolic vision. The reader realizes that the term *distance* is at once literal and metaphoric, since physical distance, the girl's height, is symbolic of temporal distance. [37] The explicit mention of the girl's age —

---

[36] The presentation of Mlle de Saint-Loup as a "time symbol" is already prepared by the preceding context stating that Mme and Mlle de Saint-Loup both give the hero "cette idée du Temps passé" (p. 1029). The narration then continues to focus on Mlle de Saint-Loup by enumerating the hero's various past experiences related to "les deux grands 'côtés'" of which Mlle de Saint-Loup is a living reminder, since she embodies "Swann's way" through her mother's side, and "Guermantes' way" through her father's. The text is devoid of metaphors and is chiefly literal and discursive except for one simile to the network of crossroads, which serves as a conceptual model for the various past experiences converging on Mlle de Saint-Loup.

[37] The simultaneous literal and metaphorical connotations of another spatial term, *volume,* likewise reveal the hero's subjective vision perceiving Albertine as a symbolic figure: "De même que le volume de cet Ange musicien était constitué par les trajets multiples entre les différents points du passé que son souvenir occupait en moi et les différents signes, depuis la vue jusqu'aux sensations les plus intérieures de mon être, qui m'aidaient à descendre jusque

"une jeune fille d'environ seize ans" — endows the tableau with the temporal precision that gives the reader a definite yardstick by which to measure time gone by. That the narrator preserves an element of humor in describing the devastating influence of time is apparent from the pun contrasting *chef-d'œuvre* and *œuvre,* referring to the young beauty and the hero's aged appearance.

The metamorphosis of the novel's characters into symbolic figures is not always accompanied by direct time references or obvious time metaphors. A far less discursive approach is the juxtaposition of two images depicting the same person in youth and old age, a descriptive device whose symbolic intentions are to be inferred by the reader. The symbolic implications of such analogies are, however, significantly reinforced by the larger context of the "Matinée Guermantes" within which they all appear. Recurrence of the same imaginal process based on sharp contrast, and the non-literal framework within which they all appear reinforce the symbolic message. This non-literal framework is due to the hero's naïve, subjective vision through which all of these images are presented to the reader. We thus participate in the hero's "optical illusion," which first leads him to believe that all the guests are disguised ("chacun semblait s'être 'fait une tête', généralement poudrée," III, 920). The extension of the travesty code, and the accumulation and frequent repetition of certain physical traits obviously referring to old age are descriptive devices that all suggest more than one level of reference within the narrative context of the "Matinée Guermantes." [38]

---

dans l'intimité du sien" (III, 372). The extension of the code (*trajets multiples, points du passé,* and *lignes* — which I believe to be the correct deciphering of the illegible word transcribed by the editors as "signes"), in conjunction with abstract expressions, reveals the second level of reference of the otherwise literal term *volume,* referring to Albertine's physical presence. The temporal content of the spatial code is clear from the genitive link *du passé.*

The explication of this passage would have to be somewhat different, of course, if the illegible word turned out to be *signes, liens,* or *sièges* (See Volume 11, pp. 84-85 of the definitive version of the Proust notebooks at the Bibliothèque Nationale).

[38] The physical traits symbolic of old age that are most frequently repeated are: "barbe blanche" (III, 920, 926, 938), "cheveux blancs" (920, 938, 940, 946), "semelles de plomb" (920, 935), and various references to bad posture and unsteady gait.

The first symbolic juxtaposition of youth and old age in a description that first seems to refer to a "travesty," is found in a passage depicting the Duc de Châtellerault: [39]

> Je fus bien plus étonné au même moment en entendant appeler duc de Châtellerault un petit vieillard aux moustaches argentées d'ambassadeur, dans lequel seul un petit bout de regard resté le même me permit de reconnaître le jeune homme que j'avais rencontré une fois en visite chez Mme de Villeparisis. A la première personne que je parvins ainsi à identifier, en tâchant de faire abstraction du travestissement et de compléter les traits restés naturels par un effort de mémoire, ma première pensée eût dû être, et fut peut-être bien moins d'une seconde, de la féliciter d'être si merveilleusement grimée qu'on avait d'abord, avant de la reconnaître, cette hésitation que les grands acteurs, paraissant dans un rôle où ils sont différents d'eux-mêmes, donnent, en entrant en scène, au public qui, même averti par le programme, reste un instant ébahi avant d'éclater en applaudissements. (III, 921)

The explicit mention of *travestissement* and the analogy to the theater reinforce our impression that we are confronted with the description of an actual disguise. The narrator's identification of the Duke as the "young man" encountered at Madame de Villeparisis' further deludes the reader, since he is led to attribute the "petit vieillard" aspect to the Duke's dexterity in disguising himself. Merely two brief remarks warn the careful reader that possibly more than a literal description is taking place. Thus the revelation that the hero's admiration for this disguise lasted "bien moins d'une seconde" is indeed surprising in a context that insists on his astonishment. The second detail that puzzles the reader is the fact that the "petit bout de regard resté le même" is the only physical trait identifying the Duke. The minimal extent of the identification, further emphasized through *petit bout,* which underlines its fragmentary nature, may lead us to suspect that more than a mere "disguise" is in question.

The key passages extending the code of disguisement are on pages 920-923, 933, 937, 938, 941, 947 and 1046.

[39] Recurrence of the same descriptive contrast emphasizing the transition from youth to old age are to be found in the passages describing Mme d'Arpajon (937), the "jeune comte de..." (938), the Vicomtesse de Saint-Fiacre (942), and Mme Swann (951).

Yet the reader, guided by the narrator's viewpoint, is deluded for some time, especially since he has not been sufficiently informed of the huge time gap between the "Matinée Guermantes" and the previous section of the novel. The brief, casual reference to the passage of time ("beaucoup d'années passèrent" [III, 854]) is not adequate preparation for the fact that people have aged, and that things have changed. This hiatus in the narrative account contributes to the reader's readiness to accept the description of the "costume party" as real, since he is hardly prepared to believe that the novel's former characters have aged to that extent. The unaware reader is not sufficiently warned by such symbolic pointers as the analogy "Ages de la Vie" to which the physical appearance of the Prince de Guermantes is likened (920-921). Nor is he completely convinced by the second, far more striking description of physical decrepitude attributed to M. d'Argencourt, whose physical decline and drastic change in behavior are repeatedly stressed in an extended passage (921-923): a series of derogatory analogies to lower forms of existence — both physical and social — emphasize the enormous change in his appearance and character (*vieux mendiant, personnage de vieux gâteux, loque en bouillie, vieux marchand d'habit ramolli, sublime gaga, molle chrysalide*). The exaggerated and derogatory nature of these analogies introduces an element of humor into the passage, while the insistence on old age (*vieux*) and feebleness (*molle, ramolli, loque en bouillie*) points to more than a literal disguise.

The repeated narrative device of descriptive passages contrasting the once proud, vigorous and well-dressed d'Argencourt to the actual senile, feeble and sloppy-looking "transformation" further emphasizes the aspect of metamorphosis and hints at the passage of time. The reader is reminded from the start of the character's former solemn, arrogant bearing while witnessing his new appearance:

> c'était un vieux mendiant qui n'inspirait plus aucun respect qu'était devenu cet homme dont la solennité, la raideur empesée étaient encore présentes à mon souvenir et qui donnait à son personnage de vieux gâteux une telle vérité que ses membres tremblotaient, que les traits détendus de sa figure, habituellement hautaine, ne cessaient de sourire avec une niaise béatitude. (III, 921-922)

The same contrast between the once haughty gentleman and the now pathetic old man is again emphasized by the following description:

> A peine, en se rappelant certains sourires d'Argencourt qui jadis tempéraient parfois un instant sa hauteur pouvait-on trouver dans l'Argencourt vrai celui que j'avais vu si souvent, pouvait-on comprendre que la possibilité de ce sourire de vieux marchand d'habits ramolli existât dans le gentleman correct d'autrefois. (III, 922)

Aside from the added emphasis on the aspect of transformation through the juxtaposition of contrasting images of former and present appearances, the narrator's explicit references to the hero's amazement at this transformation suggest that the latter does not correctly understand what has happened: "il était arrivé à être tellement différent de lui-même que j'avais l'illusion d'être devant une autre personne, aussi bienveillante, aussi désarmée, aussi inoffensive que l'Argencourt habituel était rogue, hostile et dangereux" (922).[40]

Yet, while these elements hint at the true meaning of the "costume party," other details sustain the illusion: first, a series of expressions referring specifically to the art of disguise (*clou de la matinée; art du déguisement; spectacle inénarrable et pittoresque; bénévole caricature; extraordinaire numéro*), preserve the masquerade atmosphere; second, the specific reference to two comic playwrights, and the explicit mention of *bouffe* stress the comic element of the analogy to theatrical characters — "incarnation de moribond-bouffe d'un Regnard exagéré par Labiche." Finally, the analogy to a character of children's books — the Comtesse de Ségur's *Général Dourakine* — further reduces d'Argencourt to a comic caricature.[41]

---

[40] Previously, within the same passage, the narrator already voiced his amazement at the extent of d'Argencourt's transformation: "C'était évidemment la dernière extrémité où il avait pu le conduire sans en crever; le plus fier visage, le torse le plus cambré n'était plus qu'une loque en bouillie agitée de-ci de-là" (III, 922). The remark *sans en crever*, the antithetical portrayal of former and present states, and the exaggerated reduction to *loque en bouillie* put the reader on his guard, and lead him to suspect that more than a literal description of a costume party is taking place.

[41] See *infra*, pp. 206-207 for further analysis of Argencourt's portrayal.
The use of theatre metaphors in *A la recherche* is discussed by John Gaywood Linn in *The Theater in the Fiction of Marcel Proust*, Chapter Six. The

The temporal hiatus before the "Matinée Guermantes," and these various descriptive devices are jointly responsible in deluding the reader, who consequently experiences the same shock as the hero himself when he finally realizes that he is indeed confronted with old people. The reader is given this shock rather belatedly after the detailed portraits of the Duc de Châtellerault and M. d'Argencourt — whose disguised appearance is obviously symbolic in retrospect, when the narrator explains his illusion (III, 923):

> je sentais qu'elles n'avaient plus rien de flatteur parce que la transformation n'était pas voulue, et m'avisais enfin, ce à quoi je n'avais pas songé en entrant dans ce salon, que toute fête, si simple soit-elle, quand elle a lieu longtemps après qu'on a cessé d'aller dans le monde et pour peu qu'elle réunisse quelques-unes des mêmes personnes qu'on a connues autrefois, vous fait l'effet d'une fête travestie, de la plus réussie de toutes, de celle où l'on est le plus sincèrement "intrigué" par les autres, mais où ces têtes, qu'ils se sont faites depuis longtemps sans le vouloir, ne se laissent pas défaire par un débarbouillage, une fois la fête finie.

Although the narrator occasionally reintroduces the metaphors of disguise in subsequent descriptions of the guests at the "Matinée Guermantes," the symbolic contexts that follow this explanatory passage tend towards the discursive, since they repeatedly stress the general truth just discovered.

That this discovery concerns existence within time is revealed by the time metaphors and the explicit mention of time within the following symbolic tableau. The narrator recalls the "optical illusion" and exaggerates it, since the theatrical code not only takes us to the realm of illusion, but also dehumanizes men to puppets: [42]

> Des poupées, mais que, pour les identifier à celui qu'on avait connu, il fallait lire sur plusieurs plans à la fois,

---

references to Regnard and Labiche in connection with Argencourt's portrayal are mentioned on pp. 31, 219-220.

[42] This code is introduced in the previous paragraph through an explicit analogy of M. d'Argencourt's peculiar appearance and behavior to puppets: "C'était trop de parler d'un acteur et, débarrassé qu'il était de toute âme consciente, c'est comme une poupée trépidante, à la barbe postiche de laine blanche, que je le voyais agité, promené dans ce salon, comme dans un guignol" (III, 924).

> situés derrière elles et qui leur donnaient de la profondeur et forçaient à faire un travail d'esprit quand on avait devant soi ces vieillards fantoches, car on était obligé de les regarder, en même temps qu'avec les yeux, avec la mémoire. Des poupées baignant dans les couleurs immatérielles des années, des poupées extériorisant le Temps, le Temps qui d'habitude n'est pas visible, pour le devenir cherche des corps et, partout où il les rencontre, s'en empare pour montrer sur eux sa lanterne magique. (III, 924)

The meaning of *poupées* is obvious from the preceding context of travesty, in particular the mention of marionettes (III, 923-924). The textual inclusion within this passage of "celui qu'on avait connu" and "vieillards fantoches" — whose attribute recalls their comical aspect and points to the main characteristic responsible for the metaphorical transposition from men to marionettes — at once identifies the "actors" of this drama.

The initial sentence of the quotation serves as a preparatory introduction, advising us how to view this metamorphosis: "sur plusieurs plans à la fois." The ambiguous implications of *plans* and *profondeur* are clarified through the double, discursive reference to the visual and conceptual domains: "car on était obligé de les regarder, en même temps qu'avec les yeux, avec la mémoire." The abstract mental activity that is to complement the visual perception was previously insisted upon by "travail d'esprit." The context thus explicitly denotes the passage from the actual visual perception to its symbolic implications.

The temporal notion is then obviously superimposed upon the symbolic tableau through the direct confrontation between *poupées* and Time within the same image. The genitive link *des années* directly points to the temporal content of the metaphorical expression *couleurs immatérielles des années*. And the transformation of the characters into allegorical figures is evident from the abstract temporal activity attributed to them: "des poupées extériorisant le Temps."

Further imaginal elaboration explains the temporal implications of the symbolic tableau. The personification of Time as an active agent working upon human bodies by projecting his special light (*couleurs immatérielles des années*) enacts the symbolic process in front of the reader's eyes. The analogy to *lanterne magique* particularizes the visual translation of Time's destructive influence on human bodies, and further stresses the intangible nature of this nefarious activity, since Time does not come into direct contact with bodies, but projects an image onto them. The intangible aspect of the transformation is insisted upon by the following analogy between Argencourt's appearance and the "immaterial" image of Golo projected by the magic lantern. The analogy also stresses the perceptual illusion experienced by the hero during the Matinée Guermantes: "Aussi immatériel que jadis Golo sur le bouton de porte de ma chambre de Combray, ainsi le nouveau et si méconnaissable Argencourt était là comme la révélation du Temps, qu'il rendait partiellement visible" (III, 924). This elaborated transposition into perceptual terms, and the dramatic reduction of the novel's characters into puppets strikingly emphasizes the symbolic implications of the entire "Matinée Guermantes" whose characters now obviously become participants in an allegorical drama.[43]

In a few instances the narrator relies entirely on imagery to convey the temporal notion and refrains from explanatory remarks and direct references to time. For example, one symbolic tableau reveals a particular conception of time through the accumulation of metaphors describing old people in the realm of the dead. This descriptive exaggeration turns the salon into a graveyard by replacing the "actual" setting with descriptive details from the new domain. The social gathering of the Guermantes turns into the dance of the dead, as the narrator focuses on physical debility and describes it in terms of the death code:

> Certains hommes boitaient: on sentait bien que ce n'était pas par suite d'un accident de voiture, mais à cause d'une première attaque et parce qu'ils avaient déjà, comme on dit, un pied dans la tombe. Dans l'entrebâillement de la leur, à demi paralysées, certaines femmes semblaient ne pas pouvoir retirer complètement leur robe restée accrochée à la pierre du caveau, et elles ne pouvaient se redres-

---

[43] The increasingly discursive nature of the imagery may be illustrated by focusing on the portrayal of the same character: d'Argencourt, whose old age was first hinted at by presenting him as "disguised" (III, 922-23), and who was then more explicitly likened to a "poupée" (924) is finally presented as "la révélation du Temps" (924), an analogy that clearly sets him up as an allegorical figure representing Time. This method of characterization deprives the characters of their individual traits and invests them with a general truth, thereby turning them into symbols.

ser, infléchies qu'elles étaient, la tête basse, en une courbe qui était comme celle qu'elles occupaient actuellement entre la vie et la mort, avant la chute dernière. Rien ne pouvait lutter contre le mouvement de cette parabole qui les emportait et, dès qu'elles voulaient se lever, elles tremblaient et leurs doigts ne pouvaient rien retenir. (III, 938)

As in other symbolic portrayals previously analyzed, the description begins with the mention of actual physical traits, in this case men limping and women stooping. The special focus given these selected traits through the hyperboles of the descriptive tableau points to their symbolic significance. The transposition from the literal to the metaphoric is signaled by *comme on dit*. The stereotype expression *un pied dans la tombe* introduces the new code, which at once becomes autonomous since the figurative expression is applied literally to the subsequent physical description. The cause-and-effect explanatory structure of the initial sentence (*à cause de, parce que*) supplies the key for the symbolic significance of the metaphorical transposition, since the physical trait of limping is given as the cause of poor health, which, in turn, is explained through the proximity to death conveyed through the cliché *un pied dans la tombe*. The stereotype is here restored to its full vigor within a descriptive context insisting on the material presence of the "tomb." This sudden, drastic change in milieu from salon to graveyard, striking enough in itself, is further emphasized by mixing metaphoric and literal details, insisting on the disconcerting coexistence within the same image of graveyard fixtures and the physical presence of human beings. Thus the impaired mobility and stooping posture of women is visually "explained" as a dress caught in a tombstone. The possible "optical illusion" on the observer's part is hinted at by the inclusion of *semblaient*.

The sudden comparison of physical "curvature" to an abstract concept at once points to the symbolic content of the entire setting. This intrusion of the abstract into the physical adds an obvious explanatory structure, which reveals the second level of reference to be inferred from the imagery. Thus the double semantic reference brought out by the relative clause modifying *courbe* ("une courbe qui était comme celle qu'elles occupaient actuellement entre la vie et la mort") justifies the tomb imagery whose archetypal association with death is, of course, already evident to the reader from the imagery itself. In the light of the literal and figurative meaning to be attributed to *courbe, parabole,* which extends the same image to the following sentence, is read on two levels.

The symbolic mode of narration has become entirely autonomous, when the following paragraph continues to convey extreme old age through descriptive hyperboles from the realm of death. This extension of the death code describing the physiognomy of the old in terms of the dying further insists on the symbolic significance of the "Matinée Guermantes": "Certaines figures sous la cagoule de leurs cheveux blancs avaient déjà la rigidité, les paupières scellées de ceux qui vont mourir, et leur lèvres, agitées d'un tremblement perpétuel, semblaient marmonner la prière des agonisants" (III, 938). Both of these exaggerated metaphorical descriptions work together to convey the symbolic content underlying the entire setting of the "Matinée Guermantes." Their exaggerated nature commands our attention, whereas their strong visual impact draws us into the optical illusion experienced by the hero. We thus actually "picture" the allegorical tableau and perceive extreme old age, rather than merely being told that the Guermantes gathering begins to symbolize the workings of time.[44]

The most extensive tableau portraying the novel's characters as allegorical figures symbolic of an aspect of time is found on the last three pages of the novel. As in the previous passages, the narrator finds the expressive vehicle for his temporal notion in the

---

[44] The earliest passage of *A la recherche* portraying characters as symbolic figures occurs in I, 427 where the old age of women is set in relief through the descriptive transposition from the Bois de Boulogne to "bosquets virgiliens." The abrupt transition to the mythological code underlines the observer's feeling of estrangement when first confronted with the physical phenomenon of unexpected old age. The descriptive exaggeration of the metaphorical transposition communicates this bewilderment to the reader by allowing him to feel the shock through the abrupt change of scenery. See *supra*, p. 53 for a discussion of this passage.

In a subsequent passage, which also precedes the symbolic portrayals of *Le Temps retrouvé,* the hero's grandmother becomes symbolic of an aspect of time. The narrator conveys this newly discovered truth by describing the grandmother from the viewpoint of the detached observer: we thus see her for the first time as an old woman. The symbolic content of this realistic, objective portrayal is explicitly pointed to when the narrator explains this new viewpoint: the hero's absence from home has turned the living-room into "un nouveau monde, celui du temps, celui où vivent les étrangers dont on dit 'il vieillit bien'..." (II, 141). The apposition's direct reference to "time" immediately clarifies the metaphor based on perception, *nouveau monde.*

actual physical milieu surrounding him, the guests at the "Matinée Guermantes." In this instance, the context of the symbolic tableau is extremely discursive, since explanatory remarks and didactic illustrations and analogies are interpolated into the metaphorical passages.

The narrator explicitly announces that the characters' portrayal is to be invested with a temporal dimension: "du moins ne manquerais-je pas d'y décrire l'homme comme ayant la longueur non de son corps mais de ses années, comme devant, tâche de plus en plus énorme et qui finit par le vaincre, les traîner avec lui quand il se déplace" (III, 1046). The concrete aspect of *longueur des années,* already brought out through the close syntactical link of the syllepsis joining *années* and *corps* to the same term *longueur,* is further insisted upon by the extension of the metaphorical code through *traîner.*

The following paragraph continues the discursive approach by recalling the spatial manifestation of time: "nous occupons une place sans cesse accrue dans le Temps," and "le plus simple la mesure." The narrator's insistence on clarifying the symbolic implications of the spatial code becomes didactic when he reinforces the remark "le plus simple la mesure" with an explanatory comparison: "comme il mesurerait celle que nous occupons dans l'espace." This explanatory structure is in turn reinforced by a particular illustration of man's ability to "measure" time (III, 1046).

The measurable aspect of time as revealed through human physical appearance is further insisted upon when the narrator focuses on the "Matinée Guermantes" and turns the guests into symbolic figures. This descriptive tableau extends over the novel's last two paragraphs. A series of continued metaphors portrays men as sitting on top of their years, an image that is reinforced in its concrete visual aspect when years are described in terms of "stilts." The original metaphorical transposition is direct, since the narrator does not explain which particular aspect of the "length of time lived" is responsible for the peculiar image:

> J'éprouvais un sentiment de fatigue et d'effroi à sentir que tout ce temps si long non seulement avait, sans une interruption, été vécu, pensé, sécrété par moi, qu'il était ma vie, qu'il était moi-même, mais encore que j'avais à toute minute à le maintenir attaché à moi, qu'il me sup-

portait, moi, juché à son sommet vertigineux, que je ne pouvais me mouvoir sans le déplacer. (III, 1047)

Mais encore points to the additional aspect to be conveyed, and initiates the "materialization" of the abstract. That time is suddenly to be conceived as concrete substance is conveyed through the syntactical ties between time and the verbs *attacher, supporter* and *déplacer. Sommet vertigineux* particularizes the process of materialization, while the aspect of precariousness suggested by this image is insisted upon by the repetition of *vertige* in the following imaginal extension: "J'avais le vertige de voir au-dessous de moi, en moi pourtant, comme si j'avais des lieues de hauteur, tant d'années" (1047). The prepositional phrase *au-dessous de moi* alluding to space, and *lieues de hauteur* extend the previous image, in particular the notion of height initially introduced through *sommet*, and underlined through the repeated mention of vertigo. The hesitant introduction of this image through *comme si* ("comme si j'avais des lieues de hauteur") presents the transposition as an illusion and throws its audacity into relief.

The metaphors of the final paragraph reinforce the image based on physical height. By applying it to a specific character, the Duc de Guermantes, it comes as more of a shock, since it is unexpected within the physical description portraying one of the novel's familiar characters. The exclusive focus on a particular physical aspect, the Duke's shaky legs, further emphasized through the ironic comparison to the unsteady gait of old archbishops — an analogy whose comical image underlines the physical handicap — suggests that the extended image to men "perched on top of their years" may be a descriptive hyperbole symbolic of physical instability. The precision of the image to stilts emphasizes the precarious and helpless situation to which physical debility has reduced aging characters:

> Je venais de comprendre pourquoi le duc de Guermantes, dont j'avais admiré, en le regardant assis sur une chaise, combien il avait peu vieilli bien qu'il eût tellement plus d'années que moi au-dessous de lui, dès qu'il s'était levé et avait voulu se tenir debout, avait vacillé sur des jambes flageolantes comme celles de ces vieux archevêques sur lesquels il n'y a de solide que leur croix métallique et vers lesquels s'empressent des jeunes séminaristes gaillards, et ne s'était avancé qu'en tremblant comme une feuille,

> sur le sommet peu praticable de quatre-vingt-trois années, comme si les hommes étaient juchés sur de vivantes échasses, grandissant sans cesse, parfois plus hautes que des clochers, finissant par leur rendre la marche difficile et périlleuse, et d'où tout d'un coup ils tombaient. (III, 1047-1048)

The metaphorical phrases referring back to the spatial domain are syntactically linked to the temporal code: *au-dessous de lui* is directly juxtaposed to the verbal sequence of the tenor, years ("bien qu'il eût plus d'années que moi au-dessous de lui"), whereas the image "sur le sommet peu praticable" is explicitly attributed to time through the modifying phrase *de quatre-vingt-trois années.* The final image "comme si les hommes étaient juchés sur de vivantes échasses, grandissant sans cesse" is introduced more hesitantly through *comme si,* setting up the shift in focus from actual description to conceptual analogy.

Echasses particularizes the image of "men perched on top of their years," and supplies the reader with a concrete conceptual model for the temporal notion. While the emphasis on physical height is further thrown in relief by the hyperbolic comparison to towers, the two participial phrases modifying *échasses* reveal the conceptual relationship between height and physical ability: thus "grandissant sans cesse" is linked to "finissant par leur rendre la marche difficile et périlleuse" through the verb *finir par,* which introduces a causal relationship. While these modifying phrases extend and insist on the concrete representation of the temporal notion, the chronological progression stressed by the present progressive tense and the causal sequence of the verbs reinforce the reader's awareness of the temporal implications: he is thus conscious of the double level of reference, the physical representation of men on growing stilts and the symbolic implications of men's increasing age and physical debility. We are now aware that the fall from the stilts coincides with the death of man.

Besides translating the temporal notion into concrete terms, the analogy to men on stilts raises the Duke's particular debility to a universal plight. The emphasis on just one physical trait, and the exaggerated analogies to his physical state, all point to a more than literal significance. This descriptive selection and emphasis turn the Duke into a symbolic figure, since he stands for more than himself.

METAPHORICAL EXTENSIONS 159

The universal implications of the metaphor of men on stilts are insisted upon when the narrator applies the same image to himself: "Je m'effrayais que les miennes fussent déjà si hautes sous mes pas, il ne me semblait pas que j'aurais encore la force de maintenir longtemps attaché à moi ce passé qui descendait déjà si loin" (III, 1048). The juxtaposition within the same passage of the vehicle (*miennes* and its verbal sequence refer us back to *échasses*) and tenor ("ce passé qui descendait déjà si loin") reminds the reader of the temporal aspect that originally occasioned the metaphorical transposition.

The symbolic implications of the "Matinée Guermantes" are discursively taken up when the narrator reveals how the recently discovered truth about time may be conveyed by the novelist:

> Du moins, si elle [la force] m'était laissée assez longtemps pour accomplir mon œuvre, ne manquerais-je pas d'abord d'y décrire les hommes (cela dût-il les faire ressembler à des êtres monstrueux) comme occupant une place si considérable, à côté de celle si restreinte qui leur est réservée dans l'espace, une place au contraire prolongée sans mesure — puisqu'ils touchent simultanément, comme des géants plongés dans les années, à des époques si distantes, entre lesquelles tant de jours sont venus se placer — dans le Temps. (III, 1048)

The narrator's tendency to specify an abstract temporal notion through a concrete image is again obvious when he particularizes the vague metaphor *place dans le Temps* with a brief simile: "puisqu'ils touchent simultanément, comme des géants plongés dans les années, à des époques si distantes, entre lesquelles tant de jours sont venus se placer." The analogy to giants introduces an additional image that helps us conceptualize the temporal notion in spatial terms. Within its immediate context, the simile supplies a concrete analogy to the concept of the uninterrupted accumulation of years: the "simultaneous contact with distant epochs" is thus illustrated through the image of giants. Within the larger context of the "Matinée Guermantes" the analogy to giants expands and recalls the previous continued metaphors translating years into physical height.

The simile to giants stands out within the context, since it is part of a temporal observation set off from the surrounding text by the hyphen. This obvious textual demarcation calls our attention to the disjunctive statement. The novel thus closes with a memorable image recalling the particular temporal notion developed over the last few pages.

The considerable extension and recurrence of the same image domain through similes and metaphors, and the added emphasis through explanatory literal remarks reveal the significance Proust attaches to the temporal dimension of man's existence.[45]

D. Symbolic Implications of an "Actual" Scene or Event

An explicit way of introducing a temporal notion into the description of a scene or event constituting part of the novel's plot is the direct mention of "time." When time is presented as an active force working upon the "actual" scene, the symbolic implications are evident. This obvious approach is used in two different passages describing church architecture. In the first, the narrator depicts the interior of the church of Combray in such a way as to make the time symbolism unmistakable: direct time references are preceded and followed by an accumulation of descriptive details all focusing on the worn or ancient aspect of the masonry, tombstones, stained-glass windows and tapestries.[46] Then follows a discursive statement explaining the temporal implications of the description.

The reader begins to suspect that more than a matter-of-fact description is at hand when the emphasis on the worn aspect of the stones is thrown into relief through metaphors and similes. For example, the old portico is described as "grêlé comme une écumoire . . . dévié et profondément creusé aux angles" (I, 59). The temporal notion underlying this imagery is then pointed to by a

---

[45] The extended imagery of the novel's final pages belongs to the more complex structures of metaphors and similes working together to convey an aspect of time. This category will be discussed in some detail in Chapter VII of this study.

[46] See *Chroniques*, pp. 114-122 for the same description of the interior of the church of Combray, reprinted from *Le Figaro*, 3 September, 1912. Though this version differs in many respects from the novel's, the passages conveying the temporal aspect of the church are almost exactly alike (cf. *Chroniques*, pp. 116-118).

brief reference to the church's old age ("pendant des siècles"), and the explicit revelation of time as the destructive agent of the tombstones:

> Ses pierres tombales, sous lesquelles la noble poussière des abbés de Combray, enterrés là, faisait au chœur comme un pavage spirituel, n'étaient plus elles-mêmes de la matière inerte et dure, car le temps les avait rendues douces et fait couler comme du miel hors des limites de leur propre équarrissure qu'ici elles avaient dépassées d'un flot blond, entraînant à la dérive une majuscule gothique en fleurs, noyant les violettes blanches du marbre.... (I, 59)

The liquefaction introduced into the description emphasizes time's destructive activity. By extending the code, the continued metaphors supply the reader with enough descriptive detail to allow him to participate in the visual impression, while the interpolated simile *comme du miel* reinforces the metaphorical transposition by introducing a specific image.[47] Introduced at the start of the imagery, the simile guides the reader's response to the domain of liquefaction: besides particularizing the action of *couler,* the analogy to honey prepares the visual image *flot blond.* The descriptive emphasis on the worn aspect of the tombstones, and the explicit references to time make the entire setting symbolic of the manifestation of time within the material realm.

Additional descriptive details focusing our attention on the stained-glass windows and tapestries serve the same symbolic function. Direct temporal references within this description again point to a second level of reference. For example, we are made aware of the antiquity of the windows when the narrator writes that "tous étaient si anciens qu'on voyait çà et là leur vieillesse argentée étinceler de la poussière des siècles et montrer brillante et usée jusqu'à

---

[47] A similar passage describing the worn aspect of church architecture within a context explicitly revealing "time" as the destructive agent is found in III, 646. The narrator describes the arcades of the Venice Baptistry as "soft matter": "le temps a légèrement infléchi les surfaces évasées et roses, ce qui donne à l'église, là où il a respecté la fraîcheur de ce coloris, l'air d'être construite dans une matière douce et malléable comme la cire de géantes alvéoles...." As in the above example, the description of worn stones — here introduced by an imaginal structure close to simile, namely, *avoir l'air de* — is further exaggerated through the additional analogy introduced by the simile "comme la cire de géantes alvéoles."

la corde la trame de leur douce tapisserie de verre" (I, 60). Whereas "tous étaient si anciens" explicitly states the temporal aspect, the metaphorical description "on voyait... leur vieillesse argentée étinceler de la poussière des siècles" combines the visual impression and its symbolic implications in one image: *vieillesse* and *siècles* reveal Time as responsible for the visual impression of *argentée* and *poussière*. While the century-old "dust" may be responsible for the "silvery" sheen — *argentée* would then be a transferred adjective — *vieillesse argentée* could also be interpreted as a transformation of *vieillard aux cheveux d'argent,* translating the metonymic relationship between old age and grey hair. The following emphasis on the worn aspect of the stained-glass windows through the tapestry metaphors ("brillante et usée jusqu'à la corde la trame de leur douce tapisserie de verre") further insists on the antiquity of the setting, for the notion of wear and tear is universally associated in our minds with the passage of time. What is striking in this image is the narrator's insistence on the destructive aspect of time within a monumental context, which usually serves to convey the notion of survival within time.

The century-old survival of the church, though impaired, is recalled through further emphasis on the worn aspect of the interior and its furnishings. In the following description of the threadbare tapestry the destructive work of time is again made vivid through the extended metaphors of liquefaction: "leurs couleurs, en fondant, avaient ajouté une expression, un relief, un éclairage: un peu de rose flottait aux lèvres d'Esther au delà du dessin de leur contour" (I, 61). The temporal aspect is enhanced when the narrator mentions that the donors of the precious objects within the church are all historical figures, so far removed in time from the observer, that he can only conceive them as "personnages de légende" (I, 61).

The description becomes discursive when the temporal aspect, which up to now has been suggested by the imagery and a few remarks, is directly explained: "tout cela faisait d'elle [l'église] pour moi quelque chose d'entièrement différent du reste de la ville: un édifice occupant, si l'on peut dire, un espace à quatre dimensions — la quatrième étant celle du Temps" (I, 61). The careful, explanatory nature of this theoretical translation of the abstract notion into spatial terms is thrown into relief through the transitional remark "si l'on peut dire" (transitional in the sense that it announces the metaphorical transposition), and the immediate clarification of what the fourth dimension stands for through the direct equation of "dimension" and "time": "la quatrième étant celle du Temps." The theoretical statement, however, is directly followed by images illustrating the space-time relationship.

The imaginal elaboration is by far more extensive and specific than the discursive comment briefly interpolated into the descriptive tableau of the church. This passage illustrates once more the author's preference for concrete imagery to convey an aspect of time, while the interpolated explanation allows him the use of audacious images. The above quotation directly continues with a series of descriptive phrases modifying *édifice*:

> déployant à travers les siècles son vaisseau qui, de travée en travée, de chapelle en chapelle, semblait vaincre et franchir, non pas seulement quelques mètres, mais des époques successives d'où il sortait victorieux; dérobant le rude et farouche XIe siècle dans l'épaisseur de ses murs ... élevant dans le ciel, au-dessus de la Place, sa tour qui avait contemplé saint Louis et semblait le voir encore; et s'enfonçant avec sa crypte dans une nuit mérovingienne.... (I, 61)

That the previous metaphor *dimension* is not merely a semantic conceit translating a temporal notion into spatial terms is revealed by the present descriptive elaboration disclosing the physical presence of time within the material domain of church architecture. Time is thus not, strictly speaking, a fourth and separate dimension, but is part of the existing spatial dimensions. The description conveys this by grammatically linking architectural details and temporal significance. The first textual rapprochement of the space-time relationship consists of a syllepsis: "semblait vaincre et franchir, non pas seulement quelques mètres, mais des époques successives." Whereas *semblait* announces the subjectivity of the image, the syntactical link between *mètres* and *époques* explains the conceptual relationship as a visual one: the abrupt change of architectural styles within a few feet takes the observer through time as well as space, an experience whose simultaneity is reproduced through the common semantic link of *mètres* and *époques* to *vaincre* and *franchir*. The conceptual connection between time and architectural style is further established by subsequent descriptive details, each of which explicitly identifies an architectural trait as belonging to a specific epoch, while the personification of both church (through the animating active verb forms) and time (through the personifying adjectives *rude* and *farouche* modifying *XIe siècle,* and the representation of the thirteenth century through a historical figure, Saint Louis) makes the relationship more emphatic by dramatizing it.

The symbolic implications of another scene become evident through the unexpected juxtaposition of realistic detail and the personification of Death within a familiar setting. Our impression that the description is symbolic of a general truth is reinforced through the repeated use of the impersonal pronoun *on,* and the pronouns *nous* and *vous,* which all generalize the narrative account of a personal experience. The immediate narrative framework is discursive: an explicit sentence introduces the temporal subject ("l'heure de la mort est incertaine"), and a literal explanation follows it. It is left to the narrative technique of the parable, however, to allow the reader to participate in a specific instance of the unpredictable:

> On tient à sa promenade jour avoir dans un mois le total de bon air nécessaire, on a hésité sur le choix d'un manteau à emporter, du cocher à appeler, on est en fiacre, la journée est tout entière devant vous, courte, parce qu'on veut être rentré à temps pour recevoir une amie; on voudrait qu'il fît aussi beau le lendemain; et on ne se doute pas que la mort, qui cheminait en vous dans un autre plan, au milieu d'une impénétrable obscurité, a choisi précisément ce jour-là pour entrer en scène, dans quelques minutes, à peu près à l'instant où la voiture atteindra les Champs-Elysées. (II, 314-315)

The accumulation of realistic details referring to the trivial concerns and projects that constitute an ordinary day allows the reader to enter into this experience of everyday reality. Within this familiar framework, the sudden intrusion of death as a personified abstraction comes as a shock. The narrator underlines this incongruity by specifying the presence of death within the time and space of the actual setting. The increasing temporal precision (*ce jour-là, dans quelques minutes, à peu près à l'instant où*) and the mention of the exact geographic location (*les Champs-Elysées*) convey the unexpected, abrupt nature of the hour of death through narrative suspense. This dramatic emphasis warns the reader that the description of the grandmother's last outing has universal implications: it serves to illustrate the unpredictable hour of death.

The symbolic implications are further insisted upon through the general observation about the reassuring, familiar nature of the hour of death: "elle y revêt une apparence connue, familière, quotidienne." The narrator ends the description by recalling the particular experience that is at the base of this symbolic tale: the grandmother's last outing. The sudden presence of death through the remainder of this trip is strikingly communicated through the grandmother's rapid change in attitude and physical appearance. Whereas she was preoccupied with the choice of dress and coachman at the start of the ride, she no longer deems it important to greet an old friend on the way home: "Moi qui n'étais pas encore détaché de la vie, je demandai à ma grand'mère si elle lui avait répondu, lui rappelant qu'il était susceptible. Ma grand'mère, me trouvant sans doute bien lèger, leva sa main en l'air comme pour dire: 'Qu'est-ce que cela fait? cela n'a aucune importance' " (II, 315). The abrupt change between two states of being through the sudden arrival of death is further insisted upon through the metaphorical conceits *plongée dans ce monde inconnu* (II, 316), *sombrant, glissant à l'abîme* (II, 316), and *la main de l'ange invisible avec lequel elle avait lutté* (II, 316), all appearing within the otherwise realistic description of the grandmother's changed appearance. The reader is thus allowed to witness the unsettling experience with death through the descriptive mimesis of its intrusion within an everyday setting.

In some passages the symbolic significance of an actual scene is to be inferred from the description itself, since the context is entirely devoid of discursive remarks revealing the temporal aspect. The underlying temporal notion may be suggested through the coexistence or accumulation of certain descriptive details, the temporal connotations of certain expressions or the inclusion of an obvious time metaphor.

In a passage describing the evening atmosphere at the Bois de Boulogne, the hero's subjective impression of the setting is revealed through the accumulation of various descriptive details all referring to the temporal aspect:

> au-dessus des peupliers tremblants qui rappellent sans fin les mystères du soir plus qu'ils n'y répondent, un nuage

> rose met une dernière couleur de vie dans le ciel apaisé. Quelques gouttes de pluie tombent sans bruit sur l'eau antique, mais, dans sa divine enfance, restée toujours couleur du temps et qui oublie à tout moment les images des nuages et des fleurs. (II, 385)

The exclusive focus on certain aspects of the scenery indicates that more than an objective description is at hand, and that the narrator is introducing his personal impressions. That these center on a certain temporal notion is first disclosed by the relative clause modifying *peupliers*: *rappellent* and *sans fin,* by attributing a continuous, universal function to the poplar trees, reveal the symbolic significance the hero attaches to them, whereas the genitive link *du soir* directly refers us to the time of day responsible for the impression of "mystery." The temporal aspect is further emphasized through special traits attributed to *eau*: *antique* and *divine enfance,* in stressing the continuous existence and ageless aspect of the water, present it as a symbol of eternity. The mention of *couleur du temps* supplies the reader with a key for the visual impression associated with the evening atmosphere at the Bois de Boulogne (the image reflected by the water forever corresponds to a change in weather and time of day), while *restée toujours* once more emphasizes the perennial aspect of the visual phenomenon. The introduction of the cliché *couleur du temps* reinforces our impression that the passage is written from an ironic point of view, which was already apparent when the symbolic significance of the poplar trees as representing the "mysteries of evening" was undermined by the remark *plus qu'ils n'y répondent*. The relative clause "qui oublie à tout moment les images des nuages et des fleurs" again suggests the eternal, timeless aspect of the water, since it does not attach itself to the temporal and instantaneous of which *nuages* and *fleurs* are representative phenomena.

The symbolic implications of the scene were more obvious in an earlier version of the passage, which included the following descriptive details: "Devant l'embarcadère où la petite flotille de barques attend des dîneurs qui ne viennent point, déjà le soir baigne la même pourpre immémoriale et mystérieuse qu'il ferait dans un port de Bretagne ou d'Extrême-Orient." [48] The personification of

---

[48] *Notes et Variantes,* II, 1160.

soir emphasizes the particular time of day responsible for the subjective impression, while the hour's symbolic implications are disclosed by the abstract modifiers of the dominant visual impression, *pourpre*: *même, immémoriale* and *mystérieuse*. By diverting our attention from the actual setting, the narrator suggests that it stands for more than itself, that it is symbolic within his mental context. The analogy between the evening atmosphere of the Bois and that of the harbors of Brittany or the Far East reveals the more universal implications of the unique visual impression. For the hero it is obviously symbolic of a particular time of day when it can repeatedly be observed.[49]

In another instance, a more-than-literal significance is suggested by the accumulation of certain descriptive details that insist on the withered aspect of lime flowers, and the contrasting descriptive juxtaposition of their former and present appearance. The reader is made aware of the temporal implications when the narrator explicitly attributes their physical appearance to old age: "modifiées, justement parce que c'étaient non des doubles, mais elles-mêmes et... elles avaient vieilli" (I, 52). A subsequent descriptive elaboration further emphasizes this notion by focusing on the physical metamorphosis:

> Et chaque caractère nouveau n'y étant que la métamorphose d'un caractère ancien, dans de petites boules grises je reconnaissais les boutons verts qui ne sont pas venus à terme; mais surtout l'éclat rose, lunaire et doux qui faisait se détacher les fleurs dans la forêt fragile des tiges où elles étaient suspendues comme de petites roses d'or... me montrait que ces pétales étaient bien ceux qui avant de fleurir le sac de pharmacie avaient embaumé les soirs de

---

[49] To convey that the sea at Balbec has become symbolic for him of the eternal and timeless, the narrator repeatedly introduces temporal expressions into the descriptive tableaux depicting this setting. In I, 902 he refers to the sea as "flot *immémorial*," a temporal aspect which is further clarified later on within the same passage by describing the sea as "immémoriale, encore contemporaine des âges où elle avait été séparée de la terre à tout le moins contemporaine des premiers siècles de la Grèce" (902-903).

Cf. II, 1162, footnote to p. 422, where the immemorial aspect of the sea is emphasized through the narrative analogy to mythology. In a much later passage the narrator recalls the same temporal impression associated with the Balbec sea by describing it as "plaintive aïeule de la terre" and by referring to its "immémoriale agitation" (II, 1012).

> printemps. Cette flamme rose de cierge, c'était leur couleur encore, mais à demi éteinte et assoupie dans cette vie diminuée qu'était la leur maintenant et qui est comme le crépuscule des fleurs. (I, 51-52)

The significance of the contrasting juxtaposition of the descriptive details *boules grises* and *boutons verts* is obvious from the preceding mention of metamorphosis. The narrator thus emphasizes the notion by restating it in concrete, visual terms, which have a more striking effect on the reader.

The descriptive focus on the color of the lime flowers through a series of metaphors directs the reader's attention to the key passage of the symbolic tableau. The triple accumulation modifying *éclat* (*éclat rose, lunaire et doux*) introduces the image whose particular visual aspect is reinforced by the subsequent analogy to *roses d'or,* recalling the "rose" and light content of the visual impression. The metaphor *flamme rose de cierge* evokes the rose-colored tint once more and emphasizes its brightness — previously stressed by *éclat lunaire* and *d'or* — through the analogy to fire (*flamme*). The emotional overtones of the contrasting descriptive details emphasizing the change in color — *à demi éteinte et assoupie* — and the revealing comment "dans cette vie diminuée qui était la leur maintenant" provide the reader with a key to the symbolic significance of the preceding imagery. The contrast between the former brilliance and the present dullness of color further emphasizes the phenomenon of physical metamorphosis previously stressed through the juxtaposition of the contrasting images *boules grises* and *boutons verts*. The notion of diminished life and old age is echoed once more in the final image *crépuscule des fleurs*. The context calls on both the concrete and abstract implications of this image: it expands the previous image of "diminished light" with a familiar phenomenon of the decline of light, and it reinforces the pathetic tone introduced by *éteinte* and *vie diminuée* through its abstract implications of decline.[50]

---

[50] The reader who re-examines the text of *A la recherche* may see in this passage a symbolic prefiguration of the human metamorphoses described in *Le Temps retrouvé,* and even earlier, the description of aged women in I, 427, and the aged appearance of Mme de Villeparisis and M. de Norpois in III, 630-631.

E. Symbolic Descriptions of Art

In two instances, the narrator endows descriptions of art with symbolic temporal significance. His examples are taken from drama and painting.

Within the description of the hero's visit to the theatre, the accumulation of descriptive details all referring to the ephemeral nature of dramatic performances alert the reader that the passage signifies more than a narrative account of a particular event:

> j'y sentais germer et s'épanouir pour une heure... ces individualités éphémères et vivaces que sont les personnages d'une pièce, séduisantes aussi, qu'on aime, qu'on admire, qu'on plaint, qu'on voudrait retrouver encore, une fois qu'on a quitté le théâtre, mais qui déjà se sont désagrégées en un comédien qui n'a plus la condition qu'il avait dans la pièce, en un texte qui ne montre plus le visage du comédien, en une poudre colorée qu'efface le mouchoir, qui sont retournées en un mot à des éléments qui n'ont plus rien d'elles, à cause de leur dissolution, consommée sitôt après la fin du spectacle, et qui fait, comme celle d'un être aimé, douter de la réalité du moi et méditer sur la mort.
> (II, 172-173)

Pour une heure and *éphémères* convey the brevity of the experience. The opposition between the hero's wish for permanence (*qu'on voudrait retrouver*) and the concrete images of the play's "decomposition" into separate elements illustrate the conception of the ephemeral.

The descriptive details, the change of tenses and the syntactical structure all emphasize the notion of discontinuity. While the contrasted metaphors of growth (*germer, s'épanouir*) and disintegration (*désagréger*) emphasize the abrupt change of state, the insistence on the ephemeral is further evident from the inclusion and repetition of the adverbial temporal expressions *déjà* and *ne plus*. The rapid change of tenses from the present, to the conditional and past (*admire, plaint, voudrait retrouver, se sont désagrégées*) likewise conveys the ephemeral nature of theatrical performances. The parallel syntactical structure of the triple accumulation modifying *désagrégées* gives this description a significant focus and puts all the emphasis on the aspect of metamorphosis, which is directly communicated through the syntactical juxtaposition of the new state of affairs to the former — recalled in each case by the accompanying relative clause: "qui déjà se sont désagrégées en un comédien qui n'a plus la condition qu'il avait dans la pièce, en un texte qui ne montre plus le visage du comédien, en une poudre colorée qu'efface le mouchoir...."[51]

Proust's tendency to explain his own imagery is apparent when he formulates the idea suggested by the previous tableau and reinforces it with an explanatory remark, introduced by *à cause de*: "qui sont retournées en un mot à des éléments qui n'ont plus rien d'elles, à cause de leur dissolution, consommée sitôt après la fin du spectacle." The expansion of the concept of "dissolution" through the following analogy ("comme celle d'un être aimé") focuses the reader's attention upon the underlying significance that two different experiences have in common. The idea to be inferred from the descriptive tableau becomes obvious when the final clause reveals its symbolic significance for the hero: "et qui fait ... douter de la réalité du moi et méditer sur la mort." This remark makes it certain that the description of the scene at the theatre is metaphoric of life in general. The reader is made aware of the second, more general significance through the joint effect of narrative and stylistic devices: the accumulation and special emphasis of certain descriptive details, the special syntactical disposition of salient elements, the more general content conferred on the passage through the analogy to another experience, and finally the direct translation of the symbolic significance.

Elstir's water colors take on symbolic significance when the narrator concludes his description by focusing on their temporal aspect. The abstract "idea" that this passage retrospectively finds in the description of Elstir's art, and the inclusion of certain terms referring us to literary art, suggest that the paintings and water colors were introduced for illustrative purposes, and that they constitute an artistic analogy symbolic of a general aesthetic truth:

---

[51] For a more detailed discussion of the multiple accumulations (*convergences*) appearing within this passage see Yvette Louria, *La Convergence stylistique chez Proust,* pp. 68-70.

Dans plus d'une autre, l'immense paysage (où la scène mythique, les héros fabuleux tiennent une place minuscule et sont comme perdus) est rendu, des sommets à la mer, avec une exactitude qui donne plus que l'heure, jusqu'à la minute qu'il est, grâce au degré précis du déclin du soleil, à la fidélité fugitive des ombres. Par-là l'artiste donne, en l'instantanéisant, une sorte de réalité historique vécue au symbole de la fable, le peint et le relate au passé défini. (II, 422)

The insistence on the temporal precision of Elstir's drawings through "qui donne plus que l'heure, jusqu'à la minute qu'il est," forces the reader's attention to dwell on the importance of time in Elstir's art.[52] This insistence on the temporal is explained at the end of the descriptive passage: "par là l'artiste donne, en l'instantanéisant, une sorte de réalité historique vécue au symbole de la fable, le peint et le relate au passé défini." The inclusion of the modifying phrase *en l'instantanéisant* recalls the temporal aspect, here set in relief through the rare use of the term. The cautionary expression *une sorte de,* by announcing the impending translation of an aesthetic experience into semantic terms, focuses our attention on the expected revelation *réalité historique vécue*. The main concept is underlined through the insistence on the "real" content of these drawings, as stressed by the adjectives *historique* and *vécue,* and further emphasized by the final phrase, which restates the same notion in another code: "le relate au passé défini" establishes an analogy to the literary art form, thereby introducing more general implications into the context. The more far-reaching significance is likewise suggested when the narrator refers to the mythological subject matter of Elstir's paintings as *symbole de la fable*: *symbole* implies that the artist's subject matter contains a general truth, whereas the literary terms of this statement (*symbole de la fable*; *passé défini*) introduce another art form into the description of the paintings.

---

[52] Cf. II, 421 where the significance of the temporal aspect of Elstir's paintings is explained in great detail. The significance of this aesthetic representation is explicitly revealed when the narrator explains that the temporal dimension teaches the viewer "que le plaisir finit, que la vie passe et que les instants... ne se retrouvent pas."

The earliest mention of the temporal aspect of Elstir's art may be found in I, 902 where the narrator merely describes his impression without explaining it.

The general implications suggested by the vocabulary of this observation are more obvious from an additional passage appearing in another version of the text, where the narrator illustrates the temporal notion through an account of his own experience within the Balbec landscape.[53] By clarifying his concept of the sea's timeless existence through a triple analogy to mythological times, he in fact employs the same artistic device as Elstir to communicate this notion to the reader.[54] This additional passage emphasizes, through direct illustration, what the above quotation already suggested to the reader, namely, that Elstir's art is symbolic of a general aesthetic approach, the use of analogy. The special importance Proust attaches to this aesthetic principle is evident throughout *la Recherche*. Like Elstir, he repeatedly conveys a universal truth about time through the description of a particular instance: for example, he communicates the universal fact that time ages men by focusing on a particular, contemporary setting, the "Matinée Guermantes." By introducing symbolic implications into the "story" of the hero's experiences — the plot of the novel — the narrator gives us the impression of being confronted with a "réalité historique vécue." This technique of conveying ideas allows us a more direct, striking, and memorable contact with a general truth.

---

[53] See II, 1162, footnote to p. 422.

[54] Cf. I, 708 where the narrator conveys the timeless aspect of the sea by introducing a literary analogy, *l'Orestie* of Leconte de Lisle. This analogy introduces a double temporal reference: the sea as presently viewed by the novel's hero looked the same when Leconte de Lisle wrote *l'Orestie*, and at the time of the Greek events described by him within the same setting.

Cf. I, 902-903 where the narrator views the sea as a prehistoric phenomenon, and as "contemporary of the first centuries of Greece."

CHAPTER VII

METAPHORS AND SIMILES IN THE SAME
TEMPORAL CONTEXT

Many of Proust's metaphors connected with the theme of time are accompanied by similes appearing within the same context. These similes range from a brief analogy to one extended into a tableau. In some instances, more than one comparative structure is introduced into the metaphorical context.[1] A simile may be said to play a secondary role when its brief analogy merely reinforces a descriptive detail primarily conveyed through the accompanying metaphors. Many of the similes, however, have the rather important function of either introducing or significantly reinforcing the metaphorical code. Some introduce a separate image, thereby restating the underlying temporal notion through an additional analogy. The joint presence of metaphors and similes connected with the theme of time significantly emphasizes the temporal notion, although the extent of emphasis depends on the type and length of the similes and metaphors in question.

Before beginning the analysis of individual passages, the meaning of "simile" as used within this discussion should be clarified. The term is here applied to a restricted use of the process of comparison. Whereas the term "comparison" has more general implications referring primarily to a thought process drawing an analogy

---

[1] For a categorization of the various comparative structures based on the generating element of the analogy — such as the verb, adjective or adverb — consult Danielle Bouverot's article "Comparaison et métaphore," *Le Français Moderne* (April 1969), pp. 132-147. The author further distinguishes between "qualitative" and "quantitative" comparisons (i.e. the degrees of comparison).

between two things or concepts, the term "simile" designates a comparison between two things belonging to two different domains.[2] Though the similes may or may not be from the same domain as the metaphors they accompany, they must be from a different realm of discourse than the abstract temporal notion they help to convey. For instance, such comparative structures as "ce jour-ci... plus long comme ceux du pôle" (I, 806), and "une nuit aussi courte comme les nuits du pôle" (II, 390) are not similes, as they draw an analogy between two elements from the same domain — yet we are bordering on figurative language, since *nuits du pôle* introduces a hyperbole, the archetypal short night. Grammatically and syntactically we are confronted with a comparative structure, explicitly introduced as such through the comparative links *comme* and *aussi... que*; however, the transfer from one category to another is missing.

A simile is introduced into the text through obvious grammatical links pointing at the analogy drawn between the two elements to be compared, or sometimes, contrasted.[3] It is introduced more explicitly than the metaphor, since such morphemes as *comme, ainsi que, tel que, de même que, aussi... que, plus... que* and *moins... que* announce the process of comparison. In the passages where similes reinforce or extend Proust's metaphors of time, these linking elements call the reader's attention to the mental process of analogy, thereby stressing the fact of semantic transposition.

A number of the similes reinforcing Proust's time metaphors are quite original and introduce a new insight.[4] Despite the explicit

---

[2] I am here in accordance with Joseph T. Shipley's definition of simile as given in his *Dictionary of World Literature* (New York, 1943): "The comparison of two things of different categories (thus 'John is as tall as Henry' is not a simile; but 'John is as tall as a lamppost' is) because of a point or points of resemblance, and because the association emphasizes, clarifies, or in some way enhances the original" (p. 526).

[3] Danielle Bouverot gives an oversimplified definition of "comparison" as "deux signifiants a et b réunis par un mot signalant leur ressemblance" (pp. 133-134).

[4] R. A. Sayce in his *Style in French Prose* designates such similes as "false similes," for he maintains that a true simile must "appeal to the general experience of the reader." He insists on this notion when he suggests that this general aspect constitutes "the essence of simile" (p. 65). It seems, however, that a simile drawn from the author's or hero's private experience is just as acceptable as any other, provided the figure meets the two prerequi-

nature of the comparative link, some of these similes resemble metaphor in the ambiguity of the connection made between tenor and vehicle.[5]

Before analyzing the first category of simile reinforcing metaphor, I shall study a few temporal "comparisons" that do not qualify as similes. The following comparative structures differ from the simile in that they do not introduce a new domain, but draw their analogies from the literal subject under discussion. They anchor the surrounding metaphors in the literal realm of discourse by introducing a second temporal experience stated non-figuratively:

> ces journées oisives et lumineuses qu'on passe sur la plage. Elles sont alors, et par là, bien que désœuvrées, alertes / comme des journées de travail, / aiguillées, aimantées, soulevées légèrement vers un instant prochain. (I, 830)

> nous avons donné à la journée présente une importance exceptionnelle, nous l'avons détachée des journées contiguës; elle flotte sans racines / comme un jour de départ. / (III, 354)

> cette année finale où avait commencé de changer et où s'était terminée la destinée d'Albertine, m'apparaissait remplie, diverse, vaste / comme un siècle. / (III, 484-85)[6]

The comparisons "comme des journées de travail," "comme un jour de départ," and "comme un siècle" all introduce a temporal analogy in literal terms. Within the metaphorical context, however, the abstract literal terms of the comparisons are particularized, since the semantic analogy through *comme* draws them into the metaphorical domain. For instance, the comparison "comme des journées de travail," besides reinforcing the metaphors with a conceptual parallel, transfers all the metaphorical adjectives modifying "jour-

---

sites stated above, the comparative link and the semantic transfer from one domain to another.

[5] For a discussion of the "prosaic" nature of some metaphors as opposed to the "poetic" nature of some similes consult George Whalley, in *The Princeton Encyclopedia of Poetry and Poetics*, p. 767.

[6] "Comme un siècle" reinforces the preceding metaphors through the addition of the hyperbole *siècle*.

Within each quotation, the simile or similes under discussion are set in relief by the slanted line.

nées oisives" onto "journées de travail." The metaphors thus play the double role of characterizing two separate temporal experiences at once. This double participation within the same image domain discloses the conceptual link between the two experiences. The imagery reveals that the narrator's mental connection between two separate experiences is based on a similar sensory response.

The comparisons do not reinforce the image domain of the time metaphors, nor do they aid the metaphors in conveying the abstract notion by introducing a supplementary, concrete analogy. They are literal, since they are from the same domain as the temporal notion to be conveyed. And since they are abstract, they do not play an active role in the imagery connected with the theme of time, but rather they juxtapose a parallel concept that draws on the metaphors' semantic domain.

A. Single Simile Within Metaphorical Passages

1. Simile Enhancing a Single Aspect of Metaphorical Image

Only a few similes are introduced into the metaphorical context merely to enhance a single descriptive detail. Most of them have the more important function of either establishing or particularizing the semantic domain of the metaphors, while others introduce a separate image.

Within the following personifying description of the ruins of the Guermantes château, a single simile modifying the personification emphasizes its symbolic function:

> Ce n'étaient plus que quelques fragments de tours bossuant la prairie ... passé presque descendu dans la terre, couché au bord de l'eau / comme un promeneur qui prend le frais, / mais me donnant fort à songer, me faisant ajouter dans le nom de Combray à la petite ville d'aujourd'hui une cité très différente, retenant mes pensées par son visage incompréhensible et d'autrefois qu'il cachait à demi sous les boutons d'or. (I, 167)

The analogy from the domain of human behavior ("comme un promeneur qui prend le frais") particularizes the descriptive phrase "couché au bord de l'eau" and enhances the process of personification initiated by the preceding metaphors *bossuant* and *descendu*. By endowing the past with human habits and attitudes, the simile paves the way for the audacious personifying metaphors, which are then more readily accepted by the reader: "son visage incompréhensible et d'autrefois qu'il cachait à demi sous les boutons d'or."

When a simile particularizes the action of a metaphorical verb, the analogy likewise modifies the receiver of the action, the verb's direct object:

> Si rares qu'ils devinssent, ces moments-là ne furent pas inutiles. Par le souvenir Swann reliait ces parcelles, abolissait les intervalles, coulait / comme en or / une Odette de bonté et de calme.... (I, 314)

While the metaphors *reliait ces parcelles* and *coulait* translate Swann's subjective and partial perception of Odette's character as observed over the years, the simile *comme en or* introduces an emotional dimension: the image of an Odette cast in gold reveals and emphasizes the subjective nature of Swann's point of view as modified by time. This brief analogy is directly juxtaposed to the metaphorical transposition, and its elliptical nature, by not explicitly stating all components of the analogical relationship, introduces a more direct, less discursive transposition.[7]

In the next two passages the simile accompanying a verbal metaphor serves a purely explanatory purpose. In each case, the terms of the comparison provide the key for the metaphorical expression by repeating the same verb used metaphorically within the time context in a context that explicitly states its spatial connotations:

---

[7] See Sayce, p. 61 where a similar use of *comme,* translating "as it were" rather than "as," is classified as primarily metaphoric, despite the presence of the obvious comparative link *comme*. Other comparative structures, which introduce their analogies through even less obvious semantic links, could be classified either as simile or metaphor. This is particularly true in the case of prepositional phrases drawing an analogy between two domains. See II, 350 where an analogy is introduced through a prepositional comparative structure bordering on metaphor: "Mais si nous sommes seuls, la préoccupation, en ramenant devant nous le moment encore éloigné et sans cesse attendu, / avec la fréquence et l'uniformité d'un tic-tac, / divise ou plutôt multiplie les heures par toutes les minutes qu'entre amis nous n'aurions pas comptées." The analogy, which is introduced through a prepositional phrase specifically modifying and particularizing the action of the verb *ramenant,* is closely integrated into the syntactical structure of the transposition from the literal to the metaphoric.

> Ou encore ne cachaient-ils même pas de pensée et était-ce une fatigue de ma vision qui me les faisait voir doubles dans le temps / comme on voit quelquefois double dans l'espace. / (I, 719)

> D'ailleurs, que nous occupions une place sans cesse accrue dans le Temps, tout le monde le sent... Non seulement tout le monde sent que nous occupons une place dans le Temps, mais cette place, le plus simple la mesure approximativement / comme il mesurerait celle que nous occupons dans l'espace / .... (III, 1046)

By introducing the verb of the metaphorical expression *voir doubles dans le temps* into the spatial domain, the analogy clarifies its meaning and provenance, so that the reader can be quite certain that the familiar stereotype from the realm of visual perception, *voir double,* is to be identified with the temporal experience. By juxtaposing the verb's literal meaning to its metaphoric use, the simile reinforces the metaphor's concrete, sensuous effect. The same holds true for the second example, where the verb *mesurer,* first used metaphorically, is reinforced in its literal implications by being repeated within the spatial context. Both analogies have a discursive and emphatic function: they "explain" the spatial implications of the metaphorical transposition, and they enhance the concrete nature of the image by recalling the literal context of each metaphoric term.

Most similes connected with the theme of time are concrete images giving us an insight into the nature of time. Within the present category of similes reinforcing a certain aspect of the metaphorical transposition, I have found one exception to this general tendency. Here the comparison in no way reinforces the preceding time metaphors, since it takes us from a concrete image to an abstract analogy:

> il se penchait avec une angoisse impuissante, aveugle et vertigineuse vers l'abîme sans fond où étaient allées s'engloutir ces années du début du Septennat pendant lesquelles on passait l'hiver sur la promenade des Anglais, l'été sous les tilleuls de Bade, et il leur trouvait une profondeur douloureuse mais magnifique / comme celle que leur eût prêtée un poète.... / (I, 313)

While the metaphors *abîme sans fond* and *s'engloutir* convey Swann's subjective notion about Odette's unknown past in a concrete, striking image, the following analogy to a poet's conception of such an experience is altogether vague. The simile insists on the abstract connotation of *profondeur* already stressed by the accompanying modifiers *douloureuse* and *magnifique*. *Profondeur* thus does not extend the image domain of the preceding metaphors, though it is related to them semantically through its literal implications.[8]

2. Simile Playing An Essential Role

a. *Brief Simile Specifying the Code of the Metaphorical Transposition*

Most of the similes appearing within a metaphorical context have the important function of introducing or specifying the code of the metaphorical transposition. In the following two passages, the simile introduces the image domain on which the metaphors draw to convey the temporal notion:

> Et à vrai dire, / comme dans ces calendriers que le facteur nous apporte pour avoir ses étrennes, / il n'était pas une de mes années, qui n'eût eu à son frontispice, ou intercalée dans ses jours, l'image d'une femme que j'y avais désirée.... (III, 989)

> / Comme sur un plant où les fleurs mûrissent à des époques différentes, / je les avais vues, en de vieilles dames, sur cette plage de Balbec, ces dures graines, ces mous tubercules, que mes amies seraient un jour. Mais qu'importait? en ce moment, c'était la saison des fleurs. (I, 892)

In both examples, the simile preceding the metaphorical transposition explicitly introduces the domain (*calendrier; plant*) on which the metaphors will draw. These in turn elaborate on the temporal notion by particularizing the image. Thus the metaphor *frontispice* and

---

[8] The term *profondeur* functions as a semantic link between the metaphorical and literal domains, since its material connotation is related to the metaphoric code of "abyss," whereas its figurative meaning is called upon by its abstract modifiers and the simile, which take us back to the literal domain of the actual subject under discussion: Swann's emotional state.

l'image d'une femme specify which particular aspect of calendars is responsible for the analogy between years and calendars. In the second example, the adjectives *dures* and *mous,* in stressing the aspect of dehydration and decay within the domain of plant life, particularize a general truth within a specific image and emphasize the symbolic implications of the analogy between flowers and women previously introduced by the simile. The metaphorical extension of the same image domain through "C'était la saison des fleurs" underlines the aspect of metamorphosis by introducing a contrasting image into the same domain, further emphasizing the manifestation of time within the material realm. The temporal implications of the combined imagery of simile and metaphors are significantly reinforced in this instance through the explicit temporal indications *à des époques différentes, seraient un jour,* and *en ce moment.*

In some instances, a brief simile is introduced at the start of a metaphorical transposition to particularize the code. The metaphors are then reduced to a specific domain, and their implications are far less ambiguous. The narrator's explanatory tendency is apparent in the following passage, since he first states the durational aspect in literal, aphoristic terms, and then illustrates it with a conceptual parallel from the realm of physical experience:

> Et encore, même à ce point de vue de simple quantité, dans notre vie les jours ne sont pas égaux. Pour parcourir les jours, les natures un peu nerveuses, comme était la mienne, disposent, / comme les voitures automobiles, / de "vitesses" différentes. Il y a des jours montueux et malaisés qu'on met un temps infini à gravir et des jours en pente qui se laissent descendre à fond de train en chantant. (I, 390-391)

While the initial metaphor *parcourir* initiates the metaphorical transposition, the simile specifies it and introduces a definite conceptual model into the image domain. As a result the metaphors *vitesses, gravir* and *descendre à fond de train,* which translate the hero's subjective sensibility to duration into the material realm, are all conceived within the vehicular code announced by the simile's analogy to *voitures automobiles.* The metaphorical expressions *jours montueux* and *jours en pente* expand the image by supplying concrete details that insist on the sustained analogy between the abstract notion and the material realm: while the durational aspect of days is translated into topographical terms, *malaisés* and *en chantant* introduce an emotional dimension. Considered together, the initial aphorism, the simile and the extended metaphors have a discursive function: while the general, literal statement announces the temporal subject, the combined imagery of metaphors and simile fulfills the important function of translating the subjective notion into familiar terms from the material realm, allowing the reader to participate in the hero-narrator's interior life.[9]

In the next two passages, the similes participate in the image domain established by the accompanying metaphors. The similes reinforce the metaphors by supplying an important imaginal detail that clarifies the semantic transposition. In the first example, the simile appears within the metaphorical context where it introduces a precise pictorial detail on which the subsequent metaphors elaborate:

> tout le Temps à venir qu'il portait en lui par anticipation et qui, composé de jours homogènes aux jours actuels, circulait transparent et froid en son esprit où il entretenait la tristesse, mais sans lui causer de trop vives souffrances. Mais cet avenir intérieur, ce fleuve incolore et libre, voici qu'une seule parole d'Odette venait l'atteindre jusqu'en Swann et, / comme un morceau de glace, / l'immobilisait, durcissait sa fluidité, le faisait geler tout entier; et Swann s'était senti soudain rempli d'une masse énorme et infran-

---

[9] Further examples of metaphorical contexts particularized by similes may be found in III, 979 and I, 371-372. In the latter passage, the simile illustrates Swann's emotional state by introducing a familiar image of destruction known from historical and artistic sources: the destruction of Niniveh:
> Et sous tous les souvenirs les plus doux de Swann, sous les paroles les plus simples que lui avait dites autrefois Odette... il sentait s'insinuer la présence possible et souterraine de mensonges... faisant circuler partout un peu de la ténébreuse horreur qu'il avait ressentie en entendant l'aveu relatif à la Maison Dorée, et, / comme les bêtes immondes dans la Désolation de Ninive, / ébranlant pierre à pierre tout son passé.

In III, 979 we are confronted with a comparative structure that is not a simile. There the adjectival expression *être semblable à* announces the process of comparison. The analogy introduces a conceptual model into the metaphorical context conveying the symbolization — from the point of view of the hero-narrator — of the Princess of Nassau whose eyes begin to evoke the past: "ses yeux stellaires, / semblables à une horloge astronomique taillée dans une opale, / marquèrent successivement toutes ces heures solennelles du passé si lointain qu'elle retrouvait à tout moment...."

gible qui pesait sur les parois intérieures de son être jusqu'à le faire éclater: c'est qu'Odette lui avait dit, avec un regard souriant et sournois qui l'observait: "Forcheville va faire un beau voyage, à la Pentecôte...." (I, 355-356)

The combined imagery of the metaphors and simile all from the same domain jointly "materialize" Swann's conception of time. Literal references to time accompany the metaphorical transposition, revealing the temporal notion underlying the imagery: the metaphorical apposition to *cet avenir intérieur (ce fleuve incolore et libre)* directly juxtaposes tenor and vehicle, and the relative clause modifying *Temps à venir,* by stressing the notion of homogeneity, announces the key concept to be inferred from the imagery. While the initial metaphorical transposition *circulait transparent et froid,* and the following extension and precision of the code through *fleuve incolore et libre* establish the image domain, the simile and subsequent metaphors, by extending the same domain with a contrasting image, translate the change that has taken place within Swann's concept of future time. The sudden and drastic nature of Swann's conceptual change regarding temporal homogeneity is first communicated through the simile introducing the contrasting image *morceau de glace.* The following metaphors *l'immobilisait, durcissait sa fluidité, le faisait geler tout entier* extend this image by particularizing and elaborating on the process of solidification. By supplying the continued metaphors with a precise image, an obvious antithesis to *fleuve incolore et libre,* the simile *morceau de glace* throws the change of Swann's temporal concept into relief.

The following metaphorical expansion further underlines the aspect of solidification and continues to focus our attention on the emotional consequences of Swann's new awareness: "et Swann s'était senti soudain rempli d'une masse énorme et infrangible qui pesait sur les parois intérieures de son être jusqu'à le faire éclater...." By literally applying the metaphorical image of the solidified mass to Swann's physiological make-up, the author conveys an emotional state in concrete terms: the metaphorical translation of his inner state through *jusqu'à le faire éclater* allows the reader to grasp Swann's emotional suffering through a concrete analogy from the realm of physical experience.

In a passage dealing with man's rapid change of opinions and interests, the temporal notion is first stated in literal, aphoristic terms, and then specified through the combined imagery of metaphors and simile. While the metaphors introduce the concrete image that translates the abstract notion of man's achronological existence within time, the following simile particularizes the image by delegating it to a specific domain, providing the reader with a precise image that allows him to conceptualize the abstract notion:

> Car l'homme est cet être sans âge fixe, cet être qui a la faculté de redevenir en quelques secondes de beaucoup d'années plus jeune, et qui entouré des parois du temps où il a vécu, y flotte, mais / comme dans un bassin dont le niveau changerait constamment et le mettrait à la portée tantôt d'une époque, tantôt d'une autre. / (III, 613-614)

The initial metaphorical expressions *entouré des parois du temps* and *y flotte* introduce the image domain and insist on the temporal content through the genitive link *du temps* and the qualifying phrase *où il a vécu*. The simile particularizes the metaphors by introducing a precise image: *bassin,* further modified through "dont le niveau changerait constamment," serves as a conceptual model for the temporal notion, and clarifies the metaphor *parois*. The underlying temporal content of the image is again stressed through a second genitive modifier linking the verbal sequence of the tenor to that of the vehicle: "à la portée tantôt d'une époque, tantôt d'une autre."

b. *Simile Extending to a Descriptive Tableau*

Similes play a principal part within a metaphorical context when they illustrate the temporal notion with an analogy extending to a tableau, as in the first example:

> dans la rangée des jours qui s'étendait devant moi, les jours saints se détachaient plus clairs au bout des jours mitoyens. Touchés d'un rayon / comme certaines maisons d'un village qu'on aperçoit au loin dans un effet d'ombre et de lumière, / ils retenaient sur eux tout le soleil. (II, 143)

Metaphors and simile are both responsible for translating the hero's subjective distinction between holy days and ordinary days into visual terms. The initial metaphor *rangée des jours,* reinforced by the verbs *s'étendait* and *se détachaient plus clairs,* introduces the image, whereas *des jours, jours saints* and *jours mitoyens* refer us to the temporal content. *Mitoyens* emphasizes the spatial character of *rangée,* particularly since this legal term is unexpected within a temporal context, where its effect is mainly humorous. The metaphorical attribute *touchés d'un rayon* stresses the visual translation of *jours saints.* The visual image is strikingly enhanced through the simile, interpolated between *touchés d'un rayon* and the following metaphorical extension of the same image ("retenaient sur eux tout le soleil"). The analogy between houses and holy days plays a major role within this passage. It determines our conception of the metaphorical image by particularizing it, and it impresses upon us the hero's sharp distinction between holy days and ordinary days. The analogy to the realm of sensory experience — in this instance, the visual contrast between light and dark — which refers us to a more objective, universally shared experience, serves as a key to the subjective realm of abstract concepts.

In the next two passages, a simile introducing an analogy that is extended into a tableau is solely responsible for transcribing the temporal notion into concrete terms. In the first example, the hero's awareness of the distinct difference between two contiguous emotional states is first expressed through the ambivalent metaphorical image *zone,* whereas the simile introduces a precise image, translating the concept of distinct difference into visual terms:

> La zone de tristesse où je venais d'entrer était aussi distincte de la zone où je m'élançais avec joie, il y avait un moment encore, / que dans certains ciels une bande rose est séparée comme par une ligne d'une bande verte ou d'une bande noire. On voit un oiseau voler dans le rose, il va en atteindre la fin, il touche presque au noir, puis il y est entré. / (I, 183)

Zone de tristesse où je venais d'entrer and *zone où je m'élançais avec joie* initiate the metaphorical process without, however, particularizing the image, since the metaphor *zone* is rich in connotations. The close syntactical ties between the metaphor and the verbal sequence of the tenor through the prepositional qualifying phrases *de tristesse* and *avec joie* give the reader the key to the transposition. The simile specifies the meaning of *zone* by introducing a distinct image.

The comparative link *aussi... que,* which structures the analogy around a particular part of speech — the adjective *distincte* — focuses our attention on the notion of difference between the two "zones" in question. The concept of sharp difference is further emphasized through the additional analogy *comme par une ligne,* and the extension of the tableau through the image of the flying bird. The sudden animation of the scene, repeatedly stressed through the verbs of movement, dramatizes step by step the subjective inner experience of contrasting emotional states that abruptly succeed each other.[10] The visual contrast between rose and black, and the bird's motion from one color to the other is another example of Proust's tendency to translate an inner experience into striking images.[11]

In the second passage, a simile again plays a major role in conveying the temporal notion. The analogy reinforces the descriptive context, which focuses our attention on the conceptual relationship between a specific time span and a definite sensory impression. It stresses the mental association between the sensorial impression and the specific time and place — the noon hour in the hotel room at Balbec:

> Midi sonnait, enfin arrivait Françoise. Et pendant des mois de suite, dans ce Balbec que j'avais tant désiré parce que je ne l'imaginais que battu par la tempête et perdu dans les brumes, le beau temps avait été si éclatant et si fixe

---

[10] Further on within the same passage the suddenness and regularity of this emotional change as based on the hero's subjective associations within a certain experience is conveyed through an analogy from physical experience. In this instance, the analogy is introduced by means of a prepositional qualifying phrase reinforcing a verbal metaphor: "j'ai appris à distinguer ces états qui se succèdent en moi, pendant certaines périodes, et vont jusqu'à se partager chaque journée, l'un revenant chasser l'autre, avec la ponctualité de la fièvre" (I, 183).

[11] The same notion is again translated into a visual image through another simile, structurally and functionally quite similar to the one in the above-quoted passage: "Certes, à Combray déjà j'avais vu diminuer ou grandir selon les heures, selon que j'entrais dans l'un ou l'autre des deux grands modes qui se partageaient ma sensibilité, le chagrin de n'être pas près de ma mère, aussi imperceptible, tout l'après-midi, que la lumière de la lune tant que brille le soleil..." (I, 857). As in the previous example, the analogy, which is explicitly introduced by *aussi... que,* and structured around the attribute *imperceptible,* concentrates on the principal concept.

que, quand elle venait ouvrir la fenêtre, j'avais pu toujours, sans être trompé, m'attendre à trouver le même pan de soleil plié à l'angle du mur extérieur, et d'une couleur immuable qui était moins émouvante comme un signe de l'été qu'elle n'était morne comme celle d'un émail inerte et factice. Et tandis que Françoise ôtait les épingles des impostes, détachait les étoffes, tirait les rideaux, le jour d'été qu'elle découvrait / semblait aussi mort, aussi immémorial qu'une somptueuse et millénaire momie que notre vieille servante n'eût fait que précautionneusement désemmailloter de tous ses linges, avant de la faire apparaître, embaumée dans sa robe d'or. / (I, 954-955)

The descriptive elaboration of the visual impression, in particular the insistence on its ever-present, unvaried nature through *le même pan de soleil* and *une couleur immuable,* and the introduction of the affective descriptive analogy *morne comme celle d'un émail* allows the reader an insight into the hero's sensibility and provides him with a key for the highly personal analogy that translates this impression into another domain.

The hesitant introduction of the metaphorical transposition and the attendant simile through *semblait* announces the subjective nature of the imagery. The attributes *mort* and *immémorial* emphasize hyperbolically the unchangeable and timeless aspect of the summer day, and the analogy drawn between *jour* and *momie* translates this notion into an archetypal symbol of eternal preservation. The extension of the symbolic image into a tableau — in which the summer day is personified by the details of costume — enhances the analogy's expressiveness. The narrator's consciousness of the subjective nature of the impression is once more conveyed through the conditional mood of the verb *eût fait,* which refers us to the realm of supposition and illusion. Through the introduction of a precise image symbolic of duration, the simile plays a major role in conveying the temporal notion associated with the Balbec setting.

c. *Simile Introducing a Separate Image*

Although most of the similes that cooperate with Proust's time metaphors share the same code as their adjacent metaphors, in two exceptional instances a simile introduces an image drawn from a different domain, although they complement each other in translating the same temporal notion.

Within the following passage describing the hero's sudden discovery of Balbec's historical past, the new insight is first stated literally and then emphasized through two images, each depicting a scene symbolic of temporality. The simile in this instance reinforces the metaphorical image suggesting the passage of time by an image drawn from nature. The notion to be derived from these complementary images is obvious from the preceding context. Swann's remark regarding the church of Balbec, in particular its mixture of Romanesque and Gothic architecture, is directly responsible for the hero's revised conception of Balbec: [12]

> Et ces lieux qui jusque-là ne m'avaient semblé être que de la nature immémoriale, restée contemporaine des grands phénomènes géologiques — et tout aussi en dehors de l'histoire humaine que l'Océan ou la Grande Ourse, avec ces sauvages pêcheurs pour qui, pas plus que pour les baleines, il n'y eut de moyen âge — ç'avait été un grand charme pour moi de les voir tout d'un coup entrés dans la série des siècles, ayant connu l'époque romane, et de savoir que le trèfle gothique était venu nervurer aussi ces rochers sauvages à l'heure voulue, / comme ces plantes frêles mais vivaces qui, quand c'est le printemps, étoilent çà et là la neige des pôles. / (I, 385)

The narrator reveals his first impression of Balbec as outside human history through the explicit temporal reference in *nature immémoriale,* the adjectival qualifying phrase relegating Balbec to the times of the *grands phénomènes géologiques,* and the analogy between Balbec, the "Ocean," and the "Big Dipper" as phenomena of prehuman existence — an aspect further set in relief through the following dehumanizing analogy between whales and fishermen.

The metaphor *entrés dans la série des siècles* introduces the second notion, stressing the main concept of temporal subjugation. The additional temporal indication *époque romane,* and the image *trèfle gothique,* both recall the particular temporal manifestation within the Balbec landscape, its "Romanesque-Gothic" church.

---

[12] Swann's remark, which immediately precedes the above quotation, is as follows: "L'église de Balbec, du XIIe et XIIIe siècle, encore à moitié romane, est peut-être le plus curieux échantillon du gothique normand, et si singulière!" (I, 384-385).

The image "le trèfle gothique était venu nervurer aussi ces rochers sauvages" — a descriptive metonymy of the introduction of Gothic architecture into the natural setting of Balbec — conveys the notion through a representative, pictorial detail symbolizing its two principal aspects: whereas *trèfle gothique* directly refers us to the church of Balbec as symbolic of the temporal manifestation, *rochers sauvages* recalls the second principal aspect closely associated with Balbec, its wild, uncultivated nature suggestive of prehuman existence.

The analogy to polar vegetation introduced by the simile ("comme ces plantes frêles mais vivaces qui, quand c'est le printemps, étoilent ça et là la neige des pôles") juxtaposes a second image whose visual content, like that of the previous metaphorical image, is symbolic of temporal subjugation: the punctual reappearance of the spring flowers, short lived (*frêles*) but recurring (*vivaces*), adds an element of seasonal subjugation to a polar region otherwise unmarked by time. By introducing a visual analogy from another domain, the simile reinforces the temporal notion with an additional concrete illustration, whereas the imaginal expansion further enhances it. Besides their complementary conceptual function in concretizing an abstract concept, the two images aesthetically harmonize with each other: the star-like polar florescence evoked through *étoiler* recalls the architectural "florescence" of the Gothic trefoil.[13]

3. BORDERLINE CASES BETWEEN SIMILE AND METAPHOR

a. *Être comme*

A few similes introduced through the comparative structure *être comme* are close to the process of implicit identification as found in metaphor. An analysis of the function of *être comme* within a number of passages reveals that the presence of this apparently

---

[13] A second passage where a simile introduces a suggestive image from another domain appears in III, 973: "Une simple relation mondaine, même un objet matériel, si je le retrouvais au bout de quelques années dans mon souvenir, je voyais que la vie n'avait pas cessé de tisser autour de lui des fils différents qui finissaient par le feutrer de ce beau velours inimitable des années, / pareil à celui qui dans les vieux parcs enveloppe une simple conduite d'eau d'un fourreau d'émeraude." /

explicit comparative link does not present us with a more explicit analogy between the two domains. In these passages, the analogy is not drawn between a particular characteristic shared by two domains — as is the case, for instance, when *être comme* is structured around an adjective: *il est fort comme un lion* — but rather relates the two domains in their entirety.[14] In the passages in question *être comme* comes close to translating "something like," and seems to convey the narrator's hesitancy in equating the two domains. The cautionary transitional link *être comme* alerts the reader to the semantic shift and conceptual identification.

In the following example, *être comme* does not draw an explicit analogy based on an element of similarity between two domains, but rather juxtaposes a specific sensory impression and a concrete image translating the temporal concept derived from the sensory stimulus. The analogy through *être comme,* here meaning "something like," attenuates the identification between sensory impression and the image illustrating the conceptual associations called forth by this impression. The hesitant note conveys the mystery and difficulty involved in communicating an abstract notion. The surrounding context, however, is more direct and explicit in revealing the connection between sensory impression and mental interpretation: we are told that the scent of wood fire at once evokes different settings within the hero's consciousness: Combray and Doncières are thus

---

[14] See Danielle Bouverot's article "Comparaison et métaphore" for an analysis of the various comparative structures designated as "comparaisons voilées." This category includes verbs and adjectives whose semantic implications set up an analogy based on appearance as opposed to reality, or presented as approximate or subjective. They confront us with a limited type of analogy, in other words, with an attenuated identification of *a* and *b* (pp. 144-147). The verbal list includes *on dirait, faire l'effet de, sembler, avoir l'air de, paraître,* whereas the adjectival expressions are *être pareil à, être semblable à, être comparable* and *tel.* Although Miss Bouverot does not specifically mention *être comme* in this category, the use of *être comme* without an attendant attribute does not set up a distinct analogy between two domains. Instead it functions like the veiled structures *être pareil à, être semblable à,* and *être comparable à. Être comme* fits into the schema given for this type of structure, namely "*a* + mot outil + *b*," i.e. *a* is like *b* where the adjectival or verbal expression fulfills the function of the "tool word" (p. 146). Miss Bouverot, however, makes a distinction between *être comme* and the "veiled comparaisons" in a sequel to this article where she claims that analogies structured around *être comme* seem to be halfway between the regular comparison and the above mentioned "veiled structures" (*Le Français Moderne* [October 1969], p. 306).

recalled in the midst of Paris. The hero's subjective impression of this unchronological experience constitutes the temporal subject conveyed through the imagery. While the temporal implications are stated literally through *différence d'âge* and *substitution de personne,* the analogy introduced through *être comme* is solely responsible for conveying the abstract notion in concrete terms:

> soudain ils [souvenirs] refaisaient de moi, de moi tout entier, par la vertu d'une sensation identique, l'enfant, l'adolescent qui les avait vus. Il n'y avait pas eu seulement changement de temps dehors, ou dans la chambre modification d'odeurs, mais en moi différence d'âge, substitution de personne. L'odeur dans l'air glacé des brindilles de bois, / c'était comme un morceau du passé, une banquise invisible détachée d'un hiver ancien qui s'avançait dans ma chambre / souvent striée d'ailleurs par tel parfum, telle lueur, comme par des années différentes où je me retrouvais replongé, envahi, avant même que je les eusse identifiées, par l'allégresse d'espoirs abandonnés depuis longtemps. (III, 27)

While the trope *morceau du passé* introduces the image and indicates its temporal content through the genitive link *du passé,* the following figure in apposition, *banquise invisible détachée d'un hiver ancien,* adds precision to the image and again recalls the temporal implications (*hiver ancien*). The extension of the image through *s'avançait dans ma chambre* insists on the concrete nature of the figurative statement by enhancing it with a dynamic activity. The reader's attention is thus focused on the image, which is the cognitive focus of the entire passage.

The analogy becomes autonomous and digressive when it is extended through the lengthy elaboration qualifying *chambre.* This descriptive extension primarily introduces a discursive element into the context, since it explicitly recalls the mental contiguity between sensations associated with a definite time and place. Thus the mention of different sensory impressions (*parfum, lueur*) restates the experience in more general terms, thereby shifting our attention from the specific sensation of burning wood to the general truth to be derived from this experience. The immediate juxtaposition of the literal remark *comme par des années différentes* discursively repeats the cause and effect relationship between sensory stimuli and temporal recall, as the syntactical link through the metaphor *striée par* joins *parfum, lueur* and *années.* This direct syntactical link and juxtaposition verbally reproduces the simultaneity of sensation and recall. The aspect of simultaneity is further emphasized through *replongé* and *envahi,* stressing the immediacy of the action.[15]

b. *Comme*

In a few passages, the adverbial link through *comme* draws an ambiguous analogy, because it is not clear to which part of speech *comme* refers. This more elliptical, less explicit juxtaposition of two domains makes for a simile that is less discursive, closer to metaphor, for the reader cannot be quite sure which two elements are being compared:

> le geste, l'acte le plus simple reste enfermé / comme dans mille vases clos dont chacun serait rempli de choses d'une couleur, d'une odeur, d'une température absolument différentes; / sans compter que ces vases, disposés sur toute la hauteur de nos années pendant lesquelles nous n'avons cessé de changer, fût-ce seulement de rêve et de pensée, sont situés à des altitudes bien diverses, et nous donnent la sensation d'atmosphères singulièrement variées. (III, 870)

The analogy introduces an image into the temporal context whose discursive nature it reinforces with a familiar object of specific shape and function, allowing us to conceptualize at once the notion of

---

[15] A second analogy, introduced by *être comme,* translating "something like," appears in III, 925, in a passage revealing the hero's discovery of the "Matinée Guermantes" as a living symbol of time gone by: "elle était comme ce qu'on appelait autrefois une vue optique, mais une vue optique des années, la vue non d'un moment, non [mais?] d'une personne située dans la perspective déformante du Temps." (The editors alert us that the manuscript is difficult to decipher at this point. The general sense of the passage seems to call for *mais* as opposed to *non,* which appears in the Pléiade edition.) The analogy explicitly introduced by *était comme* is further set in relief through the introductory remark "ce qu'on appelait autrefois." The two genitive links *des années* and *du Temps* assure the reader's awareness of the imagery's temporal implications. The insistence on the concrete analogy to optics seems particularly appropriate, since the entire narrative account of the "Matinée Guermantes" has revealed to us that the optical imagery is not merely a concrete translation of an abstract notion, but that it is based on an actual visual experience: the hero *sees* that time has passed when suddenly confronted with the aged looks of people he last saw as relatively young.

confinement. The linking element *comme,* however, does not draw an explicit analogy between the two realms of discourse, since the tenor is not revealed, and since the link does not specifically bind any parts of speech of either domain. *Vases clos* directly replaces the compared element (the tenor whose content the reader must infer from the surrounding context).[16] The actual notion under discussion is further clarified, however, through the enumeration of the very content in question: the descriptive elaboration qualifying *vases* — "dont chacun serait rempli de choses d'une couleur, d'une odeur, d'une température" — closely joins the domains of tenor and vehicle within one image. Thus the triple genitive link modifying *rempli de choses,* in accumulating and joining various sensorial domains, directly refers us to the mental contiguity of simultaneous sensory impressions associated with a particular experience. The reader is aware of this temporal concept from the discursive context preceding the imagery.

The imagery becomes autonomous when the domain introduced by *comme* is expanded through the temporal metaphor *hauteur de nos années,* which in turn gives rise to further imaginal precision (*altitudes, atmosphères*).[17] Although concrete, figurative language has replaced the literal, discursive narrative, we are explicitly reminded of the temporal content through the genitive link *de nos années,* and the following literal phrase "pendant lesquelles nous n'avons cessé de changer, fût-ce seulement de rêve et de pensée." The continued metaphors *altitudes bien diverses* and *atmosphères singulièrement variées,* by adding further pictorial precision to the conceptual conceit of *vases clos,* aid in specifying the nature of the temporal notion.[18]

---

[16] *Comme,* in this instance, does not translate "as" or "like," but rather approximates something like "as it were," which presents us with a comparative structure close to metaphor, as pointed out by R. A. Sayce in *Style in French Prose,* p. 61.

[17] Cf. III, 121 and III, 1046-1048 where the metaphor *hauteur* is used within a temporal context.

[18] See II, 398 where the same concept is expressed through similar imagery, likewise introduced through the comparative link *comme.* In this instance, the concept of mental isolation between memories from different periods is translated into spatial terms. See *infra,* p. 200, note 24 for an analysis of this passage.

METAPHORS AND SIMILES

A similar elliptical analogy between two realms of discourse is introduced through *comme* in the following passage, where the basis for comparison between the two domains is not directly stated. The text hesitantly marks the transition from the abstract to the concrete, figurative. This cautious mode of introduction, while apparently attenuating the analogy by signaling its approximate nature, actually emphasizes it by drawing our attention to it:

> Le cauchemar qu'avait eu Saint-Loup s'effaça un peu de son esprit. Le regard distrait et fixe, il vint me voir durant tous ces jours atroces qui dessinèrent pour moi, en se suivant l'un l'autre, / comme la courbe magnifique de quelque rampe durement forgée d'où Robert restait à se demander quelle résolution son amie allait prendre. / (II, 124)

The initial metaphor *dessinèrent* announces the concrete representation of the temporal notion, while the following analogy to a distinct aspect of staircase architecture translates it into a definite image. Introduced through *comme* — which in the present context means "something like" or "as it were" — the figure *courbe* stands as an imaginal approximation, not equivalent, of the temporal notion based on the emotional experience of *jours atroces*. The basis for the comparison between *jours* and *rampe* is not directly stated by the analogy, but only indirectly hinted at by the phrase "en se suivant l'un l'autre," which specifies the main concept of chronological continuity, thus preparing the reader's interpretation of the subsequent image. The continuation of the conceit established by *dessinèrent* and *courbe* through the specific descriptive detail *rampe durement forgée* clarifies the image. The specific reference to the ascending slope associated with staircase architecture provides us with a conceptual model from which we may intuit the subjective experience of *jours atroces*. The precise feeling or concept to be derived from this image is, however, not discursively stated.

The resumption of the literal narrative within the clause modifying *rampe durement forgée* directly links the imagery to the mental and emotional state of Saint-Loup's continued uncertainty about Rachel, thereby recalling the specific cause underlying the narrator's temporal notion. While the solid line and the ascending slope stress the concept of continuity, the unvaried aspect of the identical components constituting the ramp accents the indistinguishable nature of successive days, each continuing the uncertainty and misery of the previous one.

c. *Comme si*

An analogy introduced through the linking element *comme si* confronts us with a special type of comparative structure. Whereas *comme si* explicitly announces the coming analogy, its semantic implications and the conditional mood of the entire statement reveal the subjective, hypothetical nature of the comparison. The hesitant transition from the abstract to the concrete preserves the semantic distinction between the two domains, though the extent to which the two domains are kept apart or drawn together largely depends on the individual context.[19]

In the first example, the hypothetical analogy, reinforcing two previous metaphorical conceits, develops and clarifies the hero's abstract and subjective notion about his existence within time:

> Mais si le cadre de sensations où elles [joies et douleurs passées] sont conservées est ressaisi, elles ont à leur tour ce même pouvoir d'expulser tout ce qui leur est incompatible, d'installer, seul en nous, le moi qui les vécut. Or, comme celui que je venais subitement de redevenir n'avait pas existé depuis ce soir lointain où ma grand'mère m'avait déshabillé à mon arrivée à Balbec, ce fut tout naturellement, non pas après la journée actuelle que ce moi ignorait, mais — / comme s'il y avait dans le temps des séries différentes et parallèles / — sans solution de continuité, tout de suite

---

[19] For a discussion of the German equivalent of *comme si* (i.e. *als ob*), consult Hermann Pong's *Das Bild in der Dichtung*, I, 165-166. One may conclude from his discussion that this particular comparative structure ranges semantically from a statement close to metaphor to one approaching the more obvious proportional rapprochement of simile, depending, of course, on the particular context of the figure. It is important to account for this range of variety within comparative structures. It is a misleading oversimplification to jump to the conclusion, as does Danielle Bouverot, that analogies introduced through comparisons are more intelligible, hence "accessible to the reasoning intelligence." (*Le Français Moderne* [October, 1969], p. 305.) Miss Bouverot goes on to generalize that the code in the substitution type of metaphor is "individual and secret," whereas the standard comparison "respects the collective code" (p. 305). This is a dangerous generalization and cannot be used as a universal yardstick: similes can be original and hermetic; metaphors can be familiar and stereotype. In many instances, the surrounding context plays a significant role in rendering a figure "intelligible."

après le premier soir d'autrefois, que j'adhérai à la minute où ma grand'mère s'était penchée vers moi. Le moi que j'étais alors, et qui avait disparu si longtemps, était de nouveau si près de moi.... (II, 757)

The initial conceit based on *cadre de sensations* and *ressaisi* serves as a conceptual model for the abstract notion that concurrent sensory impressions constitute a conceptual ensemble that can be recalled through similar sensory experiences.[20] The second conceit dramatizes this notion by personifying the "revival" of a former emotional state through the animation of the *moi*.[21] This conceit further emphasizes the essence of the temporal notion by extending itself into a narrative elaboration recalling the particular time and place of the past moment suddenly "relived."

The analogy through *comme si* reinforces the previous metaphor *cadre de sensations* and serves as a second conceptual model: "Comme s'il y avait dans le temps des séries différentes et parallèles." Interpolated as a disjunctive element set off by the dash, the analogy through *comme si* is both less direct and more obvious. Introduced as an explanatory remark preceding *sans solution de continuité*, it prepares and reinforces the main concept of temporal continuity through a concrete image.[22] The two adjectives modifying the otherwise vague expression *séries* determine and specify its meaning, providing us with a conceptual image for the notion of plural chronology. The mention of *dans le temps* explicitly indicates the temporal content of the image, while the conditional mood introduced through *comme si* distinctly separates the analogy from the realm of objective reality.

Another passage where a concrete image serving as a conceptual model is introduced through the hypothetical, comparative structure *comme si* appears in I, 87. In this instance, the conditional mood reinforces the temporal notion, since the image is introduced to illustrate the narrator's falsification of the concept of mental contiguity and simultaneity by reproducing the conceptual ensemble

---

[20] Cf. I, 720-721 where the same notion is similarly expressed through *cadre d'existence*, and II, 81 where the metaphor *trame* fulfills the same conceptual function.

[21] For a discussion of the "moi" conceit see *supra*, pp. 127-133.

[22] Other conceptual models express a similar temporal experience. Cf. I, 386-387 (*supra*, pp. 75-76), II, 346, and III, 26-27 (*supra*, pp. 42-43).

through the linear mode of communication characteristic of all writing:

> c'est que mes rêves de voyage et d'amour n'étaient que des moments — que je sépare artificiellement aujourd'hui / comme si je pratiquais des sections à des hauteurs différentes d'un jet d'eau irisé et en apparence immobile / — dans un même et infléchissable jaillissement de toutes les forces de ma vie.

The analogy throws the inadequacy of the narrative method — already indicated through the previous literal remark — into relief. Whereas *jet d'eau irisé* translates the concept of indivisibility into a visual image, the hypothetical action of slicing a homogenous, indivisible whole emphasizes the impossibility of doing so. Yet the narrator is nonetheless able to reproduce in his text the notion of mental contiguity, as is apparent from the following conceptual metaphor *jaillissement,* recalling the previous image *jet d'eau.*[23]

B. Multiple Similes Within Metaphorical Passages

When the metaphors expressing a temporal concept are accompanied by more than one simile, the interrelationships of the various tropes and their combined function vary considerably within the passages that I have found. The similes may range in extent from a brief analogy to a descriptive tableau illustrating the temporal notion. Some multiple similes share the same image, whereas others are from entirely different domains.

1. Multiple Similes From the Same Domain

In the next four passages a second simile extends the code previously established by an initial one. In the first example, the

---

[23] For additional passages where an analogy introduced through the comparative link *comme si* reinforces the metaphorical time imagery, see III, 1047 ("comme si j'avais des lieues de hauteur"), and III, 1048 ("comme si les hommes étaient juchés sur de vivantes échasses, grandissant sans cesse"). Both passages were previously discussed above, pp. 156-160.

Other examples may be found in III, 386 and 947 to be discussed under multiple comparative structures, *infra,* pp. 203-204, and pp. 209-210.

brief analogy to painting introduces and particularizes the domain of the metaphors and of the second simile:

> 1. Pour un instant, du ramage réentendu qu'il avait en tel printemps ancien, nous pouvons tirer, / comme des petits tubes dont on se sert pour peindre, / la nuance juste, oubliée, mystérieuse et fraîche des jours que nous avions
> 2. cru nous rappeler, quand, / comme les mauvais peintres, / nous donnions à tout notre passé étendu sur une même toile les tons conventionnels et tous pareils de la mémoire volontaire. Or, au contraire, chacun des moments qui le composèrent employait, pour une création originale, dans une harmonie unique, les couleurs d'alors que nous ne connaissons plus.... (II, 11-12)

The combined imagery of similes and metaphors stresses the temporal concept derived by the narrator from the experience of sensory recall. The imagery is part of a long, discursive passage that serves as an explanatory anticipation of the hero's specific sensory associations with the name "Guermantes." Whereas an earlier simile draws an analogy between the faculty of memory and musical instruments retaining the sound and style of the artists who used them — thereby emphasizing and concretizing the ability of our memory to recall precise sensory impressions from the past — the metaphors reinforced by similes specify the temporal notion to be derived from such a sensory recall. *Ramage réentendu* indicates the sensory domain of auditory recall. The very nature of the recall is then particularized through an analogy to painting: *petits tubes* refers us to a specific domain, and gives a concrete translation of the notion of mental contiguity based on simultaneous sensory impressions. The following metaphors participate in the same code and transcend it: the semantic flexibility of *nuance* allows the term to participate at once in the auditory code introduced by *ramage,* and the visual domain interpolated by the analogy to painting. The genitive link modifying *nuance* in turn enhances its semantic ambivalence, since it refers us to an additional domain: the explicit mention of *des jours* points to the temporal implications of the preceding and following imagery. The adjectival accumulation modifying *nuance* extends both the established image from painting and the temporal domain syntactically linked to it through *des jours.*

198 METAPHORIC NARRATION

The extension of the analogy from painting — carefully reintroduced through the second simile (*comme les mauvais peintres*), and in turn extended through additional metaphors (*passé étendu sur une même toile, tons conventionnels et tous pareils*) — further explains the temporal notion through the descriptive precision of an extended image. By representing the former, erroneous concept in terms of the same image domain, the author compels us to focus on the main aspect of the newly discovered truth: the two antithetical images strikingly portray the discrepancy between the former and present conception.

The abstract concept is further translated into concrete terms by the following metaphors *création originale, harmonie unique* and *couleurs d'alors,* which further extend the previous image from painting. The direct inclusion of the temporal expressions *passé, chacun des moments,* and *d'alors,* and the mention of *mémoire volontaire* explicitly point to the temporal subject under discussion.

The temporal concept thrown into relief through the combined imagery of metaphors and similes is further reinforced through the narrative account of a particular incident: the sudden resurgence of the hero's childhood impressions connected with the Guermantes, called forth by the sensory recall of the specific ring that name once had for him.

In the second passage, the temporal notion derived from the hero's experience of forgetfulness is first expressed through the combined imagery of metaphors and similes, and then stated more directly through the inclusion of a literal elaboration revealing the temporal dimension. This example differs from the previous one in that an initial metaphorical transposition introduces the image domain. The accompanying similes reinforce and explain the imagery by drawing a double analogy between space and time:

  et mon regret d'Albertine et la persistance de ma jalousie, qui avaient déjà dépassé par leur durée mes prévisions les plus pessimistes, n'auraient sans doute jamais changé beaucoup si leur existence, isolée du reste de ma vie, avait seulement été soumise au jeu de mes souvenirs, aux actions et réactions d'une psychologie applicable à des états immobiles, et n'avait pas été entraînée vers un système plus
1. vaste où les âmes se meuvent dans le temps / comme les corps dans l'espace. /
2.   / Comme il y a une géométrie dans l'espace, il y a

une psychologie dans le temps, / où les calculs d'une psychologie plane ne seraient plus exacts parce qu'on n'y tiendrait pas compte du Temps et d'une des formes qu'il revêt, l'oubli; l'oubli dont je commençais à sentir la force et qui est un si puissant instrument d'adaptation à la réalité parce qu'il détruit peu à peu en nous le passé survivant qui est en constante contradiction avec elle. (III, 557)

The initial metaphorical transposition is closely linked to the literal context through direct syntactical ties: the metaphorical clause "où les âmes se meuvent dans le temps" directly modifies and particularizes the abstract statement "entraînée vers un système plus vaste." The juxtaposed simile reinforces the dynamic aspect of the verb *meuvent* by drawing an analogy between time and space. This analogy serves as a conceptual model, for the reader is familiar with the movement of bodies in space, whereas the concept of movement within time may be totally alien to him. Thus the metaphorical action attributed to time and the immediate reinforcement of the image through the analogy to space jointly concretize and accentuate the abstract temporal notion of man's emotional flexibility. That this flexibility is to be attributed to time is clear from the temporal indication *dans le temps*.

The expansion of the space analogy through the second simile further particularizes the temporal concept. The prepositional modifiers of the figures *géométrie dans l'espace* and *psychologie dans le temps* recall the two domains drawn together by the conceptual analogy. The following metaphor *psychologie plane* directly grows out of the time-space analogy: *plane* is immediately identified as a semantic transfer from the domain of geometry. The established analogy between geometry and psychology enables us to transfer the conceptual distinction between *géométrie dans l'espace* as opposed to *géométrie plane* onto *psychologie dans le temps* as opposed to *psychologie plane*. In the light of this analogy, the inacceptability of *psychologie plane* points to the main concept to be derived from the imagery, the multi-dimensional aspect of the temporal experience.

The context becomes discursive when the same sentence begins to explain the temporal notion in literal terms: "parce qu'on n'y tiendrait pas compte du Temps et d'une des formes qu'il revêt, l'oubli. . . ." The direct mention of *Temps,* and the extra "dimension" in question, *l'oubli,* clearly indicate the precise content of the concept first stated indirectly, but concretely, by the preceding space analogy. While the metaphors and similes jointly establish a conceptual parallel between the abstract temporal notion and the more familiar spatial domain, the subsequent literal elaboration illustrates the notion with a specific account from the hero's personal experience.

A similar function of conveying an abstract notion about man's perception within time by translating it into concrete terms is carried out by the metaphors and similes of the following passage. The expansion and precision of the image through the combined effort of the various tropes again emphasizes the temporal notion:

> il y avait plusieurs duchesses de Guermantes, comme il y avait eu, depuis la dame en rose, plusieurs madame Swann, séparées par l'éther incolore des années, et de l'une à l'autre
> 1. desquelles / je ne pouvais pas plus sauter que si j'avais eu à quitter une planète pour aller dans une autre planète que l'éther en sépare. / Non seulement séparée, mais différente, parée des rêves que j'avais en des temps si diffé-
> 2. rents, / comme d'une flore particulière, qu'on ne retrouvera pas dans une autre planète / , , , , (III, 990) [24]

The juxtaposition of two similar experiences from the hero's life through the initial analogy between the Duchess and Madame

---

[24] The same temporal notion regarding the conceptual gulf between memories from different years is translated into concrete terms through the combined imagery of similes and metaphors within the following passage: "si nous revivons un autre souvenir prélevé sur une année différente, nous trouvons entre eux, grâce à des lacunes, à d'immenses pans d'oubli, / comme l'abîme d'une différence d'altitude /, / comme l'incompatibilité de deux qualités incomparables d'atmosphère respirée et de colorations ambiantes" / (II, 397-398). The metaphors *lacunes* and *immenses pans d'oubli* initiate the spatial code, which is further expanded by the figure "abîme d'une différence d'altitude" of the first comparative structure. The direct syntactical juxtaposition of the second comparative structure, particularizing and explaining the genitive link of the initial simile ("abîme d'une différence d'altitude"), introduces a discursive tone. The genitive links of the second comparison ("d'atmosphère respirée et de colorations ambiantes") point to the actual subject underlying the imagery, namely the conceptual contiguity between simultaneous sensory impressions according to which memories are related or divorced within our mental context.

METAPHORS AND SIMILES 201

Swann reveals that the passage is getting at a general truth drawn from experience. The plural existence that our conceptual faculties attribute to the same person over a period of time is first translated into more concrete terms through the phrase modifying "plusieurs duchesses de Guermantes": "séparées par l'éther incolore des années." While the metaphorical transposition introduces the image and attributes it to the hero-narrator's notion of the Duchess's plural existence, and, by analogy, of Madame Swann's, the following simile expands and particularizes the image. This far-fetched analogy between planets and the plural appearance of women strikingly emphasizes the idea of the discontinuity in the hero's temporal experience, implicit in the initial metaphorical image *éther incolore des années.*

The expansion of the same image domain by a second simile, again illustrating the idea of temporal discontinuity in spatial terms, draws the reader further into the realm of the imaginary: "comme d'une flore particulière, qu'on ne retrouvera pas dans une autre planète." The additional concept to be derived from this elaboration is explicitly revealed through the literal statement that precedes it. The simultaneous presence of figurative language and the literal mention of the actual subject at hand makes for a discursive passage and emphasizes the temporal notion.

A number of similes stress the symbolic implications of the metaphors they accompany.[25] For instance, the following metaphor *neige,* a descriptive metonymy of the physical manifestations of old age, is explained and emphasized through similes:

> on ne croirait pas que ceci peut avoir jamais été cela, que la matière de cela est elle-même, sans se réfugier ailleurs, grâce aux savantes manipulations du temps, devenue ceci, que c'est la même matière n'ayant pas quitté le même corps, si l'on n'avait l'indice du nom pareil et le témoignage affirmatif des amis, auquel donne seule une apparence de vraisemblance la rose, étroite jadis entre l'or des épis, étalée maintenant sous la neige.
> 1. / Comme pour la neige d'ailleurs, / le degré de blancheur des cheveux semblait en général comme un signe de

---

[25] Several examples were already included in the above discussion of metaphors symbolic of the manifestations of time within the narrative context of old age: see *supra,* Chapter VI, Part C, pp. 135-139; 153-160.

2. la profondeur du temps vécu, / comme ces sommets montagneux qui, même apparaissant aux yeux sur la même ligne que d'autres, révèlent pourtant le niveau de leur altitude au degré de leur neigeuse blancheur. / (III, 940)

The temporal implications underlying the physical description of old age are apparent from the explanatory remark "grâce aux savantes manipulations du temps." While the metaphorical image introduces the striking descriptive focus on a particular aspect of aging — the visual contrast between *l'or des épis* and *neige* accentuates the aspect of physical metamorphosis — the following explicit analogy between snow and white hair at once explains the metaphorical image and extends it. It becomes clear from the elaboration of the analogy that the basis for comparison resides in *degré de blancheur*. The initial comparative structure sets up the analogy between snow and white hair, whose symbolic implications are explicitly stated through *semblait comme* relating whiteness of hair to age (*profondeur du temps vécu*).[26] The second simile extends into a visual tableau and clarifies the initial analogy to snow through its descriptive elaboration: the expansion of the analogy to snow, by focusing on a particular descriptive detail that relates the two key concepts of depth (*niveau; profondeur*) and whiteness, translates the temporal notion into one distinct image. *Niveau* recalls and further concretizes the temporal notion expressed through the time metaphor *profondeur du temps vécu*. As in the previous examples, the similes particularize the metaphors' image and introduce an explanatory note. The considerable extent of the image through the joint effort of metaphors and similes focuses our attention on the temporal notion.

2. Multiple Similes From Different Domains

Some similes appearing within the same passage introduce analogies from different domains, reinforcing the metaphors with separate images. The function and extent of each simile may vary con-

---

[26] Cf. III, 946 where the metaphorical analogy between "gray hair" and "autumn" likewise emphasizes, though less explicitly, the symbolic manifestations of time within the realm of physical experience.

siderably. For instance, frequently one of the similes introduces a brief analogy interpolated for explanatory reasons, whereas the second analogy enhances the temporal subject by introducing an evocative image or tableau.

In the first example of this type, the initial simile introduces a brief image that emphasizes the main concept to be conveyed by the following time metaphor. The second comparative structure fulfills a less obvious function: it reinforces the temporal notion by juxtaposing two evocative, symbolic images that suggest the same concept already expressed by the previous imagery. The similes and metaphor reinforce each other in conveying the hero's subjective notion about Albertine, whose unknown past gradually turns her into a symbol of the unfathomable, the infinite:

> 1. Alors sous ce visage rosissant je sentais se réserver / comme un gouffre / l'inexhaustible espace des soirs où je n'avais pas connu Albertine. Je pouvais bien prendre Albertine sur mes genoux, tenir sa tête dans mes mains, je pouvais la caresser, passer longuement mes mains sur elle,
> 2. mais, / comme si j'eusse manié une pierre qui enferme la salure des océans immémoriaux ou le rayon d'une étoile, / je sentais que je touchais seulement l'enveloppe close d'un être qui par l'intérieur accédait à l'infini. (III, 386)

While the analogy to *gouffre* emphasizes and particularizes the following metaphorical expression *inexhaustible espaces des soirs,* the two images introduced through the second comparative structure — the qualifying images modifying *pierre* — both function as concrete illustrations of the hero's feeling towards Albertine. The linking element *comme si* announces the analogy, while the conditional mood stresses its hypothetical nature. Our attention is drawn to it, since it interrupts the flow of the main sentence, and takes us unexpectedly from the literal to the figurative. The juxtaposition of images from two entirely different domains points to the main concept inherent within both: the saltiness of oceans and the ray of a star each symbolize the unfathomable, the unattainable. While we first infer this notion from the tautological message of the juxtaposed images, the remainder of the main sentence, which follows this interpolated illustration, spells it out discursively: "je sentais que je touchais seulement l'enveloppe close d'un être qui par l'intérieur accédait à l'infini."

The insistence on the idea that Albertine embodies for the hero informs us that she is beginning to stand for more than herself. The narrator continues to reveal the symbolic implications when an additional metaphor is directly followed by a simile that overtly states the hero's temporal notion: "ce personnage dont tout le monde ignorait qu'il tenait enfermée dans une bouteille la Princesse de la Chine; m'invitant sous une forme pressante, cruelle et sans issue, à la recherche du passé, elle était plutôt comme une grande déesse du Temps" (III, 386-387).[27]

Similes and metaphors jointly communicating the same temporal notion may appear within different syntactical frameworks. Within one passage, an initial explanatory simile introduces the subject, while a second simile follows an intervening narrative digression and extends into a tableau that is primarily responsible for translating the abstract notion into concrete terms.

Similes and metaphors work together to convey the abstract concept of the influence of forgetfulness on our concept of time. The combined imagery is introduced into the context after an aphoristic literal statement announcing the notion in terms of a general law. The initial transposition is carried out by a single metaphor translating the abstract notion into perceptual terms (*erreurs optiques dans le temps*). The figure's provenance is immediately explained by the accompanying analogy to space: "il reste que c'est le temps qui amène progressivement l'oubli, l'oubli n'est pas sans altérer profondément la notion du temps. Il y a des erreurs optiques dans le temps / comme il y en a dans l'espace" / (III, 593).

After a brief description of "optical illusions" not related to the process of forgetting, the time imagery is taken up once more to deal with "optical illusions" in physical terms. The metaphor *espaces vides* reintroduces the spatial code, which is extended by a number of additional metaphors later on within the same passage. This metaphoric extension, however, is preceded by a simile that illustrates the concept of optical illusion with a brief tableau depicting an ocean fog. This particular image determines our interpretation of the surrounding metaphors:

---

[27] For other references to passages where Albertine is portrayed as a symbolic figure, see *supra*, p. 141, n. 32.

cet oubli de tant de choses, me séparant, par des espaces vides, d'événements tout récents qu'ils me faisaient paraître anciens... c'était son interpolation, fragmentée, irrégulière, au milieu de ma mémoire — / comme une brume épaisse sur l'océan, et qui supprime les points de repère des choses / — qui détraquait, disloquait mon sentiment des distances dans le temps, là rétrécies, ici distendues, et me faisait me croire tantôt beaucoup plus loin, tantôt beaucoup plus près des choses que je ne l'étais en réalité. (III, 593-594)

This pictorial simile, emphasized as a disjunctive element set off by dashes, constitutes the imaginal focus of the passage.

Within each of the following three passages, metaphors and similes work together in drawing up a symbolic tableau dramatizing the ephemeral nature of life. In the first, the temporal notion to be inferred from the symbolic portrayal of one of the novel's characters, Mme d'Arpajon, is conveyed through two separate images, each of which is clarified and particularized by a brief simile: [28]

1. Cet aspect était si différent de celui que je lui avais connu qu'on eût dit qu'elle était un être condamné, / comme un personnage de féerie, / à apparaître d'abord en jeune fille, puis en épaisse matrone, et qui reviendrait sans doute bientôt en vieille branlante et courbée. Elle semblait, / comme
2. une lourde nageuse qui ne voit plus le rivage qu'à une grande distance, / repousser avec peine les flots du temps qui la submergeaient. (III, 937)

The initial analogy to the theatre clarifies the symbolic archetypes dramatizing the successive stages of life (*jeune fille, épaisse matrone, vieille branlante et courbée*). The narrative shift from the description of the present state of affairs to past and future implications abruptly changes the point of view from the particular to a more objective observation where the particular instance is symbolic of a general truth. By emphasizing the process of aging instead of merely describing Mme d'Arpajon's middle-aged appearance, the narrator stresses the symbolic significance, thereby turning the character into an allegorical manifestation of time. The addition of the

---

[28] See Chapter VI, Section C, pp. 133-160 for a discussion of the role of metaphors within the symbolic portrayal of the novel's characters.

following metaphorical transposition to the preceding sketch of the "three Ages of Life" further emphasizes the symbolic significance of the portrayal. The simile accompanying the metaphors establishes their image domain by supplying them with a specific tableau. The metaphor *flots du temps,* in mentioning "time" provides us with a key for the temporal notion underlying the symbolic description of both images. The renewal of the stereotype through additional descriptive details from the same domain (*nageuse, rivage, submergeaient*), which insist on the imaginal transposition of the vehicle *flots,* throws the key element into relief. That more than a realistic description is at hand is further evident from the careful transitional remarks preceding each symbolic image (*on eût dit qu'elle était; elle semblait*), signaling the subjective, illusional nature of the observer's perception.

The two similes of another passage play a major role in communicating the temporal notion otherwise only briefly expressed by a single, initial metaphor. The figures are from different domains, but reinforce each other in the symbolic portrayal of one of the novel's characters, M. d'Argencourt.[29] The extent and expressive nature of each simile introduces an imaginal focus into the context, which stresses the symbolic process. While the initial analogy reinforces the metaphor with a concrete image whose function it is to emphasize the underlying cognitive content, the second simile consists of a short dramatic sketch that is primarily responsible for revealing the symbolic significance of d'Argencourt's portrayal:

1. l'aspect tout nouveau d'un être comme M. d'Argencourt m'était une révélation frappante de cette réalité du millésime, qui d'habitude nous reste abstraite, / comme l'apparition de certains arbres nains ou de baobabs géants nous avertit du changement de méridien. /
2. Alors la vie nous apparaît / comme le féerie où on voit d'acte en acte le bébé devenir adolescent, homme mûr et se courber vers la tombe. / (III, 926)

The symbolic significance to be derived from d'Argencourt's portrayal becomes apparent from the explicit nature of the metaphor-

---

[29] See pp. 149ff. for other aspects of d'Argencourt's portrayal.

ical transposition: the direct syntactical link — through the copula — between d'Argencourt's appearance and *millésime* overtly announces what he symbolizes for the observer. The expressiveness of *millésime* because of the technical implications and relatively rare use of the term underscores the key notion, while the accompanying simile clarifies its meaning by juxtaposing a concrete analogy from the realm of physical reality, which stresses the principal concept to be inferred from the tropes.[30] The illustration of abrupt change from the geographical domain, by stressing the aspect of change in d'Argencourt's appearance, focuses the reader's attention on the main concept.

The most striking reinforcement, however, is due to the second simile, whose hyperbolic dramatization through the abrupt juxtaposition of the successive stages of life illustrates and emphasizes the symbolic message by concentrating it into a brief, exaggerated sketch. The outside analogy to the theatre provides us with a conceptual framework, and the descriptive elaboration into a dramatic *mise en scène* focuses all our attention on the analogy. This dramatic "representation" of life throws the symbolic message into relief: the accelerated process of aging directly points to time's manifestation within a human life. The interpolation of this symbolic sketch, by introducing a general, universal truth into the portrayal of d'Argencourt, deprives the character of his individuality and turns him into an allegorical symbol.

The third passage in which metaphors and similes constitute a symbolic tableau dramatizing time's manifestation in the physical realm appears in *A l'Ombre des jeunes filles en fleurs*. The two similes within this passage have a discursive, preparatory function. Each introduces an analogy to another realm of discourse. Both domains are then merged and extended by the following symbolic tableau, which includes the time metaphors:

1. c'est que je n'étais pas situé en dehors du Temps, mais soumis à ses lois, / tout comme ces personnages de roman qui, à cause de cela, me jetaient dans une telle tristesse quand je lisais leur vie, à Combray, au fond de ma guérite d'osier. / Théoriquement on sait que la terre tourne, mais

---

[30] For a similar use of *millésime* within a temporal context, see *supra*, pp. 51-52.

2. en fait on ne s'en aperçoit pas, le sol sur lequel on marche semble ne pas bouger et on vit tranquille. / Il en est ainsi du Temps dans la vie. / Et pour rendre sa fuite sensible, les romanciers sont obligés, en accélérant follement les battements de l'aiguille, de faire franchir au lecteur dix, vingt, trente ans, en deux minutes. Au haut d'une page on a quitté un amant plein d'espoir, au bas de la suivante on le retrouve octogénaire, accomplissant péniblement dans le préau d'un hospice sa promenade quotidienne, répondant à peine aux paroles qu'on lui adresse, ayant oublié le passé. (I, 482)

Similes, metaphors and symbolic tableau all work together to express the hero's sudden discovery of his subjugation to time. The extent of the imaginal elaboration, and its emphatic nature stress this notion within the narrative context. The first simile briefly introduces the main conceptual framework for the following symbolic dramatization of life. The analogy to space set up by the second simile serves to concretize another aspect of the newly discovered notion: its imperceptibility. The nature of this additional analogy is primarily explanatory, since the conceptual parallel between the temporal and spatial domains is introduced through an explicit, syntactical equation: "Il en est ainsi du Temps dans la vie." The resumption of the conceptual framework introduced by the initial analogy to fictional characters, and its considerable elaboration constitute the symbolic focus of the entire passage. The metonymical reference (through *en accélérant follement les battements de l'aiguille*) to a time-measuring device (*aiguille de cadran*), which in the light of the previous conceptual parallel to space alludes also to a geographical measuring device (*aiguille aimantée d'une boussole*) translates the notion of flight into a concrete image. The indirect reference to time and space through a well-known object, and the insistence on the dynamic activity of the mechanism through *accélérant follement,* emphatically stress the notion of "flight."

The elaboration of the conceit of the "novel within the novel" through the narrative focus on the process of aging — greatly exaggerated through the abrupt juxtaposition of youth and old age — throws the symbolic content into relief. The particular emphasis on some aspects of old age adds further intensity to the message. This descriptive focus introduces a pathetic note, since the accelerated presentation of the ages of man depicts life as a melodrama. The effect on the reader is one of shock, for the sudden portrayal of old age is totally unexpected within the account of the hero's youth.

The imagery, which interrupts the narrative account of *Jeunes Filles,* transcends the realm of the hero's experience: it not only emphasizes his particular plight of temporal subjugation by anticipating its full implications, but also imparts a universal truth, applicable to all men. The universal nature of the message is quite obvious from the generalizing novelistic outline that diverts the reader's attention from the hero's exploits and focuses it on a more far-reaching truth.

The specific reference to novelistic techniques within an early passage of the long cyclical work is a prefiguration — a symbolic parallel — of the novel's overall structure: the narrative, which begins with early childhood, closes with endless portrayals of old age.[31]

Some metaphors appear within a comparative structure where they fulfill a purely secondary function. For example, in one passage three similes are primarily responsible for conveying the temporal notion: the initial simile illustrates the narrator's vantage point by supplying a concrete, perceptual image, while the following two analogies introduce brief explanatory statements, which further clarify the notion to be derived from the already established image domain:

>   D'ailleurs, même chez les hommes qui n'avaient subi qu'un léger changement, dont la moustache était devenue blanche, etc., on sentait que ce changement n'était pas posi-
> 1. tivement matériel. / C'était comme si on les avait vus à travers une vapeur colorante, un verre peint qui changeait l'aspect de leur figure mais surtout, par ce qu'il y ajoutait de trouble, montrait que ce qu'il nous permettait de voir "grandeur nature" était en réalité très loin de nous, / dans
> 2. un éloignement / différent, il est vrai, de celui de l'espace, /

---

[31] The abrupt movement from youth to old age is particularly obvious in the original conception of the novel, as announced by Proust in the 1913 edition of *Swann*: the two additional volumes were to be *Le Côté de Guermantes* and *Le Temps retrouvé.*

The reader of the final, greatly expanded version is, however, still confronted with the same abruptness: the narrative hiatus between the "Matinée Guermantes" and what precedes unexpectedly portrays as extremely aged those characters we previously knew as relatively young.

3. mais du fond duquel, / comme d'un autre rivage, / nous sentions qu'ils avaient autant de peine à nous reconnaître que nous eux. (III, 947)

The introduction of several similes into the descriptive context of old age emphasizes the hero's subjective temporal notion and guides our conception of his particular visual impression. The considerable extension of the analogies to vapor and glass allows the reader a concrete grasp of the perceptual phenomenon, and reveals the novel's tendency to elaborate, to restate one experience in terms of another, which may be more familiar to the reader.

This explanatory tendency is pursued by the following analogies, introduced to clarify the implications of the metaphors *loin, éloignement* and *fond*. The particular meaning of *loin* is emphasized through the metalinguistic commentary contrasting space and time, and the continued metaphor *fond* is particularized through an additional analogy to space: *comme d'un autre rivage*.

The similes appearing within the following two passages fulfill a less obvious function. They help to clarify a descriptive tableau symbolic of an aspect of time, but devoid of time metaphors and explicit temporal indications. The imagery is suggestive, not discursive, since the reader has to intuit the temporal notion from it.

In the first example, similes, symbolic images and certain key words jointly convey the hero's subjective impression of temporal manifestations within the material world. The passage must be quoted at length to reveal the symbolic portrayal of the Duc de Guermantes:

> Il n'était plus qu'une ruine, mais superbe, et moins encore qu'une ruine, cette belle chose romantique que peut être un rocher dans la tempête. Fouettée de toutes parts par les vagues de souffrance, de colère de souffrir, d'avancée montante de la mort qui la circonvenaient, sa figure, effritée comme un bloc, gardait le style, la cambrure que j'avais toujours admirés; elle était rongée comme une de ces belles têtes antiques trop abîmées mais dont nous sommes trop heureux d'orner un cabinet de travail. Elle paraissait seulement appartenir à une époque plus ancienne qu'autrefois, non seulement à cause de ce qu'elle avait pris de rude et de rompu dans sa matière jadis plus brillante, mais parce qu'à l'expression de finesse et d'enjouement avait succédé une involontaire, une inconsciente expression, bâtie par la

maladie, de lutte contre la mort, de résistance, de difficulté à vivre. Les artères ayant perdu toute souplesse avaient donné au visage jadis épanoui une dureté sculpturale. Et sans que le duc s'en doutât, il découvrait des aspects de nuque, de joue, de front, où l'être, comme obligé de se raccrocher avec acharnement à chaque minute, semblait bousculé dans une tragique rafale, pendant que les mèches blanches de sa magnifique chevelure moins épaisse venaient souffleter de leur écume le promontoire envahi du visage. Et comme ces reflets étranges, uniques, que seule l'approche de la tempête où tout va sombrer donne aux roches qui avaient été jusque-là d'une autre couleur, je compris que le gris plombé des joues raides et usées, le gris presque blanc et moutonnant des mèches soulevées, la faible lumière encore départie aux yeux qui voyaient à peine, étaient des teintes non pas irréelles, trop réelles au contraire, mais fantastiques, et empruntées à la palette, à l'éclairage, inimitable dans ses noirceurs effrayantes et prophétiques, de la vieillesse, de la proximité de la mort. (III, 1017-1018) [32]

During the course of the description, the Duke is dehumanized, not only because his appearance is primarily depicted through continued metaphors drawn from the realm of nature (*rocher dans la tempête*), but also because the description, instead of being a faithful reproduction, focuses on certain aspects of the physiognomy. This descriptive emphasis and the inclusion of certain key words (attached to the imagery through the genitive link — avancée montante *de la mort,* l'éclairage ... *de la vieillesse,* proximité *de la mort* — or explicitly presented as a causal explanation — *bâtie par la maladie, de lutte contre la mort, de résistance, de difficulté à vivre*) reveal the hero's subjective impression of the struggle against time and death, which the Duke begins to symbolize for him and for the reader. The elaborate nature of the imagery allows us to participate in the hero's personal vision and guides our conceptual interpretation of the tableau. The temporal dimension underlying the symbolic portrayal is explicitly indicated through *une époque plus ancienne qu'autrefois,* and the temporal adverb *jadis.* The descriptive precision and variety through the multiple analogies to

---

[32] The specific mention of hardened arteries as a significant visual detail within the symbolic portrayal of a character already appeared in III, 998. The passage is analyzed *supra,* pp. 137-138.

ruins, weather-beaten rocks, stone, and antique sculpture — all hyperboles concretizing the concepts of old age and struggle — help us comprehend these abstractions.[33]

The second symbolic tableau conveys the hero's subjective notion of the Guermantes' antiquity. The similes within this context reinforce the symbolic content of the description and aid us in decoding the message to be derived from the textual juxtaposition of two different domains: the Guermantes and a series of Gothic cathedrals. This descriptive juxtaposition of separate domains without any guidelines revealing the purpose of the rapprochement is an example of a less discursive symbolic process.[34] The hero's private notion of antiquity, illustrated for him by the Guermantes' lineage is translated into more universal terms through the multiple descriptive analogies, all familiar archetypes of long-term existence:

> puis ç'avait été la terre héréditaire, le poétique domaine
> 1. où cette race altière de Guermantes, / comme une tour jaunissante et fleuronnée qui traverse les âges, / s'élevait déjà sur la France, alors que le ciel était encore vide là où devaient plus tard surgir Notre-Dame de Paris et Notre-Dame de Chartres; alors qu'au sommet de la colline de
> 2. Laon la nef de la cathédrale ne s'était pas posée / comme l'Arche du Déluge au sommet du mont Ararat, emplie de Patriarches et de Justes anxieusement penchés aux fenêtres pour voir si la colère de Dieu s'est apaisée, emportant avec elle les types des végétaux qui multiplieront sur la terre, débordante d'animaux qui s'échappent jusque par les tours où des bœufs, se promenant paisiblement sur la toiture, regardent de haut les plaines de Champagne; / alors que le voyageur qui quittait Beauvais à la fin du jour ne voyait pas encore le suivre en tournoyant, dépliées sur l'écran d'or du couchant, les ailes noires et ramifiées de la cathédrale.
> (II, 13-14)

The temporal implications of the description become obvious through the accumulation of archetypal representatives of the Gothic era — the cathedrals of Paris, Laon, Beauvais — and the repeated

---

[33] For an extensive analysis of the symbolic portrayal of the Duc de Guermantes, consult Gottfried Wäber's article "Die Bedeutung der Proustschen Metapher, aufgezeigt an der Darstellung des gealterten Herzogs," *Die Neueren Sprachen,* 14 (1965), 431-437.

[34] Other examples of this descriptive process were previously discussed in Chapter VI, Sections C through E.

mention of their temporal relationship in regard to the racial antiquity of the Guermantes, carefully delineated each time through adverbial expressions of time underlining the Guermantes' priority in time.

The temporal aspect is further stressed through the analogy to Noah's Ark. Within the context of Gothic art, the archetypal "Ship" presents us with an architectural analogy — drawn from earliest Biblical times — to the immense naves of ogival cathedrals. The extension of the analogy to the Biblical event reinforces the description of the Guermantes' antiquity with a symbolic tableau from another domain, dramatizing the notion of remoteness in time.[35]

Whereas the mention of various cathedrals and the analogy to Noah's Ark all draw on traditional associations to translate the hero's subjective notion into more universal terms, the initial simile functions more explicitly. It points to the conceptual analogy between the ancient race of the Guermantes and the age-old tower, both representative of perennial existence. Besides illustrating and concretizing the concept of antiquity in terms of another domain, the initial simile contains the only direct temporal indication: the relative clause *qui traverse les âges* provides us from the start with a key to the main concept to be derived from the combined imagery of symbolic archetypes and similes.

The various combinations of similes and metaphors all have the main function of translating the abstract into concrete terms. Imaginal extensions and multiple images clarify the temporal concept by accumulating descriptive details that add up to a precise image.

Precision and extension of the imagery through the joint presence of similes and metaphors almost always reveal Proust's tendency to be exact when dealing with an important concept.[36] This tendency is further evident when the temporal notion is made ex-

---

[35] The comparison between Noah's Ark and the cathedral of Laon seems particularly appropriate, since Proust, in elaborating the analogy, has chosen those characteristics that find parallels in both: like the archetypal Ark filled with animals, the cathedral has oxen looking out from its towers, and a host of sculpted figures — some "leaning forward" like the Patriarchs and the Just of Noah's Ark — adorn the portals.

[36] In twenty-seven of the forty passages analyzed in this chapter the semantic precision of the vehicle through the combined effort of metaphors and similes aids our identification and comprehension of the tropes.

plicit through the precision of the tenor, or through syntactical structures that closely relate the verbal sequence of tenor and vehicle. The discursive nature of some passages is also obvious from the type of image used: some of them function as "conceptual models" whose graphic nature illustrates and emphasizes the salient idea.[37]

The frequency of the imaginal elaborations and the stylistic emphasis thus introduced into the narrative account point to the importance the author attaches to the description of the hero's increasing awareness of Time. We begin to realize that images are introduced into a temporal passage to help us grasp these discoveries. This is particularly evident when figures drawn from different domains are juxtaposed: the multiple vehicles are organized around the abstract concept, since their only relationship is their joint function in translating mental discoveries into concrete terms.

The generalizing observations accompanying some images lend more universal implications to the narrative account of the hero's exploits. They give us the impression that *A la recherche* is not simply dealing with a "story" written to divert the reader, but that it also contains a number of "truths" to be gleaned by each one of us. The narrator is obviously telling us that the hero's discoveries are applicable to our lives as well.

---

[37] Sixteen passages studied in this chapter have images functioning as "conceptual models."

CONCLUSION

The role of Proust's time metaphors is not to dazzle the reader but to instruct him. Although most of them are original, they are not simply expressive literary devices whose departure from the norm catches our attention. They have a primary function in telling the story, and in conveying its meaning.

If we examine them within the narrative context of *A la recherche du temps perdu,* we realize that Proust's metaphors show us a world in the process of being shaped by the hero's sensibility and insights, that they allow us to witness his growing artistic awareness while they emphasize and exemplify artistic creation. Their important function is underlined by the care Proust takes in introducing them into the narrative account, and in developing them. To make certain that they are understood, he roots them in a surrounding context that discloses the specific associations that prompted a particular semantic transfer, while guiding our interpretation through careful links between the domains of tenor and vehicle, through extensions of the metaphoric code, or through explanatory statements.[1]

That Proust's metaphors have a cognitive as well as a narrative function, is clear from those that provide the reader with "concep-

---

[1] Among the syntactical structures that relate tenor and vehicle, the most frequent — used in almost half of the passages examined in previous chapters — was the genitive link through *de,* either joining the vehicle to the tenor, or to a term metonymically related to it. As we have seen, a variety of prepositional and clausal constructions were used to reveal the semantic relationships between the verbal sequences of the two domains. Other, more obvious devices used included apposition, where tenor and vehicle are juxtaposed, and the explicit equation through the copula *être* (A *is* B).

Metaphorical extensions that specified the semantic domain of the vehicle appeared in two out of three passages analyzed. Quite as often we were also given information specifying the tenor, or guiding our interpretation of it.

tual models." After focusing our attention on what the hero perceives or discovers, they initiate us into an analysis of the nature of perception by providing us with an object or schema that serves as a model construct for grasping the abstract notion. The repeated pause, during the course of the narrative, in order to introduce such images makes us aware of the emphasis on certain ideas or concepts. At such points in the text we realize — especially if the metaphorical image is accompanied by generalizing statements, or a sudden change in narrative voice from the first person to the more inclusive *on* or *nous* — that the focus has shifted from the hero's exploits to the more universal subject of the workings of the human mind.

Besides the narrator's tendency to introduce conceptual metaphors, he uses certain narrative techniques that contribute to the discursive mode of *A la recherche,* and underline its farther-reaching implications. For instance, some metaphors appear within a context where he draws an analogy between several experiences, mainly because each one exemplifies the same temporal notion. In such passages, the emphasis is clearly on the idea to be conveyed, while the individual experiences are of secondary significance, since they are used to illustrate a concept.[2]

The predominantly cognitive function of other metaphorical passages becomes evident when Proust uses two separate images to convey one and the same temporal notion. Though this approach is more expressive than discursive, since we have to infer the temporal notion from two separate images, the double transposition stresses the concept and commands our attention.

The cognitive function is also apparent when recurrent metaphors and their variants are always associated with the same idea. The metaphorical image then gradually begins to stand as an emblem for the temporal concept it repeatedly conveys. When the reader becomes aware of the recurrent identification between image and idea, he realizes that the metaphor has added significance, that it is one of the novel's conceptual constants.

---

[2] Gérard Genette uses the term *récit itératif* to refer to passages in which a particular narrative account refers to a number of recurrences of the same experience, or to similar experiences related in the hero's mind ("Discours du récit" in *Figures III* [Paris: Editions du Seuil, 1972], pp. 145-156).

CONCLUSION

Time metaphors, in particular those dealing with the nature of perception, play an important part in the narrative account: they focus our attention on the hero's major mental discoveries, and aid us in grasping complex insights. In the earlier parts of the novel, where the hero repeatedly views life as divided into separate, unrelated moments, a number of metaphors are introduced that emphasize this notion by translating it into concrete terms. Thus *porte fermée, monde nouveau, fil coupé, vase, cloison,* and its variant *parois* all stress the concept of separation.[3] The complementary notion that each experience is characterized by its own distinct atmosphere, activities, and thoughts — so that we are bound to remember it as a closely knit unit — is expressed by such metaphors as *réseau, assemblage,* and *vase,* each translating the close conceptual relationship.[4]

Subsequent narrative accounts stress the hero's second important discovery, namely that time can be recaptured, that experiences can be recalled and related through sensory analogies. That such experiences give continuity to life — a type of continuity that has nothing to do with chronological sequence — is conveyed through metaphors stressing the notion of anachronism. While the narrative context reveals the cause of the chronological reversal — a present sensory perception evokes a past experience characterized by the same sensation — the metaphors refer us to concrete objects that illustrate the abstract notion.[5]

---

[3] The conceit based on *porte fermée* first appears in I, 347. It is used with the verb *rouvrir* in III, 25 to express the sudden discovery of continuity between the present moment and the past. Cf. the metaphor *entrée* in I, 537. *Monde nouveau* is used in II, 141; II, 346; III, 404. The variant *planète différente* conveys a similar concept in II, 398 and III, 990. *Cloison,* another image for the idea of separation, appears in I, 634-635 and II, 397, and the variant *parois* in III, 613-614. *Vase,* as a model of enclosure, also stresses the idea of separation (I, 135). A drastic change in point of view is expressed through the image *zone* in I, 809 and 182.

[4] *Réseau* appears in I, 345-346; I, 407, and III, 1030. Cf. III, 848 for a metonymical reference to the same image through *fil* in connection with the verb *tisser. Assemblage* is used in I, 426; *vase* in III, 870, 889, and p. 1136, Footnote 1 to page 885. Other metaphors translating intricate conceptual relationships include *écran diapré* (I, 84), *jet d'eau irisé* (I, 87), *cohésion* (I, 539), and *amorce* (I, 721).

[5] The book metaphor is used several times in this context: *calendrier* appears in I, 386-387; II, 756, and III, 989; *évangile* in III, 26. Metaphors from other domains include *cadre* (I, 721), and *séries* (II, 757).

Another important function of Proust's metaphors is to give us insight into the novel's narrative techniques. Just as many networks of time metaphors are verbal translations of the multiple aspects of an experience, so many of Proust's complex sentences are held together by the logic of a unique personal insight: various levels of awareness and numerous associations are accounted for by an intricate syntactical structure and frequent digressions and elaborations. In addition, the conceptual metaphors give us significant clues for understanding the novel's narrative ordering. For instance, *réseau* and *vases clos,* as concrete images of how the mind perceives the world, provide us with a key to the narrative context in which they appear. The sequential accounts of the two childhood walks towards Méséglise and Guermantes (I, 134-165; 165-186) are elucidated by the metaphor *vases clos* (I, 135), which dramatizes the hero's view of life as divided into separate, unrelated moments. The metaphor *réseau,* on the other hand, prefigures a complex narrative account of closely related impressions, activities and thoughts.

The reader who has travelled through Proust's novel has come to see that the metaphors of time have a major function in telling the story, and in guiding our interpretation of it. They focus our attention on the major "events" in the hero's life, and they emphasize that these events are mental. Since they record and explain the central character's insights into the nature of time, they have both a narrative and didactic function.

We may conclude that close analysis of metaphors, within their immediate context and the larger context of the entire novel, reveals that the metaphoric process is not only the substitution of a lexical term from one semantic domain (the vehicle) for that from another (the tenor), but also the integration of the metaphoric term into syntactic, thematic, descriptive, and narrative structures. While on the level of the sentence lexical transformation and syntactical correlations set up the semantic relationships, other internal relationships within the larger narrative framework also come into play and orient our interpretation.

BIBLIOGRAPHY

Since this list contains the titles only of those works actually consulted in the preparation of my study, it cannot pretend to comprehensiveness. Those seeking more complete bibliographies should consult the following. For references to Proust's own published and unpublished writings:

Bonnet, Henri. *Le Progrès spirituel dans l'œuvre de Marcel Proust.* 2 vols. Paris: Vrin, 1946, 1949. II, 261-277.
———. *Marcel Proust de 1907 à 1914.* 2nd ed., rev. Paris: Nizet, 1971, pp. 204-323. Bibliographie complémentaire II. Paris: Nizet, 1976.
Chantal, René de. *Marcel Proust: Critique littéraire.* Montreal: Les Presses de l'Université de Montréal, 1967. II, 645-713.
Graham, Victor E. *Bibliographie des études sur Marcel Proust et son œuvre.* Geneva: Droz, 1976.
Kolb, Philip and Larkin B. Price. Ed. *Marcel Proust: Textes retrouvés.* Urbana: Univ. of Illinois Press, 1968, pp. 262-290.

For a more complete listing of studies of Proust's work, consult pages 718-737 of Volume Two of René de Chantal's book. Additional entries covering some of the lesser known studies up to 1940, including many articles and reviews, are listed in the extensive bibliography of Douglas W. Alden's *Marcel Proust and his French Critics* (Los Angeles: Lymanhouse, 1940, pp. 171-257).

I. WORKS BY PROUST

A la recherche du temps perdu. "Bibliothèque de la Pléiade." Ed. Pierre Clarac and André Ferré. 3 vols. Paris: Gallimard, 1954.
"A propos du style de Flaubert." *La Nouvelle Revue Française,* 14, No. 76 (1 January, 1920), 72-90.
Chroniques. Paris: Gallimard, 1927.
"Contre l'obscurité." *La Revue Blanche,* 11, No. 75 (15 July, 1896), 69-72.
Contre Sainte-Beuve. Suivi de nouveaux mélanges. Paris: Gallimard, 1954.
Contre Sainte-Beuve. Précédé de *Pastiches et mélanges* et suivi de Essais et articles. Ed. Pierre Clarac and Yves Sandre. Paris: Gallimard, 1971.
Jean Santeuil. 3 vols. Paris: Gallimard, 1952.
Jean Santeuil. Précédé de *Les Plaisirs et les jours.* Ed. Pierre Clarac and Yves Sandre. Paris: Gallimard, 1971.
Les Pastiches de Proust. Ed. Jean Milly. Paris: A. Colin, 1970.

Pastiches et mélanges. Paris: Gallimard, 1919.
Les Plaisirs et les jours. 1896; rpt. Paris: Gallimard, 1924.
"Pour un ami" (Remarques sur le style). *Revue de Paris,* 6 (15 November, 1920), 270-280.
Textes retrouvés. Ed. Philip Kolb and Larkin B. Price. Urbana: Univ. of Illinois Press, 1968. Rev. ed. Paris: Gallimard, 1971.
"Voyage en zigzags dans la république des lettres." *Les Annales Politiques et Littéraires,* 78 (26 February, 1922), 236.

Prefaces by Proust

Blanche, Jacques-Emile. *Propos de peintre. De David à Degas.* Paris: Emile-Paul, 1919, pp. i-xxxv.
Morand, Paul. *Tendres Stocks.* Paris: Gallimard, 1921, pp. 9-37.
Ruskin, John. *La Bible d'Amiens.* Trans. Marcel Proust. Paris: Mercure de France, 1947.

Correspondence

Corrèspondance de Marcel Proust: I, 1880-1895. Ed. Philip Kolb. Paris: Plon, 1970. 2nd rev. ed., 1976. II, 1896-1901. III, 1902-1903. Paris: Plon, 1976.
Correspondance générale de Marcel Proust. Published by Robert Proust and Paul Brach. 6 vols. Paris: Plon, 1930-36.
Marcel Proust et Jacques Rivière: Correspondance, 1914-22. Ed. Philip Kolb. Paris: Plon, 1955.
Lettres à Reynaldo Hahn. Ed. Philip Kolb. Paris: Gallimard, 1956.

II. STUDIES ABOUT PROUST

Alden, Douglas William. *Marcel Proust and His French Critics.* Los Angeles: Lymanhouse, 1940.
Bailey, Ninette. "Symbolisme et composition dans l'œuvre de Proust." *French Studies,* 20, No. 3 (July 1966), 253-266.
Bardèche, Maurice. *Marcel Proust romancier.* 2 vols. Paris: Les Sept Couleurs, 1971.
Barthes, Roland. "Proust et les noms." In *To Honor Roman Jakobson: Essays on the Occasion of his Seventieth Birthday.* The Hague: Mouton, 1967. I, 150-158.
Bédé, Jean-Albert. "Chateaubriand et Marcel Proust." *Modern Language Notes,* 49 (June 1934), 353-360.
Bersani, Leo. *Marcel Proust: The Fictions of Life and of Art.* New York: Oxford University Press, 1965.
———. "Proust and the Art of Incompletion." In *Aspects of Narrative.* Ed. J. Hillis Miller. New York: Columbia Univ. Press, 1971, pp. 119-142.
Beznos, Maurice J. "Aspects of Time According to the Theories of Relativity in Marcel Proust's *A la recherche du temps perdu*: A Study of the Similitudes in Conceptual Limits." *The Ohio University Review,* 10 (1968), 74-102.
Black, Carl John Jr. "Albertine as an Allegorical Figure of Time." *Romanic Review,* 54 (Oct. 1963), 171-186.
Blanc, Georges. "Une Bibliographie." *Europe,* 48, Nos. 496-497 (August-Sept. 1970), 264-266.

Bloch-Sakai, Françoise. "Remarques sur la métaphore proustienne." *Etudes de Langue et de Littérature Française*, No. 10 (March 1967), 104-116.
Bolle, Louis. *Marcel Proust ou le complexe d'Argus*. Paris: Grasset, 1967.
Bonnet, Henri. *Marcel Proust de 1907 à 1914*. 2nd ed., rev. Paris: Nizet, 1971.
―――. *Le Progrès spirituel dans l'œuvre de Marcel Proust*. 2 vols. Paris: Vrin, 1946-1949.
Brée, Germaine. "Un nouvel aperçu sur les problèmes de composition dans *A la recherche du temps perdu*." *Romanic Review*, 38 (February 1947), 43-52.
―――. *Du temps perdu au temps retrouvé*. Paris: Société d'Edition "Les Belles Lettres," 1950.
Cattaui, Georges. *Marcel Proust*. Paris: Editions Universitaires, 1958.
―――. *Proust perdu et retrouvé*. Paris: Plon, 1963.
―――. *Proust et ses métamorphoses*. Paris: Nizet, 1972.
Centenaire de Marcel Proust. Europe, 48, Nos. 496-497 (August-September 1970).
Chantal, René de. *Marcel Proust, critique littéraire*, 2 vols. Montreal: Presses de l'Université de Montréal, 1967.
Chernowitz, Maurice Eugene. *Proust and Painting*. New York: International Univ. Press, 1945.
Clark, Charles N. "Love and Time: The Erotic Imagery of Marcel Proust." *Yale French Studies*, No. 11 (1953), pp. 80-90.
Cocking, J. *Proust*. New Haven: Yale Univ. Press, 1956.
Cook, Albert. "Proust: The Invisible Stilts of Time." *Modern Fiction Studies*, 4 (1958), 118-126.
Curtius, Robert Ernst. *Französischer Geist im Neuen Europa*. Stuttgart: Deutsche Verlags-Anstalt, 1925.
―――. *Marcel Proust*. Trans. Armand Pierhal. Paris: Revue Nouvelle, 1928.
Czoniczer, Elizabeth. *Quelques antécédants d' 'A la recherche du temps perdu.'* Geneva: Droz, 1957.
Daniel, Georges. *Temps et mystification dans 'A la recherche du temps perdu.'* Paris: Nizet, 1963.
Daube, Uwe. "Dechiffrierung und strukturelle Funktion der Leitmotive in Marcel Prousts *A la Recherche du temps perdu*." Inaugural Dissertation. Heidelberg, 1963.
Deleuze, Gilles. *Marcel Proust et les signes*. 4th ed. Paris: Presses Universitaires de France, 1976.
Dentan, Michel. "La Structure métaphorique d'*Un Amour de Swann*." *Etudes de Lettres*, 4, No. 4 (October 1971), 15-28.
Devoto, Giacomo. "Il tempo proustiano: Uno studio stilistico." *Letteratura*, 9, No. 6 (1947), 102-121.
Entretiens sur Marcel Proust. Ed. Georges Cattaui and Philip Kolb. Paris: Mouton, 1966.
Feuillerat, Albert. *Comment Marcel Proust a composé son roman*. Yale Romanic Studies, 7. New Haven: Yale Univ. Press, 1934.
Fiser, Emeric. *L'Esthétique de Marcel Proust*. Paris: Revue Française, 1933.
―――. *Le Symbole littéraire: Essai sur la signification du symbole chez Wagner, Baudelaire, Mallarmé, Bergson et Proust*. Paris: Corti, 1941.
Genette, Gérard. "Discours du récit." In *Figures* III. Paris: Seuil, 1972, pp. 70-273.

Genette, Gérard. "Métonymie chez Proust, ou la naissance du Récit." *Poétique,* No. 2 (1970), pp. 156-173.

———. "Proust et le langage indirect." In *Figures II: Essais.* Paris: Seuil, 1969, pp. 223-294.

———. "Proust palimpseste." In *Figures: Essais.* Paris: Seuil, 1966, pp. 39-67.

———. "Time and Narrative in *A la recherche du temps perdu.*" In *Aspects of Narrative.* Ed. J. Hillis Miller. New York: Columbia Univ. Press, 1971, pp. 93-118.

Goebel, Gerhard. "Die 'Mémoire involontaire,' die fünf Sinne und das verlorene Paradies in Prousts *A la recherche du temps perdu.*" *Romanistisches Jahrbuch,* 20 (1969), 113-129.

Gouézec, Annick. "La composition poétique du *Côté de chez Swann.*" *Le Français Moderne,* 36, No. 3 (July 1968), 186-208.

Graham, Victor E. *The Imagery of Proust.* Language and Style Series, 2. Ed. Stephen Ullmann. Oxford: Basil Blackwell, 1966.

Green, Frederick Charles. *The Mind of Proust: A Detailed Interpretation of 'A la recherche du temps perdu.'* Cambridge, England: Cambridge Univ. Press, 1949.

Gülich, Elisabeth. "Die Metaphorik der Erinnerung in Prousts *A la recherche du temps perdu.*" *Zeitschrift für Französische Sprache und Literatur,* 75 (1965), 51-74.

Hachez, Willy. "La Chronologie et l'âge des personnages de *A la recherche du temps perdu.*" *Bulletin Société Marcel Proust,* No. 6 (1956), pp. 198-207.

———. "Retouches à une chronologie." *Bulletin Société Marcel Proust,* No. 11 (1961), pp. 392-398.

Hindus, Milton. *The Proustian Vision.* New York: Columbia Univ. Press, 1954.

Hommage à Marcel Proust. Les Cahiers Marcel Proust, No. 1. Paris: Gallimard, 1927.

Houston, J. P. "Temporal Patterns in *A la recherche du temps perdu.*" *French Studies,* 16 (January 1962), 33-44.

———. "Thought, Style and Shape in Proust's Novel." *Southern Review,* 5, No. 2 (1969), 987-1003.

Jauss, Hans Robert. *Zeit und Erinnerung in Marcel Prousts 'A la recherche du temps perdu': Ein Beitrag zur Theorie des Romans.* Heidelberg: Carl Winter, 1955.

Johnson, Theodore, Jr. " 'La Lanterne magique': Proust's Metaphorical Toy." *L'Esprit Créateur,* 11, No. 1 (Spring 1971), 17-31.

King, Adele. *Proust.* London: Oliver and Boyd, 1968.

Kostis, Nicholas. "Albertine: Characterization through Image and Symbol." *PMLA,* 84, No. 1 (January 1969), 125-135.

Kumar, Shiv K. "Bergson and Proust's 'souvenir involontaire.' " *Canadian Modern Language Review,* 2 (1959), 7-10.

Layton, Monique J. "Structures de certaines métaphores rencontrées dans Proust." *Révue d'Esthétique,* 25 (October 1972), 425-441.

Lewis, Philip E. "Idealism and Reality." *Yale French Studies,* No. 34 (June 1965), pp. 24-28.

Linn, J. C. "Notes on Proust's Manipulation of Chronology." *Romanic Review,* 52 (1961), 210-225.

———. "Proust's Theatre Metaphors." *Romanic Review,* 49, No. 3 (October 1958), 179-190.

———. *The Theater in the Fiction of Marcel Proust.* Ohio State University Press, 1966.

Louria, Yvette. *La Convergence stylistique chez Proust.* Geneva: Droz, 1957.
Macksey, Richard and Gerald Kamber. " 'Negative Metaphor' and Proust's Rhetoric of Absence." *Modern Language Notes,* 85 (1970), 858-883.
March, Harold. *The Two Worlds of Marcel Proust.* Philadelphia: Univ. of Pennsylvania Press, 1948.
Matoré, Georges. "Proust linguiste." In *Festschrift: Walther von Wartburg zum 80. Geburtstag.* Ed. Kurt Baldinger. Tübingen: Max Niemeyer Verlag, 1968. I, 279-292.
Maurois, André. *A la recherche de Marcel Proust.* Paris: Hachette, 1949.
Mein, Margaret. *Proust's Challenge to Time.* Manchester: Manchester Univ. Press, 1962.
Milly, Jean. "Proust et l'image." *Bulletin Société Marcel Proust,* No. 20 (1970), pp. 1031-43.
———. *Proust et le style.* Paris: Minard, 1970.
Mindlin, Iris G. "Marcel Proust: A Contribution towards a Bibliography." *Bulletin of the New York Public Library,* 70 (June 1966), 369-388.
Monnin-Hornung, Juliette. *Proust et la peinture.* Geneva: Droz, 1951.
Moss, Howard. *The Magic Lantern of Marcel Proust.* New York: MacMillan, 1962.
Mouton, Jean. *Le Style de Marcel Proust.* Paris: Corrêa, 1948.
———. *Le Style de Marcel Proust.* rpt. Paris: A.G. Nizet, 1968.
Muller, Marcel. "Romananfang und Romanschluss bei Marcel Proust." In *Romananfänge: Versuch zu einer Poetik des Romans.* Ed. Norbert Miller. Berlin: Literarisches Colloquium, 1965.
———. *Les Voix narratives dans la 'Recherche du temps perdu.'* Geneva: Droz, 1965.
Murray, Jack. "Proust's Views on Perception as a Metaphoric Framework." *French Review,* 42, No. 3 (February 1969), 380-394.
Nitzberg, Howard. "*A la recherche du temps perdu*: Mirror-Image as a Level of Extratemporal Existence." *French Review,* 34 (1961), 440-444.
O'Brien, Justin. "La Mémoire involontaire avant Marcel Proust." *Revue de Littérature Comparée,* 19 (January 1939), 19-36.
———. "Proust et 'le joli langage.' " *PMLA,* 80 (1965), 259-265.
———. "Proust's Use of Syllepsis." *PMLA,* 69, No. 4 (Sept. 1954), 741-752.
Ortega y Gasset. "Le Temps, la distance et la forme chez Marcel Proust." In *Hommage à Marcel Proust. Cahiers Marcel Proust,* No. 1. Paris: Gallimard, 1927, pp. 287-299.
Painter, George Duncan. *Proust: The Early Years.* Boston: Little, Brown, 1959.
———. *Proust: The Later Years.* Boston: Little, Brown, 1965.
Pardee, W. Hearne. "The Images of Vision." *Yale French Studies,* No. 34 (June 1965), pp. 19-23.
Pfeiffer, Jean. "Proust et le Livre." *L'Arc,* No. 47 (1971), pp. 74-83.
Picon, Gaëtan. *Lecture de Proust.* Paris: Gallimard, 1963.
Pierre-Quint, Léon. *Comment travaillait Marcel Proust.* Paris: Editions des Cahiers Libres, 1926.
———. *Marcel Proust: Sa vie, son œuvre.* Paris: Editions du Sagittaire, 1935.
Pistorius, George. "Proust en Allemagne, 1960-1964: Bibliographie." *Bulletin Société Marcel Proust,* No. 16 (1966), pp. 441-447.
Pommier, Jean Joseph Marie. *La Mystique de Marcel Proust.* Geneva: Droz, 1968.
Poulet, Georges. *L'Espace proustien.* Paris: Gallimard, 1963.
———. *Etudes sur le temps humain.* Paris: Plon, 1950, pp. 364-405.

Price, Larkin B. "Bird Imagery Surrounding Proust's Albertine." *Symposium,* 26, No. 3 (Fall 1972), 242-259.
Proust. A Collection of Critical Essays. Ed. René Girard. Englewood Cliffs, New Jersey: Prentice Hall, 1962.
Remâcle, Madeleine. *L'Elément poétique dans 'A la recherche du temps perdu' de Marcel Proust.* Bruxelles: Palais des Académies, 1954.
Richard, J. P. *Proust et le monde sensible.* Paris: Seuil, 1974.
Rogers, B. G. *Proust's Narrative Techniques.* Geneva: Droz, 1965.
Sandre, Yves. "Pour une esthétique au jour le jour: D'après la correspondance de Marcel Proust." *Europe,* 48, Nos. 496-497 (August-September 1970), 52-74.
Shattuck, Roger. *Marcel Proust.* New York: Viking Press, 1974.
———. *Proust's Binoculars: A Study of Memory, Time, and Recognition in 'A la recherche du temps perdu.'* New York: Random House, 1963.
Silva Ramos, G. da. "Bibliographie proustienne." *Cahiers Marcel Proust,* No. 6 (1932), pp. 29-70.
Simon, P.-H. "Stylistique proustienne." *Journal de Genève,* 13-14 (July 1957), 10-15.
Slater, Maya. "Some Recurrent Comparisons in *A la recherche du temps perdu.*" *Modern Language Review,* 62, No. 4 (October 1967), 629-632.
Spillner, Bernd. *Symmetrisches und asymmetrisches Prinzip in der Syntax Marcel Prousts*: Ein Beitrag zur Geschichte des französischen Prosastils. Meisenheim am Glan: Anton Hain, 1971.
Sticca, Sandro. "Anticipation as a Literary Technique in Proust's *A la recherche du temps perdu.*" *Symposium,* 20, No. 3 (Fall 1966), 254-262.
Stockwell, H. C. "L'Image dans l'œuvre de Proust." *Modern Languages,* December 1944, pp. 10-15.
Strauss, Walter A. *Proust and Literature: The Novelist as Critic.* Cambridge, Mass.: Harvard Univ. Press, 1957.
Tadié, Jean-Yves. *Proust et le roman.* Paris: Gallimard, 1971.
Tiedtke, Irma. *Symbole und Bilder im Werke Marcel Prousts.* Hamburg: Paul Evert Verlag, 1936.
Torres Bodet, Jaime. *Tiempo et memoria en la obra de Proust.* Mexico: Editorial Porrua, 1967.
Uitti, Karl D. "*Le Temps retrouvé*: sens, composition et langue." *Romanische Forschungen,* 75, Nos. 3-4 (1963), 332-361.
Ullmann, Stephen. "L'Esthétique de l'image dans *Contre Sainte-Beuve* de Marcel Proust." In *Festschrift: Walther von Wartburg zum 80. Geburtstag.* Ed. Kurt Baldinger. Tübingen: Max Niemeyer Verlag, 1968. I, 267-278.
———. "Les Idées linguistiques de Proust dans *Jean Santeuil.*" *Revue de Linguistique Romane,* No. 31 (January-June 1967), pp. 134-146.
———. *The Image in the Modern French Novel.* 1960; rpt. New York: Barnes and Noble, 1963, pp. 124-238.
———. "Images of Time and Memory in *Jean Santeuil.*" In *Currents of Thought in French Literature: Essays in Memory of G. T. Clapton.* Oxford: Basil Blackwell, 1965, pp. 209-226.
———. "Proust's Ideas on Language and Style as Reflected in his Correspondence." In *The French Language: Studies Presented to Lewis Charles Harmer.* Ed. T. G. S. Combe and P. Rickard. London: Harrap, 1970.
———. *Style in the French Novel.* 1957; rpt. New York: Barnes and Noble, 1964.

Virtanen, Reino. "Proust's Metaphors from the Natural and Exact Sciences." *PMLA*, 69 (December 1954), 1038-1059.
Wäber, Gottfried. "Die Bedeutung der Proustschen Metapher, aufgezeigt an der Darstellung des gealterten Herzogs." *Die Neueren Sprachen*, 14, No. 9 (1965), 431-437.
Zaeske, Kaethe. *Der Stil Marcel Prousts*. Emsdetten (Westf.): Heinrich und J. Lechte, 1937.
Zeblewski, Elfi. "Zur Bildersprache in Marcel Prousts *Jean Santeuil*." *Die Neueren Sprachen*, No. 6 (1958), pp. 324-337.

III. STUDIES IN LANGUAGE, STYLE AND LITERARY THEORY

Abbou, André. "Problèmes et méthode d'une stylistique des images." *Le Français Moderne*, 37, No. 3 (July 1969), 212-223.
A Presentation of 'The Rule of Metaphor' by Paul Ricoeur. *Philosophy Today*, 21, No. 4/4 (Winter 1977).
Aristotle. *The Art of Rhetoric*. Trans. J. H. Freese, Cambridge, Mass.: Harvard Univ. Press, 1949.
L'Analyse structurale des récits. *Communications*, No. 8 (1966).
Antoine, Gérald. "Pour une méthode d'analyse stylistique des images." *Langue et Littérature*. Actes du VIIIe Congrès de la Fédération Internationale des Langues et Littératures Modernes. Paris: Les Belles Lettres, 1961, pp. 151-164.
Auerbach, Erich. *Mimesis: The Representation of Reality in Western Literature*. Trans. Willard Trask. 1953; rpt. New York: Doubleday, 1957.
Bally, Charles. *Le Langage et la vie*. Paris: Payot, 1926.
———. *Traité de stylistique française*. 2 vols. 3rd. ed. Paris: C. Klincksieck, 1951.
Barfield, Owen. *Poetic Diction: A Study in Meaning*. New York: McGraw-Hill, 1964.
Barthes, Roland. *Le Degré zéro de l'écriture*. Paris: Seuil, 1953.
———. *S/Z*. Paris: Seuil, 1970.
Beardsley, Monroe C. "The Metaphorical Twist." *Philosophy and Phenomenological Research*, 22 (March 1962), 293-307.
Benveniste, Emile. *Problèmes de linguistique générale*. Paris: Gallimard, 1966.
———. "La Forme et le sens dans le langage." In *Le Langage*. Neuchâtel: La Baconnière, 1967, pp. 27-40.
Berggren, Douglas. "The Use and Abuse of Metaphor." *Review of Metaphysics*, 16, No. 1 (Dec. 1962), 237-258; (March 1963), 450-472.
Black, Max. *Models and Metaphors: Studies in Language and Philosophy*. Ithaca: Cornell Univ. Press, 1962.
Bouverot, Danielle. "Comparaison et métaphore." *Le Français Moderne*, 37, Nos. 2, 3, and 4 (April, July, October 1969), 132-147; 224-238; 301-316.
Brisson, Luc. "Sémantique de la métaphore." *Dialogue*, 15 (1976), 256-281.
Booth, Wayne C. *A Rhetoric of Irony*. Chicago: Univ. of Chicago Press, 1975.
Brooke-Rose, Christine. *A Grammar of Metaphor*. London: Secker and Warburg, 1965.
Cohen, Jean. *Structure du langage poétique*. Paris: Flammarion, 1966.
———. "Théorie de la figure." *Communications*, No. 16 (1970), pp. 3-25.
Crosman, Inge Karalus. "The Status of Metaphoric Discourse: Paul Ricoeur: *La Métaphore vive*." *Romanic Review*, 68, No. 3 (May 1977), 207-216.

Culler, Jonathan. *Structuralist Poetics*. Ithaca: Cornell Univ. Press, 1975.
Dictionary of World Literature. Ed. Joseph T. Shipley. New York: The Philosophical Library, 1943.
Dubois, J., et al. *Rhétorique générale*. Paris: Larousse, 1970.
Dubois, Philippe. "La Métaphore filée et le fonctionnement du texte." *Le Français Moderne*, 43, No. 3 (1975), 202-213.
Ducrot, Oswald and Tzvetan Todorov. *Dictionnaire encyclopédique des sciences du langage*. Paris: Seuil, 1972.
Empson, William. *The Structure of Complex Words*. Ann Arbor: Univ. of Michigan Press, 1967.
Encyclopedia of Poetry and Poetics. Ed. Alex Preminger. Princeton: Princeton Univ. Press, 1965.
Essays on the Language of Literature. Ed. Seymour Chatman and Samuel R. Levin. Boston: Houghton Mifflin, 1967.
Fish, Stanley. "How to Do Things With Austin and Searle: Speech-Act Theory and Literary Criticism." *Modern Language Notes*, 91, No. 5 (October 1976), 983-1023.
Fontanier, Pierre. *Les Figures du discours*. Paris: Flammarion, 1968.
Frye, Northrop. *Anatomy of Criticism: Four Essays*. 1957; rpt. New York: Atheneum, 1966.
Genette, Gérard. *Figures III*. Paris: Seuil, 1972.
―――. "La Rhétorique restreinte." *Communications*, No. 16 (1970), pp. 158-171.
Goodman, Nelson. *The Languages of Art: An Approach to A Theory of Symbols*. Indianapolis, New York: Bobbs-Merril Co., 1968.
Greimas, A. J. *Sémantique structurale*. Paris: Larousse, 1966.
Grice, Paul. "Meaning." *Philosophical Review*, 64 (1957), 377-88.
―――. "Utterer's Meaning, Sentence-Meaning and Word-Meaning." *Foundations of Language*, 4 (August 1968), 225-42.
Guenther, Franz. "On the Semantics of Metaphor." *Poetics*, 4, Nos. 2/3 (August 1975), 199-220.
Hardt, Manfred. *Das Bild in der Dichtung: Studien zu Funktionsweisen von Bildern und Bildreihen in der Literatur*. Munich: W. Fink, 1966.
Hausser, Michel. "Un aspect de la fonction poétique: la fonction impressive." *Le Français Moderne*, 36, No. 2 (April 1968), 105-132.
Henel, Heinrich. "Metaphor and Meaning." In *The Disciplines of Criticism*. Ed. Peter Demetz, Thomas Greene, and Lowry Nelson, Jr. New Haven: Yale Univ. Press, 1968, pp. 93-123.
Henry, Albert. *Métonymie et métaphore*. Paris: Klincksieck, 1971.
Hesse, Mary B. "The Explanatory Function of Metaphor." In *Models and Analogies in Science*. Notre Dame: Univ. of Notre Dame Press, 1966; 1970, pp. 157-177.
Hester, Marcus B. *The Meaning of Poetic Metaphor*. The Hague: Mouton, 1967.
Hinderer, Walter. "Theory, Conception, and Interpretation of the Symbol." In *Perspectives of Literary Symbolism*. Ed. Joseph Strelka. University Park: Pennsylvania State Univ. Press, 1968, pp. 87-98.
Hirsch, E. D. *The Aims of Interpretation*. Chicago: Univ. of Chicago Press, 1976.
―――. *Validity in Interpretation*. New Haven: Yale Univ. Press, 1967.
Hornstein, Lillian Herlands. "Analysis of Imagery: A Critique of Literary Method." *PMLA*, 57 (1942), 638-653.

Les Jeux de la métaphore. Littérature, 5, No. 17 (February 1975).
Jakobson, Roman and Morris Halle. *Fundamentals of Language.* The Hague: Mouton, 1956.
―――. "Linguistics and Poetics." In *Style in Language.* Ed. Th. Sebeok. Cambridge, Mass.: M.I.T. Press, 1964, pp. 350-377.
―――. *Questions de poétique.* Paris: Seuil, 1973.
Köller, Wilhelm. *Semiotik und Metapher. Untersuchungen zur grammatischen Struktur und kommunikativen Funktion von Metapher.* Stuttgart: J. B. Metzler, 1975.
Konrad, Hedwig. *Etude sur la métaphore.* Paris: Vrin, 1958.
Kumar, Shiv K. *Bergson and the Stream of Consciousness Novel.* New York: New York Univ. Press, 1963.
Kuentz, Pierre. *La Stylistique.* Paris: Klincksieck, 1970.
Lämmert, Eberhard. *Bauformen des Erzählens.* Stuttgart: J. B. Metzler, 1967.
Lavis, Georges. "Le Statut sémantique de la métaphore, de la métonymie et du symbole. A propos d'un livre récent." *Cahiers d'Analyse Textuelle,* 16 (1974), 86-108.
Leakey, F. W. "Intention in Metaphor." *Essays in Criticism,* 4, No. 1 (1954), 191-198.
Le Guern, Michel. *Sémantique de la métaphore et de la métonymie.* Paris: Larousse, 1973.
Lehmann, A. G. *The Symbolist Aesthetic in France: 1885-1895.* Oxford: Basil Blackwell, 1950.
Levenston, Edward A. "Metaphor, Speech Act and Grammatical Form." *Poetics,* 5, No. 4 (1976), 383-402.
Lodge, David. *Language and Fiction.* New York: Columbia Univ. Press, 1966.
Loewenberg, Ina. "Identifying Metaphors." *Foundations of Language,* 12 (1975), 315-338.
―――. "Truth and Consequences of Metaphors." *Philosophy and Rhetoric,* 6, No. 1 (Winter 1973), 30-46.
Lüdi, Georges. *Die Metapher als Funktion der Aktualisierung.* Bern: Francke Verlag, 1973.
Mack, Dorothy. "Metaphoring as Speech Act." *Poetics,* 4, Nos. 2/3 (August 1975), 221-256.
Marouzeau, Jules. *Lexique de la terminologie linguistique.* Paris: Geuthner, 1933.
―――. *Précis de stylistique française.* Paris: Masson, 1959.
McCall, March H. *Ancient Rhetorical Theory of Simile and Comparison.* Cambridge, Mass.: Harvard Univ. Press, 1969.
Mendilow, A. A. *Time and the Novel.* New York: Humanities Press, 1965.
La Métaphore. Le Français Moderne, 43, No. 3 (1975).
Meyerhoff, Hans. *Time in Literature.* Berkeley: Univ. of California Press, 1955.
Müller, Günther. "Über das Zeitgerüst des Erzählens." *Deutsche Vierteljahrsschrift,* 24 (1950), 1-32.
Nesselroth, Peter W. "The Stylistic Analysis of the Literary Image." In *Problems of Textual Analysis.* Ed. Pierre R. Léon et al. Montreal: Didier, 1971, pp. 123-131.
Onimus, Jean. "L'Expression du temps dans le roman contemporain." *Revue de Littérature Comparée,* 28 (July-Sept. 1954), 299-317.
On Metaphor. New Literary History, 6, No. 1 (1974).

Pavel, Toma. "Notes pour une description structurale de la métaphore poétique." *Cahiers de Linguistique Théorique et Appliquée*, No. 1 (1962), pp. 185-207.
Peirce, Charles Sanders. "Logic as Semiotic: The Theory of Signs." In *Philosophical Writings of Peirce*. Ed. Justus Buchler. New York: Dover Publications, 1955, pp. 98-119.
Pongs, Hermann. *Das Bild in der Dichtung: Versuch einer Morphologie der metaphorischen Formen*. I. 2nd ed. rev. Marburg: N. G. Elwert, 1960.
―――. *Das Bild in der Dichtung: Voruntersuchungen zum Symbol*. II. 2nd ed. rev. Marburg: N. G. Elwert, 1963.
Pouillon, Jean. *Temps et roman*. Paris: NRF, 1946.
Poulet, Georges. *Etudes sur le temps humain*, IV: *Mesure de l'instant*. Paris: Plon, 1968.
Pratt, Mary Louise. *Toward A Speech Act Theory of Literary Discourse*. Bloomington: Indiana Univ. Press, 1977.
Quine, Willard Van Orman. *From a Logical Point of View*. 2nd ed. rev. Cambridge: Harvard Univ. Press, 1971.
―――. *Word and Object*. Cambridge: M.I.T. Press, 1973.
Quintilian, Marcus Fabius. *Institutio oratoria*. Trans. H. E. Butler. 4 vols. Cambridge, Mass.: Harvard Univ. Press, 1958-60.
Reinhart, Tanya. "On Understanding Poetic Metaphor." *Poetics*, 5, No. 4 (1976), 383-402.
Rhétorique et herméneutique. *Poétique*, 6, No. 23 (1975).
Richards, I. A. *The Philosophy of Rhetoric*. London: Oxford Univ. Press, 1936.
―――. *Principles of Literary Criticism*. New York: Harcourt, Brace, 1925.
Ricoeur, Paul. "Metaphor and the Main Problem of Hermeneutics." *New Literary History*, 6, No. 1 (Autumn 1974), 95-110.
―――. *La Métaphore vive*. Paris: Seuil, 1975. English trans. *The Rule of Metaphor*. Trans. Robert Czerny. Toronto: Univ. of Toronto Press, 1977.
Riffaterre, Michael. "Criteria for Style Analysis." *Word*, 15 (1959), 154-174.
―――. *Essais de stylistique structurale*. Paris: Flammarion, 1971.
―――. "Fonctions du cliché dans la prose littéraire." *Cahiers de l'Association Internationale des Etudes Françaises*, No. 16 (March 1964), pp. 81-95.
―――. "Intertextual Scrambling." *Romanic Review*, 68, No. 3 (1977), 197-206.
―――. "La métaphore filée dans la poésie surréaliste." *Langue Française*, September 1969, pp. 46-60.
―――. "Semantic Overdetermination in Poetry." *PTL*, 2, No. 1 (1977), 1-19.
―――. "The Self-Sufficient Text." *Diacritics*, Fall, 1973, pp. 39-45.
―――. "Sémantique du poème." *Cahiers de l'Association Internationale des Etudes Françaises*, 23 (1971), 125-43.
―――. *Le Style des Pléiades de Gobineau: Essai d'application d'une méthode stylistique*. New York: Columbia Univ. Press, 1957.
―――. "Stylistic Context." *Word*, 16 (1960), 207-218.
Ruwet, Nicolas. "Synecdoques et métonymies." *Poétique*, 6, No. 23 (1975), 371-388.
Saussure, Ferdinand de. *Cours de linguistique générale*. Paris: Payot, 1922.
Sayce, R. A. *Style in French Prose: A Method of Analysis*. 1953 rpt. Oxford: Clarendon Press, 1965.
Schrader, Ludwig. *Sinne und Sinnesverknüpfungen*. Heidelberg: Carl Winter, 1969.

Searle, John R. "The Logical Status of Fictional Discourse." *New Literary History*, 6, No. 2 (Winter 1975), 319-332.
Shibles, Warren A. *An Analysis of Metaphor*. The Hague: Mouton, 1971.
———. *Metaphor: An Annotated Bibliography and History*. Whitewater, Wisc.: Language Press, 1971.
Soublin, F. and J. Tamine. "Métaphores et cadres syntaxiques: la juxtaposition." *Le Français Moderne*, 41, No. 3 (July 1973), 240-255.
———. "Le Paramètre syntaxique dans l'analyse des métaphores." *Poetics*, 4, Nos. 2/3 (August 1975), 311-338.
Spitzer, Leo. *Stilstudien*. II: *Stilsprachen*. Munich: Max Hueber, 1961.
Stanford, W. B. *Greek Metaphor*. Oxford: Univ. Press, 1936.
———. "Synaesthetic Metaphor." *Comparative Literature Studies*, 6-7 (1942), 26-30.
Stierle, Karlheinz. "Aspekte der Metapher." In *Text als Handlung. Perspektiven einer systematischen Literaturwissenschaft*. Munich: Fink, 1975.
Stutterheim, Cornelis Ferdinand Petrus. *Het Begrip Metaphoor: Een Taalkundig en wijsgerig Onderzvek*. Amsterdam: H. J. Paris, 1941.
Style in Language. Ed. Thomas A. Sebeok. Cambridge, Mass.: M.I.T. Press, 1960.
Tamba-Mecz, Irène. "Système de l'identification métaphorique dans la construction appositive." *Le Français Moderne*, 43, No. 3 (1975), 234-255.
Tamine, Joëlle. "L'Interprétation des métaphores en *de*. Le feu de l'amour." *Langue Française*, 30 (May 1976), 34-43.
Thomas, Owen. *Metaphor and Related Subjects*. New York: Random House, 1969.
Theory of Metaphor. Poetics, 4, Nos. 2/3 (August 1975).
Tindall, William York. *The Literary Symbol*. New York: Columbia Univ. Press, 1955.
Todorov, Tzvetan. "Introduction à la symbolique." *Poétique*, No. 11 (1972), pp. 273-308.
———. "Problèmes actuels de la recherche rhétorique." *Le Français Moderne*, 43, No. 3 (1975), 193-201.
———. "Recherches sur le symbolisme linguistique." *Poétique*, No. 18 (1974), pp. 215-245.
———. "Synecdoques." *Communications*, No. 16 (1970), pp. 26-35.
———. "Tropes et figures." In *To Honor Roman Jakobson*. The Hague: Mouton, 1967. III, 2006-2023.
Traugott, Elizabeth. "Generative Semantics and the Concept of Literary Discourse." *Journal of Literary Semantics*, 2 (1973), 5-22.
Turbayne, Colin Murray. *The Myth of Metaphor*. New Haven: Yale University Press, 1962. Rev. ed. Columbia: Univ. of South Carolina Press, 1970 (Appendix: "Models, Metaphors, and Formal Interpretations").
Ullmann, Stephen. *The Image in the Modern French Novel*. 1960; rpt. New York: Barnes and Noble, 1963.
———. "L'Image littéraire: Quelques questions de méthode." *Langue et Littérature*. Actes du VIIIe Congrès de la Fédération Internationale des Langues et Littératures Modernes. Paris: Les Belles Lettres, 1961, pp. 41-59.
———. *Language and Style*. New York: Barnes and Noble, 1964.
———. *Meaning and Style*. Oxford: Basil Blackwell, 1973.
———. *The Principles of Semantics*. 2nd ed. rev. Oxford: Basil Blackwell, 1959.

Ullmann, Stephen. *Semantics: An Introduction to the Science of Meaning.* Oxford: Basil Blackwell, 1962.
———. "Simile and Metaphor." In *Studies in Greek, Italic, and Indo-European Linguistics.* Eds. Anna Morpugo Davies and Wolfgang Meid. Innsbruck: Inst. für Sprachwissen. der Univ. Innsbruck, pp. 425-30.
———. *Style in the French Novel.* 1957; rpt. New York: Barnes and Noble, 1964.
Urban, Willbur Marshall. *Language and Reality.* New York: Macmillan, 1961.
Uspensky, Boris. *A Poetics of Composition.* Berkeley: Univ. of California Press, 1973.
Van Dijk, Teun A. "Formal Semantics of Metaphorical Discourse." *Poetics,* 4, Nos. 2/3 (August 1975), 173-198.
Vigh, A. "Comparaison et similitude." *Le Français Moderne,* 43, No. 3 (1975), 214-233.
Weinrich, Harald. "Münze und Wort: Untersuchungen an einem Bildfeld." In *Romanica: Festschrift Gerhard Rohlfs.* Halle: Max Niemeyer, 1958, pp. 508-521.
———. "Semantik der kühnen Metapher." *Deutsche Vierteljahrsschrift für Literatur und Geistesgeschichte,* 37, No. 3 (1963), 325-344.
———. *Tempus: Besprochene und erzählte Welt.* Stuttgart: W. Kohlhammer, 1964.
———. "Typen der Gedächtnismetaphorik." *Archiv für Begriffsgeschichte,* 9 (1964), 23-26.
Wellek, René. *Concepts of Criticism.* Ed. Stephen G. Nichols, Jr. New Haven: Yale Univ. Press, 1965.
Wellek, René and Austin Warren. *Theory of Literature.* New York: Harcourt, Brace, 1956.
Wheelright, Philip. *The Burning Fountain.* Bloomington: Indiana Univ. Press, 1954.
———. *Metaphor and Reality.* Bloomington: Indiana Univ. Press, 1962.
Wimsatt, W. K. *The Verbal Icon: Studies in the Meaning of Poetry.* Lexington: Univ. of Kentucky, 1954.

NORTH CAROLINA STUDIES IN THE ROMANCE LANGUAGES AND LITERATURES

I.S.B.N. Prefix 0-8078-

Recent Titles

POETRY AND ANTIPOETRY: A STUDY OF SELECTED ASPECTS OF MAX JACOB'S POETIC STYLE, by Annette Thau. 1976. (No. 158). *-005-X.*

FRANCIS PETRARCH, SIX CENTURIES LATER, by Aldo Scaglione. 1975. (No. 159).

STYLE AND STRUCTURE IN GRACIÁN'S "EL CRITICÓN", by Marcia L. Welles, 1976. (No. 160). *-007-6.*

MOLIERE: TRADITIONS IN CRITICISM, by Laurence Romero. 1974 (Essays, No. 1). *-001-7.*

CHRÉTIEN'S JEWISH GRAIL. A NEW INVESTIGATION OF THE IMAGERY AND SIGNIFICANCE OF CHRÉTIEN DE TROYES'S GRAIL EPISODE BASED UPON MEDIEVAL HEBRAIC SOURCES, by Eugene J. Weinraub. 1976. (Essays, No. 2). *-002-5.*

STUDIES IN TIRSO, I, by Ruth Lee Kennedy. 1974. (Essays, No. 3). *-003-3.*

VOLTAIRE AND THE FRENCH ACADEMY, by Karlis Racevskis. 1975. (Essays, No. 4). *-004-1.*

THE NOVELS OF MME RICCOBONI, by Joan Hinde Stewart. 1976. (Essays, No. 8). *-008-4.*

FIRE AND ICE: THE POETRY OF XAVIER VILLAURRUTIA, by Merlin H. Forster. 1976. (Essays, No. 11). *-011-4.*

THE THEATER OF ARTHUR ADAMOV, by John J. McCann. 1975. (Essays, No. 13). *-013-0.*

AN ANATOMY OF POESIS: THE PROSE POEMS OF STÉPHANE MALLARMÉ, by Ursula Franklin. 1976. (Essays, No. 16). *-016-5.*

LAS MEMORIAS DE GONZALO FERNÁNDEZ DE OVIEDO, Vols. I and II. by Juan Bautista Avalle-Arce. 1974. (Texts, Textual Studies, and Translations, Nos. 1 and 2). *-401-2; 402-0.*

GIACOMO LEOPARDI: THE WAR OF THE MICE AND THE CRABS, translated, introduced and annotated by Ernesto G. Caserta. 1976. (Texts, Textual Studies, and Translations, No. 4). *-404-7.*

LUIS VÉLEZ DE GUEVARA: A CRITICAL BIBLIOGRAPHY, by Mary G. Hauer. 1975. (Texts, Textual Studies, and Translations, No. 5). *-405-5.*

UN TRÍPTICO DEL PERÚ VIRREINAL: "EL VIRREY AMAT, EL MARQUÉS DE SOTO FLORIDO Y LA PERRICHOLI". EL "DRAMA DE DOS PALANGANAS" Y SU CIRCUNSTANCIA, estudio preliminar, reedición y notas por Guillermo Lohmann Villena. 1976. (Texts, Textual Studies, and Translation, No. 15). *-415-2.*

LOS NARRADORES HISPANOAMERICANOS DE HOY, edited by Juan Bautista Avalle-Arce. 1973. (Symposia, No. 1). *-951-0.*

ESTUDIOS DE LITERATURA HISPANOAMERICANA EN HONOR A JOSÉ J. ARROM, edited by Andrew P. Debicki and Enrique Pupo-Walker. 1975. (Symposia, No. 2). *-952-9.*

MEDIEVAL MANUSCRIPTS AND TEXTUAL CRITICISM, edited by Christopher Kleinhenz. 1976. (Symposia, No. 4). *-954-5.*

SAMUEL BECKETT. THE ART OF RHETORIC. edited by Edouard Morot-Sir, Howard Harper, and Dougald McMillan III. 1976. (Symposia, No. 5). *-955-3.*

DELIE. CONCORDANCE, by Jerry Nash. 1976. 2 Volumes. (No. 174).

FIGURES OF REPETITION IN THE OLD PROVENÇAL LYRIC: A STUDY IN THE STYLE OF THE TROUBADOURS, by Nathaniel B. Smith. 1976. (No. 176). *-9176-2.*

A CRITICAL EDITION OF LE REGIME TRESUTILE ET TRESPROUFITABLE POUR CONSERVER ET GARDER LA SANTE DU CORPS HUMAIN, by Patricia Willett Cummins. 1977. (No. 177).

THE DRAMA OF SELF IN GUILLAUME APOLLINAIRE'S "ALCOOLS", by Richard Howard Stamelman. 1976. (No. 178). *-9178-9.*

When ordering please cite the *ISBN Prefix* plus the last four digits for each title.

Send orders to: University of North Carolina Press
                  North Carolina 27514
                  Chapel Hill
                  U. S. A.

NORTH CAROLINA STUDIES IN THE ROMANCE LANGUAGES AND LITERATURES

I.S.B.N. Prefix 0-8078-

Recent Titles

A CRITICAL EDITION OF "LA PASSION NOSTRE SEIGNEUR" FROM MANUSCRIPT 1131 FROM THE BIBLIOTHEQUE SAINTE-GENEVIEVE, PARIS, by Edward J. Gallagher. 1976. (No. 179). -9179-7.

A QUANTITATIVE AND COMPARATIVE STUDY OF THE VOCALISM OF THE LATIN INSCRIPTIONS OF NORTH AFRICA, BRITAIN, DALMATIA, AND THE BALKANS, by Stephen William Omeltchenko. 1977. (No. 180). -9180-0.

OCTAVIEN DE SAINT-GELAIS "LE SEJOUR D'HONNEUR", edited by Joseph A. James. 1977. (No. 181). -9181-9.

A STUDY OF NOMINAL INFLECTION IN LATIN INSCRIPTIONS, by Paul A. Gaeng. 1977. (No. 182). -9182-7.

THE LIFE AND WORKS OF LUIS CARLOS LÓPEZ, by Martha S. Bazik. 1977. (No. 183). -9183-5.

"THE CORT D'AMOR". A THIRTEENTH-CENTURY ALLEGORICAL ART OF LOVE, by Lowanne E. Jones. 1977. (No. 185). -9185-1.

PHYTONYMIC DERIVATIONAL SYSTEMS IN THE ROMANCE LANGUAGES: STUDIES IN THEIR ORIGIN AND DEVELOPMENT, by Walter E. Geiger. 1978. (No. 187). -9187-8.

LANGUAGE IN GIOVANNI VERGA'S EARLY NOVELS, by Nicholas Patruno. 1977. (No. 188). -9188-6.

BLAS DE OTERO EN SU POESÍA, by Moraima de Semprún Donahue. 1977. (No. 189). -9189-4.

LA ANATOMÍA DE "EL DIABLO COJUELO": DESLINDES DEL GÉNERO ANATOMÍSTICO, por C. George Peale. 1977. (No. 191). -9191-6.

RICHARD SANS PEUR, EDITED FROM "LE ROMANT DE RICHART" AND FROM GILLES CORROZET'S "RICHART SANS PAOUR", by Denis Joseph Conlon. 1977. (No. 192). -9192-4.

MARCEL PROUST'S GRASSET PROOFS. *Commentary and Variants*, by Douglas Alden. 1978. (No. 193). -9193-2.

MONTAIGNE AND FEMINISM, by Cecile Insdorf. 1977. (No. 194). -9194-0.

SANTIAGO F. PUGLIA, AN EARLY PHILADELPHIA PROPAGANDIST FOR SPANISH AMERICAN INDEPENDENCE, by Merle S. Simmons. 1977. (No. 195). -9195-9.

BAROQUE FICTION-MAKING. A STUDY OF GOMBERVILLE'S "POLEXANDRE", by Edward Baron Turk. 1978. (No. 196). -9196-7.

THE TRAGIC FALL: DON ÁLVARO DE LUNA AND OTHER FAVORITES IN SPANISH GOLDEN AGE DRAMA, by Raymond R. MacCurdy. 1978. (No. 197). -9197-5.

A BAHIAN HERITAGE. An Ethnolinguistic Study of African Influences on Bahian Portuguese, by William W. Megenney. 1978. (No. 198). -9198-3.

"LA QUERELLE DE LA ROSE: Letters and Documents", by Joseph L. Baird and John R. Kane. 1978. (No. 199). -9199-1.

TWO AGAINST TIME. *A Study of the very present worlds of Paul Claudel and Charles Péguy*, by Joy Nachod Humes. 1978. (No. 200). -9200-9.

TECHNIQUES OF IRONY IN ANATOLE FRANCE. Essay on *Les sept femmes de la Barbe-Bleue*, by Diane Wolfe Levy. 1978. (No. 201). -9201-7.

THE PERIPHRASTIC FUTURES FORMED BY THE ROMANCE REFLEXES OF "VADO (AD)" "PLUS INFINITIVE, by James Joseph Champion. 1978 (No. 202). -9202-5.

THE EVOLUTION OF THE LATIN /b/-/ṷ/ MERGER: A Quantitative and Comparative Analysis of the B-V Alternation in Latin Inscriptions, by Joseph Louis Barbarino. 1978 (No. 203). -9203-3.

METAPHORIC NARRATION: THE STRUCTURE AND FUNCTION OF METAPHORS IN "A LA RECHERCHE DU TEMPS PERDU", by Inge Karalus Crosman. 1978 (No. 204). -9204-1.

When ordering please cite the *ISBN Prefix* plus the last four digits for each title.

Send orders to: University of North Carolina Press
Chapel Hill
North Carolina 27514
U. S. A.

The Department of Romance Studies Digital Arts and Collaboration Lab at the University of North Carolina at Chapel Hill is proud to support the digitization of the North Carolina Studies in the Romance Languages and Literatures series.

www.ingramcontent.com/pod-product-compliance
Lightning Source LLC
Chambersburg PA
CBHW022013220426
43663CB00007B/1067